CW01455984

EREBUS AND THE DRAGONFLY

NEW ZEALAND AIR PIONEERS AND THE ACCIDENT INSPECTORS

ROBIN FAUTLEY

About the Author

Robin Fautley qualified as a Chartered Accountant in 1970. During training he worked at Prout Brothers, catamaran builders and designers. After qualifying he encountered James Wharram's Polynesian Catamarans, eventually building three. This is his second book; the first was on sailing and building Polynesian Catamarans.

His accountancy business required him to visit many distant clients and this led to Robin learning to fly and obtaining a Private Pilot's licence. Further flying experience led to Night and Instrument Certification (IMC).

His thoughts are always drawn back to the flight with Brian Chadwick in 1962 who disappeared just a few days later with all his passengers in the 'Bermuda Triangle' of New Zealand.

Robin lives in Essex and is married with four stepchildren and ten grandchildren whom he adores.

Published by Robin Fautley

© Robin Fautley 2024

The right of Robin Fautley to be identified as the author of this work has been asserted in accordance with the Copyright Designs and Patents Act,1988.

This book is sold subject to the condition that it shall not, by way of trade or otherwise, be lent, resold, hired out, or otherwise circulated without the publisher's prior consent in any form of binding or cover other than that in which it is published and without a similar condition including this condition being imposed on the subsequent purchaser.

First Published 2024

All rights reserved. No part of this publication may be reproduced in any material form (including photocopying or storing it in any medium by electronic means and whether or not transiently or incidentally to some other use of this publication) without the written permission of the copyright owner except in accordance with the provisions of the Copyright Designs and Patents Act 1988. Applications for the copyright owner's written permission to reproduce any part of this publication should be addressed to the publisher.

Printed by AquaPress Ltd
25 Farriers Way, Temple Farm Industrial Estate,
Southend-on-Sea, Essex, SS2 5RY
www.aquapressbooks.co.uk

ISBN: 978-1-0687353-0-1

This book is dedicated to all those passengers and air crew whose stories have been related within this epistle who have perished. Likewise in remembrance of two men who took on a whole nation's legal, political and aviation establishments to make Air Travel as safe as possible – Alwyn Gordon Vette and his Hon. Peter Thomas Mahon

ACKNOWLEDGEMENTS

Many people in New Zealand, Australia and the United Kingdom have willingly given me assistance, shared information and lent photographs. Their generosity is greatly appreciated.

Special thanks go to the Reeve family (Bobbie, Llynnelley, Adam and Simon) who were the first to realise the significance of the unique 8mm film and then spent such a massive amount of time cleaning it up frame by frame, Gavin Grimmer of findlostaircraft.co.nz, Lew Bone of DH90.info, and John King. These New Zealanders forbearance of this POME (Prisoner Of Mother England) over such a time has been appreciated. Then without the help given by Alec and Richard Waugh, I would never have considered this book. Finally, the immense help with the manuscript from Stuart Macfarlane, Ian Hambly, Arthur Cooper and again Richard Waugh whose help cannot be overstated.

There are other persons who wish to remain anonymous but have exchanged and provided information that has never seen the light of day before due to the need for confidentiality but trust me to relate their story accurately and in confidence. I appreciate their fears that their licences were at risk due to the ever-vengeful respective CAAs of their country taking retribution in the way that Rod Lovell was treated by his Australian CAA They know who they are, and I thank them profusely.

As well as those persons acknowledged above, there have been so many others who I have exchanged emails and phone calls with who have been so encouraging, all wanting the whole truth to be related sometimes at their own discomfort on occasions. All have been so encouraging, even without realising or appreciating how helpful they have been. So I would like to thank: Brian Andrews, Ron Ark, Russell Bartlett, Ian Blake, Hanneke Boon, Michael Briggs, Tim Bromhead, Jeremy Burfoot, Tim Burfoot, Mark Chadwick, Don Cheetham, Emily Clark, John Cooper, Bruce Crosbie, Ron Cuskelly, Mary Durham, Martin Fautley, Matthew Fautley, John Gemmell, Brian Grant, Anne Hunt, John Keir, Henry Labouchere, Stuart Leighton, Graham Lister, Rod Lovell, Graeme McConnell, Ross Jamie McDermott, Colin Monteath, Sarah Norris, Lizzie Oakes, Pip and Debbie Patterson, Lex Perriam, Russell Pickup, Graham Pudney, Peter Rhodes, John Rowan, Chris Rudge, Dan Ryan, Joey Sheehan, Bill Simpson, Colin Tuck, Kynan Yu, Jamie Wharram, Mike White, Jeff Williams and Michael Wright.

I give a special thanks to Chris Davey of AquaPress who has been so helpful designing this book. Any glaring errors and poor layout are where his advice has not been followed. His base just happens to be less than one mile as the crow flies of the home of the Dragonfly pilot's parents with whom my parents and I first shared the 8mm cine film of Brian Chadwicks flying in 1962. The Dragonfly has come home to roost!

Finally, I am grateful to my wife Helen, family and friends who have put up with me over such a long time whilst my mind has been stuck 13,000 miles away.

Robin Fautley. April 2024

Southend on Sea.

CONTENTS

FOREWORD BY REV DR RICHARD WAUGH QSM

You may be wondering why a Chartered Accountant from England's Southend-on-Sea in Essex has written a book about mainly New Zealand-related air accidents, including the Mt. Erebus DC-10 disaster in Antarctica.

Robin Fautley is a remarkable man. He has longtime senior chartered accountancy experience, including analysing many legal cases at the highest levels. He is also an accomplished yachtsman with considerable knowledge, involving maritime navigation and publishing. Then there is his private flying, with night rating and IMC rating.

He is a most intelligent and versatile person. Remarkably his aviation interest was forever piqued by a New Zealand flight in 1962 when he was a young teenager. It was in a de Havilland biplane over the Southern Alps, flown by the redoubtable Captain Brian Chadwick, ex RAF, and one of the post-war pioneers of provincial and scenic flying in the South Island. I doubt Robin would have written this book if it wasn't for that memorable flight all those years ago; just weeks before Captain Chadwick and his four passengers disappeared without trace. Take a look again at the rear cover photograph of this book with young Robin standing next to Chadwick.

Writing a foreword for Robin's new book is a privilege. Maybe I was asked because my parents were born and raised in England with my father, Brian Waugh, serving in the RAF every day of World War II, and later a flying colleague and friend of Brian Chadwick? Or because my research and writing over 30 years about New Zealand airlines includes several airliner accidents? Perhaps due to my instigating role for the Erebus National Memorial? More likely, the reason can be found in my book, LOST … without trace? Brian Chadwick and the missing Dragonfly, where I posed a cautionary sentence, "Reading this book may give you Dragonfly Fever; a condition of nervous enthusiasm when thinking about the Dragonfly ZK-AFB. Can lead to a compulsion to try and find it!" I would say Robin Fautley has a severe dose of Dragonfly Fever! Yet he has put such preoccupation to very good use indeed. In this new book Robin investigates in innovative and insightful ways the surprising interwoven links between various air accidents. It all makes for sobering reading due to the serious nature of the subject, the human suffering which resulted from each of the accidents, and lessons still to be learnt. The author knowledgeably and skillfully analyses the various accidents and describes many serious failures by accident investigators. In years past "Blame the Pilot" was an all too common fall-back opinion, and the author challenges such contentions with careful scrutiny, new information and important reflections.

Yes, Robin does reminisce back to his memorable flight with Brian Chadwick, as well as making a lucid and impassioned case about the Aero Commander accident and discerning studies about other air accidents too. But the heart of this book is about the Mt. Erebus DC-10 accident. It is clear to me as an airline historian that as the years and decades have passed since the 1979 Mt. Erebus air accident, we now have a much better perspective and more correct interpretation of the key events. Not only because of the passage of time but because of new information now available – and not accessible to the Royal Commission and Judge Mahon. We now live in a different context compared with the 1980s, 1990s and early 2000s, and in the face of new evidence and more accurate analysis, rational conclusions can be drawn. There is now much less heat and much more reason when considering the causes of the Antarctica air accident. In fact today I would doubt that there are any reputable aviation commentators who would seek to defend Chief Inspector Ron Chippindale's report or the actions of Air New Zealand and some of the airline staff of the time.

This book examines the Erebus accident in new and creative ways. The author's comments about Judges McMullin and Woodhouse and their biased behaviour is quite arresting, as is Diplock's forgetfulness regarding his own earlier judgement on natural justice. Then there is the basic change made to ICAO annex 13 reporting from the proximate cause of a crash to a review of all the circumstances that led to the accident, including the human mindset. Another factor is the recognition of and treatment of PTSD. Once again the intransigence of Ron Chippindale is revealed. It is patently unjust that his report with so many fundamental errors still continues to have some official standing today.

We are very soon approaching the 45th anniversary of the Mt. Erebus DC-10 accident. Robin Fautley's book contributes new insights and information for aviation safety and proper air accident investigation practices. So its content is opportune and relevant.

In a previous publication I contended that it behoves all air accident investigators to be persistent in their search for accurate causes of air accidents, and not pre-occupied with the last stages of an accident timeline, so that pertinent lessons can be learnt and changes made for improved aviation safety. Sometimes in subsequent years, with deeper understanding, new evidence, and through taking a broader perspective, it can be shown that an air accident report has been sub-standard or even incorrect in significant ways. In such situations there should be ready and transparent rectification. There is no place in air accident investigation for pride, secrecy or arrogance. The search for truth and a just culture must be paramount and unrelenting.

Rev. Dr Richard Waugh QSM

Aviation Historian, Christchurch, New Zealand
February 2024

FOREWORD BY STUART MACFARLANE

In his research for this book Robin made a startling discovery about the Privy Council judge (Lord Diplock) who wrote that court's decision. It started when Mahon said in his report the Air New Zealand witnesses had told him an orchestrated litany of lies. The New Zealand Court of Appeal said that although they would not decide whether in fact the witnesses had or had not told him an orchestrated litany of lies, the law did not permit him to say so. The court said:

> Once the thesis of such a conspiracy had emerged in the Commissioner's thinking as something upon which he might report, he would have had power, if that question were indeed reasonably incidental to his terms of reference, to reconvene the hearing if necessary so that the alleged conspirators could be fairly confronted with the allegation.

> All these considerations suggest that the Commission was bound by the broad requirements of natural justice. These included a reasonable opportunity of meeting the unformulated allegation of organised deception and concealment that was apparently passing through the Commission's mind.

Diplock (in the Erebus appeal to the Privy Council) agreed. So I asked Mahon why he had not done what the courts said he should have done. Mahon replied that he had only followed the binding precedent in the English Court of Appeal case of Maxwell v. Department of Trade. That had held he did not need to do so.

The disturbing fact which Robin discovered was that Diplock, in the House of Lords case of Hoffmann La Roche, had agreed with Maxwell v. Department of Trade. Therefore Diplock, in Erebus, should have held that Mahon was correct, and did not need to do what the New Zealand Court of Appeal said he should have done.

Stuart Macfarlane

Formerly a senior lecturer in law at the University of Auckland

INTRODUCTION

I had never thought about writing a book until two brothers living in New Zealand recognised that I had a remarkable story to tell. It was the emergence of an ancient film on the flight of one person who had been at the heart of their family's historic aviation connections which caught their imagination. As the film was seen by more and more folk interested in New Zealand aviation, I was blessed by their new information arising from memories triggered by the film. In February 2023, I was asked to give a presentation, albeit from afar, to a meeting of over 100 people still interested in the subject of that film. That was some 61 years after the disappearance of Captain Brian Chadwick, his three Australian and one New Zealander passengers in the DH90A Dragonfly ZK-AFB on 12th February 1962.

This book is a result of that interest within Australian and New Zealand aviation circles. That interest was reawakened following the discovery of my 8mm cine film of Brian Chadwick who was at the centre of innovatory post-war tourist flights through the spectacular scenery of the Southern Alps of the South Island. I had scanned and transmitted the film to New Zealand showing the trip in the other Air Charter's aircraft, Dominie DH89 – ZK-BCP. I cannot thank enough those who have helped, not least being Richard and Alec Waugh, the Reeve family, Gavin Grimmer and Lew Bone.

The film in question was made in 1962 by my father and mother, Albert and Daisy Fautley. I was fortunate to accompany them as a young teenager. When the film was first seen in New Zealand in 2021, it was quickly recognised as the only film of that pilot, Brian Chadwick – and his pioneering trans alpine flying. About three weeks after my flight, Chadwick and his passengers disappeared on a flight in Air Charter's other aircraft DH90A Dragonfly ZK-AFB with the same end destination as that filmed by my parents.

This new evidence, albeit more than 60 years old, has helped inspire more searches. The latest official search and rescue exercise by the NZ police was carried out in February 2023. Some further private searches have recommenced.

In the course of distribution of the film and contact with many noted aviators and writers, I have had the privilege of being the recipient of so much new information not disclosed before with respect to New Zealand aviation. I acknowledge Reverend Dr Richard Waugh QSM and his brother retired Police Superintendent Alec Waugh who first recognised the unique position I found myself in and the information I had been given. Originally, I wrote the manuscript not so much for a book but for a series of presentations for interested aviation parties. Therefore, it was intended as a verbal script to go with those presentations.

The selection of the eight cases that I intended for those meetings selected themselves but they are in so many ways all linked in fascinating ways. They show that many aviation lessons have not been learnt. These cases, included the largest aerial search at the time and still continuing (unsuccessful so far) in New Zealand history for a missing aircraft, for that Dragonfly of Chadwick, as well as what is still the worst aircraft accident in the Southern Hemisphere in terms of numbers of souls lost, the Mt Erebus accident with 257 fatalities. The air hours spent searching for the Dragonfly was only superseded by the two-week-old search for a helicopter of Michael Erceg ZK-HTF in 2005. Erceg was one of the richest New Zealanders and virtually every helicopter available was thrown into the search. Hence the air-hours far exceeded the search for the Dragonfly. I provide more details of that search in chapter eight as most of the search time for that helicopter was an uncoordinated complete waste of time and to compare that with the search for the Dragonfly, most unreasonable.

Initially, the links may not be that obvious but when you add the names of the pilots, the reasons for the accidents and the controversies from the resulting air accident investigations by the respective chief inspectors of accidents, it is clear that new action is necessary, particularly in view of ICAO and annex 13. Are prosecutions under health and safety acts appropriate and could they hinder air safety improvements, contrary to the aims of ICAOs Annex 13?

I must also apologize for inconsistencies in the spelling of some names, principally that of one CIAA inspector who appears in most of the investigations, and that is Ron Chippindale. I also apologize to those whose log books and emails record his name being spelled as Chippendale. One of the principal websites show that his report to the New Zealand Minister of Transport 79-139 dated 31 May 1980 and approved by that minister, Colin McLachlan, on 12 June 1980 record the Inspector's name as R. Chippendale on page 3. As one main cause of the accident in Antarctica was also a typographical error, namely the recording of a coordinate of 166.48 as being 164.48, greater care should have been taken regarding typos. But then later, in another international investigation into the accident that caused the death of President Machell, again there was another conflicting spelling of Chippindale's name. Or was it Chippendale?

The printed report of the Royal Commission of Inquiry into the Erebus tragedy, the Mahon Report, contained typos, such as that on page 89 when important numbers had been misprinted, 160 instead of 169 for a coordinate and 1969 being shown in place of 1979. So when you come across any of my missed typos, my defence is that I may be trying to retain the tradition of the typo club with a deliberate mistake. I hope it does not spoil the reading.

My sources of information.

Whilst a number of books have been studied in the quest to research the loss of Captain Brian Chadwick as well as all the many tomes on the Mt. Erebus saga, it has been the other source of information, personal contact via the internet that has proved most interesting. Other sources include New Zealand newspaper articles, podcasts particularly Lizzie Oakes and her website -erebusengravedonourhearts.co.nz, not forgetting the 2019 White Silence by Mike Wright, and Erebus Flight 901; Litany of Lies 2019, John Keir director. I am indebted to the Rev Dr. Richard Waugh not least for his many books but also prolific articles. Considering that it was first published in 1995, John King's NZ Tragedies Aviation Accidents and Disasters has excellent summaries of some crashes that are also my subject incidents, not least Erebus. Finally, without "Erebus Papers" by Stuart Macfarlane, no comments on the legal issues that arose after the Mt. Erebus accident can be made without some reference to this excellent book.

I have exchanged emails with so many of those involved directly in some of these air accidents. These communications have constantly proved to contain so many more elements of the missing jigsaw pieces that sometime show a new or different picture to many books published earlier and newspaper articles, finally not least the transcripts of the associated court cases. The emails have provided the most valuable contributions to the contents of this book. Official Reports require revision.

With regard to the Dragonfly mystery, a key source of previously unpublished information, has come from Dragonfly searchers that I know of and have communicated with. The Reeve family, Gavin Grimmer and Lew Bone are currently at the head of the list of searchers. Some folk have been kind enough to add comments to the brief YouTube clip of the 1962 rare film of Chadwick's flight in the Dominie to Milford and Queenstown, returning to Christchurch.

There were many others in connection with the Erebus saga who have added their personal stories which explain so much that went on behind the headlines. These insights have helped assist my new viewpoints on various aspects of aviation, especially in New Zealand. In particular, pilots who were involved in the original 1962 search for the Dragonfly. Later, one accompanied the Chief Accident Inspector to Antarctica in 1979, and tried to take on Air New Zealand CEO Morrie Davis during the subsequent Mahon Inquiry.

Likewise, via YouTube, I have come across comments posted by Roger, a son of one of the executive pilots, Maynard Hawkins. This gave me another viewpoint of Erebus and the contradictions prevailing in some New Zealand aviation circles. Erebus was and still is so important for all the lessons to be learnt. The parallels of flight TE901 to the Ice of Antarctica and the earlier Dominie/Dragonfly flights over the Ice of the Glaciers and mountains of New Zealand are so plain, as well as the continuing importance of finding that missing Dragonfly with the data that it hides.

Both flights were pure sightseeing. Fuel levels and the aircraft respective ranges were the only restrictive factors. One was a modern DC-10 jet, the other was a deluxe, albeit pre-war, de Haviland biplane, once considered to be the ultimate in personal executive transport.

Some names crop up from New Zealand history in interesting ways. In 1855 a James Mackenzie stole 1,000 sheep from Rhodes's farm at Timaru. Rhodes searched for Mackenzie who was caught at Lindis Pass. Mackenzie was subsequently convicted. But the area was thereafter named Mackenzie country, not Rhodes. In 1962 another Rhodes, Peter, searched in the Mackenzie country for Brian Chadwick and his Dragonfly, but that search was not so successful.

All these accidents, even spread from one side of the world to the other are all linked more closely than anyone can realise. What are the lessons that can be learnt from each of them? I will share what I have learnt and illustrate what lessons were missed.

CHAPTER CASE LINKS

What are the links between the case studies chapters and why were these air accidents selected for specialist study? They are arranged in date order of the incidents, which led to the accident investigation. The first chapter sets the scene for the central character whose family have been involved in some of the following incidents in one way or another. That character was Brian Waugh whose first accident was in 1954 in a pre-war de Havilland biplane. His accident was caused by a wrong digit supplied in the pilot's weather forecast. Fortunately, no lives were lost when the DH89 Rapide accumulated ice. The pilot believed the icing level was 15,000 feet when it was only 1,500 feet (chapter.1.)

Contrast this with the loss of 257 lives in Antarctica due to a coordinate with the number four replacing the number six into the navigation system of the DC-10 and its untimely reversal (chapter 6). The pilot of the Rapide, after being prosecuted for unsafe flying, moved to New Zealand to fly early regional air routes.

The second chapter, although that took place in 1961 is still subject of much controversy. The accident was in the centre of North Island, New Zealand again on the slopes of a volcano. The study shows the differing global standards of air accident investigation. The United Nations agency, namely the International Civil Aviation Organisation (ICAO) has Annex 13 which is the basis for the standard of reporting of those accidents. The aim of Annex 13 is the prevention of repetition of Air Accidents by the investigation concentrating on the cause of an accident and not the allocation of blame.

The success of Annex 13 has been the improvement in the safety of air transport over other means of transport. The standard of reporting under Annex 13 is variable and the case of New Zealand's standard of investigation in study no.2 is a prime example of failure to achieve the aims of ICAO. Three chief inspectors were involved covering the period 1961 through to 1998. None of them achieved an accurate report of the 1961 accident and continued to attribute the accident to pilot error. To this day New Zealand's responsible agency for transportation accident investigation has yet to show it is now capable of recognising a repeat of a similar cause of air accidents. It is now the Transport Accident Investigation Commission (TAIC).

The third chapter involves two ancient biplanes, de Havilland DH89 and DH90 designs. The pilot was a friend of Brian Waugh with similar RAF service and origins in the north of England and then in New Zealand. They were employees of the same two small airlines until Brian Chadwick set up his own independent charter business. I was one of Chadwick's last passengers just two or three weeks prior to his disappearance in February 1962. Our flight was recorded on film by my parents as well as the photograph taken by my father being included in the biography of Chadwick's former colleague. That biography was "Turbulent Years" written by Brian Waugh, and finally published in 1991. The manuscript was edited and published by Waugh's son Richard, who in turn became one of New Zealand's foremost civil aviation historians. It was only by chance that my parents had been introduced to Chadwick's Air Charter by the parents of the pilot of chapter no.2, Salvation Army Brigadier and Mrs Albert Bartlett of Christchurch. Pure coincidence.

The fourth case chapter is that of the accident on the Kaimai Range involving the ubiquitous DC-3 that had occurred in 1963. I have selected this incident for a number of reasons, not least that it was responsible for the greatest loss of life, 23 souls, on New Zealand soil. Another reason is that the accident investigation was also followed by a formal inquiry, not unlike the situation of Erebus. I had believed that the inquiries led to improvements in safety with changes to navigation beacons as well as installation of upgraded beacons so that there would not be a repetition of that accident. That is exactly the purpose of ICAO Annex 13 investigations. It was only when I came across the interpretation of the accident by the Air Traffic Control officer who had radio contact with the DC-3 from Auckland airport at Whenuapai until handover to the ATCs at Tauranga, just two minutes before the aircraft hit the highest point of the Kaimai Range. It made me curious about a possible cover-up by the authorities and pressure on individuals to withhold the truth. Erebus included the repetition of threats against employees for telling the truth which may have been the main cause of an accident.

An interesting side issue arising from the Kaimai tragedy was the construction 40 years later of a memorial in remembrance of the victims and their relations. Closure for these friends and relations can never be complete. However, being able to make contact with a physical memorial where one can touch that friend or relation's name has a certain spiritual warmth and importance of remembrance. The memorial, instigated by Richard Waugh, Graeme McConnell and fellow historians in 2003 was based on the seating plan which showed the places of the passengers of flight 441. When the memorial was being constructed, the names of the crew and passengers were displayed showing those positions. When the relatives visit the memorial site, seeing and touching the names of the loved ones and their neighbouring passengers has a comforting effect on those relatives. Sadly, the similar memorial being planned for the victims of the Erebus tragedy has yet to be settled both as to design and location. The Waugh family are well aware of the benefits of these memorials and have been working hard in raising awareness as well as implementation. Richard Waugh is chaplain to the guild, now "Honourable Company", of airline pilots and in that role has been in the forefront of planning of many air accident memorials.

The fifth chapter involved once again the same pilot who was the centre of case study no.1, Brian Waugh. Waugh's son, Richard, had the presence of mind that the archive of letters to and from the Air Accident Inspector Ted Harvie would make a useful reference book, being based on the actual exchanges between a pilot under investigation and the accident inspector. In 1967, air accident investigation had improved globally by comparison with the fifties and early sixties. But not in New Zealand. Harvie was a highly respected figure in NZ aviation having been a pioneer aviator himself, and had flown with notables in NZ history like George Bolt and Francis Chichester. Due to Harvie's reputation, when "Blame the Pilot" attribution was being considered by Harvie, Brian Waugh was at a disadvantage initially. It took a lot of hard investigating over a period including a reference to the Ombudsman that the ditching into the Shotover River, short of the Queenstown runway, was not labelled as pilot error.

Waugh's tangle with the Shotover River in 1967 was well before the ditching into Botany Bay by DC-3 pilot Rod Lovell in 1994 and the similar but higher profile ditching in New York's Hudson River in January 2009 of the A320 Airbus of Sully Sullenberger. However, all three incidents involved loss of useable engine power for various reasons. The first two being poor maintenance and lack of appropriate supervision by the authorities. That led to cover-ups by employees of those authorities. The third case was bird strike and the ingestion of geese into both jet engines shortly after take-off. The remarkable thing of all three incidents was that the considerable skill of the pilots was such that there was no loss of life. However, even Sullenberger's decision making when he had just 208 seconds was questioned at first with a possible blame the pilot attribution. As for Lovell, he had even less time, only 46 seconds. In Waugh's situation, possibly even less. Sullenberger was fortunate by comparison due to the facilities and expertise of the investigators with their simulators' assistance.

There is a somewhat tenuous connection between Brian Waugh and the Erebus tragedy. The judge whose precedent decision that should have been followed was Lord Denning. He came to fame for his Inquiry into the Profumo affair and breaches of national security at Cliveden House alongside the Thames. Christine Keeler, Mandy Rice-Davis, Lord and Lady Astor, a Russian spy and osteopath Stephen Ward and their parties were all catered for by the services of the Waugh family, specifically the grandfather of Brian Waugh being in charge of the electricity and utility services in such a great house. It was at Cliveden House and the Profumo affair that Denning's reputation was first brought to major public attention. He would not have achieved such a high legal profile that covered the Maxwellisation common law of natural justice that addressed the legal issues on which Mahon was right to report in his stylish way the lying in chapter 6.

The sixth chapter involved the Erebus accident and the loss of 257 lives in the DC-10 crash in November 1979. At the time it was the fourth worst loss of life in an air accident. Even now, it is the worst air accident in the Southern Hemisphere. How can this catastrophe have any direct connection with the earlier case studies? There were two direct links with the search for the DH90 Dragonfly of Brian Chadwick on 12th February 1962. The search for the missing Dragonfly ZK-AFB once involved the largest search for a missing aircraft, until just exceeded by the 2005 Erceg extravagant use of uncoordinated helicopter searches, in New Zealand's history.

Brian Waugh never stopped looking for his erstwhile friend Chadwick whenever he was flying his DH89 Dominie but the Government organised search party was led by RNZAF pilots in two Harvard aircraft with other air support for communications with high-flying Constellations and DH Devons. Two of those young pilots became pilots for Air New Zealand, they were Roger Dalziell and Peter Rhodes. They were central characters in the Erebus story. Dalziell was the only Antarctica pilot who did not take his passengers over the Antarctic research stations and Scott's hut on Ross Island. He had to divert to the South Magnetic Pole. No doubt that was a disappointment for his fare paying passengers on the 7th November 1979 trip and subsequent pilots, including Collins and Cassin, were under some pressure not to disappoint their passengers. The other young pilot who searched extensively for Chadwick was Peter Rhodes. There were many other widespread searches by light aircraft as well as the Harvard's of Rhodes and Dalziell. Almost certainly, those hours of aerial search times expended were not fully recorded during the official search period. Thereafter, many pilots continued to look for their "buddy" Chadwick during their routine commercial flights. Not least by Brian Waugh.

Rhodes was one of the pilots in the search for the Dragonfly, during which he had to devise a safe method of searching the valleys in the Southern Alps around Mounts Tasman and Cook. Rhodes later became invaluable as the most up to date trained air accident investigator. He had participated in training courses in Australia which caused the postponement of his promotion to a full captain from being a First Officer for the Air NZ DC-10 fleet. Rhodes was Chippindale's choice of assistant from ALPA alongside the controversial Ian Gemmell, who was chief pilot for Air New Zealand. During the Royal Commission into the Erebus Inquiry, Rhodes was the only witness called by both sides of the Mahon inquiry. His investigations were both on the ice in Antarctica, then at the US McMurdo Station and the New Zealand Scott Base. His subsequent evidence to the Royal

Commission was central to Mahon's report and Rhodes controversial evidence reviewed within the judgments of the judicial reviews in the NZ Court of Appeal and again at the Privy Council, so important was his technical and visual evidence.

The seventh chapter was on the other side of the globe to New Zealand. It involved the only scheduled passenger helicopter flights linking the enchanted Isles of Scilly with the mainland at Penzance. Scilly had been a noted favourite playground for Brian Waugh for his air charter work in 1953. Scilly is almost as beautiful as the South Island of New Zealand. But pilots can be fooled by visual phenomena when flying VFR. Despite years of experience and deep knowledge of Scilly, the two helicopter pilots had been unaware of the sea fog masking the fact that they were inadvertently descending and so hit the water at cruising speed. 20 out of 26 passengers and crew on board were killed. This was in 1983 and the full benefits from the accident reports of the tragedy at Erebus were not yet known. I refer to visual illusions highlighted by Gordon Vette's studies. Vette's contribution to air safety was delayed, due in part to the controversies with the judicial reviews still to be settled at the Privy Council later that same year.

Had the input from Captain Gordon Vette's investigation on visual phenomena been available for study by pilots worldwide, the Isles of Scilly air accident may never have happened. It was only by coincidence that I was on a subsequent flight that year with a survivor's sibling, that another version of what may have happened emerged. The loss of 20 souls, most of whom were islanders with a permanent population of about 2,000 was devastating. It still is remembered to this day.

My eighth and final chapter was that of another helicopter disappearance in 2004 in the Southern Alps of New Zealand. Its occurrence became the trigger for the search for my parents' old holiday film of Chadwick and his biplanes. Nearly nine years later, the missing helicopter was discovered just two miles from its last reporting point. To my extended family, it had personal connections as the passenger was my stepson and daughter-in-law's family friend. They were living in New Zealand at the time. Only recently when I look at the films of my stepson's wedding did I realise that the passenger was one of the guests, together with other members of her family and seeing her on the wedding video as well as her name on the table plans at the subsequent reception brought it home to me of the effect any air accident has on the family and friends, irrespective of whether just two or 257 lives are lost. There has to be a lesson learnt from this case. How it was eventually found has to provide a lesson for those other missing aircraft in the Southern Alps. The purpose for including this air accident is that the failure to find the missing aircraft in such a restricted search area has to question the search methods and organisation. What lessons were learned from this case that may assist the search for the other missing aircraft in that same inhospitable region? Two New Zealand aviation authors, Chris Rudge and Gavin Grimmer, make this one of their main reasons for writing about these incidents.

Anything that can be done to avoid making the same mistakes has to be foremost. On a review of the accident reports, the old blame the pilot attribution has been used too often to cover up previous systemic failure by the same organisation carrying out the investigation. There are artificial independence walls separating the functions of the accident inspectorates with the Civil Aviation Authorities but at the end of the day, funding is still required by the same state's authority and its taxpayers. Justice must be done, and seen to be done! Particularly after the scandalous Mt. Erebus first accident report.

CHAPTER 1

AN ADDED ZERO

Details for chapter 1 -Rapide G-AFMF 19 February 1954 Newcastle to Dublin. The pilot Brian Waugh. Icing levels.

Background

The Pilot was an experienced aviator for the time and had been flying for a few years based in the North of England. In 1951, he flew from Woolsington, now Newcastle Airport, and whilst there he became a friend of fellow pilot, Brian Chadwick, who will become a familiar name later. The weather was always poor in the North of England in those days for light aircraft charter flying and Waugh's experience and ability to fly IFR (Instrument Flight Rules) in IMC conditions was more than useful. Like all pilots of the time, he enjoyed flying VFR (Visually) out of cloud within sight of the ground and well ahead.

One of his most memorable flights took place in 1953. That was to the Isles of Scilly, an archipelago just 28 miles from the UK's Land's End. They are one of the most enchanted group of islands anywhere in the world, almost as good as the most scenic parts of New Zealand. Whilst there, he became a member of the famous Scillonian Mal de Mers club, playing football, cricket and most importantly Golf, winning the scratch cup. Years later, I too became a country member of that same golf club. The problem for aviation in the early fifties in the UK was however, its weather. Waugh's log book showed mainly instrument flying until he approached the enchanted Isles of Scilly.

Richard Waugh has kindly supplied the details of one such charter from his father's log book of the time. I have summarised these log book entries as follows:

30.9.53 Newcastle to Elmdon (now Birmingham International Airport) 2.15 flying hours, charter 5 passengers. (178 miles)

30.9.53 Elmdon to Cardiff 1.10 flying hours (instrument flying 0.10) 100 miles.

30.9.53 Cardiff to Scillies 2.15 flying hours (instrument flying 0.30) 170 miles – [This indicates that he must had had quite a strong headwind.]

3.10.53 Scillies to St Just .15 flying hours, private.

3.10.53 St Just to Scillies .20 flying hours, private

7.10.53 Scillies to Elmdon 2.25 flying hours, charter 6 passengers (instrument flying 0.30) [268 miles]

7.10.53 Elmdon to Newcastle 1.40 flying hours, charter 5 passengers (instrument flying 0.10) [178 miles]

Other than around Scilly there was no VFR flying on that trip But what a welcome break it was.

Synopsis of Accident

On 19th February 1954, Waugh had a charter party with the DH89 Rapide G-AFMF - to fly the boxing team from Durham University. There were seven in the team flying from Newcastle to Dublin. Pre-flight checks were carried out and weather reports obtained. These included the statistic that the freezing level, which is always an important factor when flying light aircraft in the English winter, was stated to be 15,000 feet. At least, that was the figure written on Waugh's weather report as he later vehemently attested. Despite some misgivings that this may have been unusually high for winter, Waugh accepted this at face value, so he flight-planned for 6,000 feet above cloud. However, the true freezing level was 1,500 feet. The flight should not have taken place. After take-off, the Rapide rapidly accumulated ice, became uncontrollable and crashed.

In the official inquiry (CAP 122) it was claimed that the actual weather report given to the pilot was snow and sleet on hills with a freezing level of 1500 ft. Two reports alluding to icing were alleged to have been shown to the pilot who filed a flight plan with a cruising level of 6000ft. When he took off, the cloud base was 500ft. The pilot could not make contact with Preston on his radio and believing this to be due to his low altitude he climbed. At 3,000ft. he noticed the windscreen was icing until it became opaque. He also saw that the air speed indicator readings were fluctuating. In order to see out the pilot opened the side panels and then observed that thick ice was forming on the wing edges and on the inter-plane bracing.

Waugh was in fact very lucky that when he closed the engines again, almost immediately the aircraft became out-of-control and struck the ground. It hit soft moorland at a spot 220m above sea level and bounded six metres and then caught fire. It seemed that the aircraft had a low forward speed and as the aircraft was almost level, that must have cushioned the impact in ground effect.

Fortunately, the members of the Durham University boxing team were not badly hurt and only three were in hospital for a short time. One can speculate that these were strong, tough, fit, young athletes, and somehow, despite the aircraft spinning into the ground, such fitness proved their salvation.

Not so for the pilot. His long-lasting injury was to his smashed ankle and many years later, in 1967, another crash and injury to the other ankle caused Waugh's final retirement from flying (chapter 5) ZK-AKT 16/04/1967. The investigation began with the usual assumption of blame the pilot. This being the starting point for most accident inspectors. In those days, Waugh relates some of the details in his book "Turbulent Years". I believe that this was the origin of the Waugh family's enthusiasm for book writing but modesty forbids son Richard Waugh taking any credit for his father's readable masterpiece of New Zealand aviation history.

Whilst the name of the ministry inspector from that Newcastle UK Accident Investigation Department is unknown, Waugh labelled him a real gestapo type and thereafter was critical of the ability of most accident inspectors he encountered later in New Zealand. The inspector appeared to be the typical retired officer from the Royal Air Force who found his niche in the Civil Service. That inspector issued an official report and the court basically accepted that the experienced pilot should have known that icing starting at 15,000 feet was wrong. If this sounds a familiar description of a character involved in subsequent case studies, that is no accident. A reminder of a certain Ron Chippindale, see later studies. The true cause of the crash had been icing at 1,500 feet.

Waugh's claim about the weather report of 15,000 feet icing level was not accepted or believed. The meteorologist lied about the 15,000 feet typo and produced a forged carbon copy indicating 1500 feet. But carbon copies were not made before the incident with G-AFMF. Without the hard documentary evidence of the piece of paper that had been burnt in the crash, Waugh was prosecuted in a court of law. He said "I was the first commercial pilot to be charged in a civil court after an air crash — what fame !!!" The judgment of the civil court statement was as follows:

> A pilot holding a commercial licence should have suspected some mistake because of the earlier forecast of icing above 600m (2,000 ft.) The Court concluded that the pilot was in error in making the flight.

It is noticed that an official inquiry was held (CAP 122). It sounded as if the pilot was always to be blamed when it comes to icing. If the pilot has no de-icing equipment, he ought to foresee when icing is likely and not make the flight. The lesson is never to trust a weather forecast which appears suspect. Interestingly, Brian Waugh went on after his 1967 accident to become a member of the meteorological service and trained at Christchurch. Hopefully he never added an incorrect zero to pilots' weather forecasts.

Fast forward 50 years, the first Drone pilot to be prosecuted in New Zealand was one of the foremost hunters for the Dragonfly ZK-AFB. I refer to Simon Reeve of the White Bus Family, film-makers from Christchurch. However, in Reeve's case, common-sense was used by the judge as the precise rules for flying drones in New Zealand had not yet been developed sufficiently to warrant a conviction. There were also doubts about the veracity of the helicopter pilot who complained. Not long after that incident, the helicopter pilot was himself killed in an air accident. So a donation to charity was substituted by the judge in place of a formal conviction.

There are important lessons here. The change of one digit in data received by a pilot can lead to catastrophic results. In Brian Waugh's case the 15,000 including the addition of that incorrect 0 (zero) when in fact icing commenced at 1,500 feet.

In chapter 6, the reverse of the coordinate figures 166 to 164 back to 166 was in the simplest terms the main factor of the Erebus crash with the loss of 257 lives. The Dan Air flight 1008 in April 1980 at Tenerife had a similar typo problem, with the loss of 146 lives. See later comments in chapter 6 re Erebus but that involved a seemingly minor verbal error by Spanish ATC. The Spanish ATC had indicated a holding pattern that was not possible for a Boeing 727 to fly.

It is clear that the unfair UK prosecution of Brian Waugh of 1954 was the last straw for him and his family, so that the temptation of a fantastic life in New Zealand promised by his former flying colleague, Brian Chadwick, could not possibly be turned down (chapter 3). That was the commencement of the Waugh dynasty in New Zealand. That dynasty was not just flying aircraft, but the beginning of a production line of aviation publications starting with "Turbulent Years" written by Brian Waugh himself. One of Brian's sons - Rev. Dr Richard Waugh, followed with numerous books, and Richard is now established as a respected civil aviation historian. Everyone I have had contact with during the writing of this book say that he is one of the foremost aviation historians in New Zealand. He is currently President of the respected Aviation Historical Society of New Zealand. Past Presidents include Brian Lockstone, former Press Secretary to the notorious former New Zealand Prime Minister Robert Muldoon, heavily involved in the Mt. Erebus saga (Chapter 6).

There was a book published in 1958 "Danger in the Air" by Oliver Stuart. Early as that was in aviation, there was a chapter on Icing and the effect it has on airframes and engines. Lessons were not learned in a number of accidents. The Mahon Inquiry did lead to massive changes in the way all accidents were subsequently investigated. That included the methods of investigation of different types of accidents, not just aviation-based accidents. For example, ICAO refers to Bhopal Gas, Union Carbide 1984, Chernobyl 1986, Kings Cross fire 1987, and the rail disaster at Clapham Junction 1988., all as a result of the Mahon and Vette improved studies of accident reporting.

Currently the largest air accident in Canada was that of the Arrow Air Flight 1285 on 12th December 1985 with a DC-8. The loss of life was 256, all due to carelessness in de-icing. Oliver Stuart's book should have provided the lessons but a similar problem arose at Dryden in Canada due to poor de-icing procedures. That case on 10th March 1989 was blessed by the investigation of Virgil Moshansky, using similar techniques to that by Mahon, except that Moshansky was not aware of the methods of Mahon in 1989. The Mahon report was only officially recognised and made available world-wide by ICAO many years later in 1999 when the Hon. Maurice Williamson was able to have the report accepted in the New Zealand Parliament.

By chance, Durham was the university of choice for one step-daughter and so far two grandsons. I was even briefly a temporary coach for one ladies rowing team. That embarrassed my step-daughter who was in that team, but they won the cup.

Main source of information

"Turbulent Years" – A Commercial Pilots Story by Brian Waugh.
Subsequent email exchanges with two of his sons, the Reverend Dr Richard Waugh and Alec Waugh his brother.
"Danger in the Air" by Oliver Stewart quoting Official Inquiry CAP 122 of 1954.

Some Waugh books come with a warning as to the consequences of reading them, such as "Dragonfly Fever" being the urge to search for the Dragonfly and Chadwick after reading the "Lost without Trace?" book. Turbulent Years did not! When I first started to read, it was impossible to put on one side to get on with my work. When I complained to his son, Richard Waugh, I was admonished as follows:

> *"The name of the publishers should have warned you – Hazard Press."*

CHAPTER 2

WING FRACTURES

Details for chapter 2 - ZK-BWA Mt Ruapehu 21/11/1961– Bay of Plenty Airways
Captain Alf Bartlett – Aircraft Aero Commander Persons on board 5 + Bartlett.
Review of accident report by E F (Ted) Harvie on 11 April 1972 revision released
by Chippindale on 16/1/1984

Synopsis.

This was a flight from Wellington to Rotorua and Tauranga. A wing spar fractured and the
starboard wing fell off as the aircraft flew through severe turbulence near the summit of
Mt Ruapehu. The accident was witnessed by an experienced pilot Roy Turner. Years later
Turner himself disappeared near Franz Josef Glacier with his family in a Cessna C172
– ZK-CSS. Photographs recovered from the crash had been taken by Mr Irvine Down, a
passenger who was sitting next to the pilot, Alf Bartlett. Those photographs assisted the
competent experts called in during the 1970s and 1980s. Particularly photograph no.4.

For many years, Alfred William Bartlett, who was a friend of Brian Waugh, had been
blamed for the crash and was accused of flying too close to Mt Ruapehu. In 1961/2 the
CIAA (chief inspector of Air Accidents) was Wing Commander Paddy O'Brien. He was
assisted by Ted Harvie, more of him later. It took a number of the pilot's colleagues who
could not believe Bartlett was careless, to try to bring justice for the reputation of the ill-
fated pilot. Fast forward to the DC-10 1979 crash in Antarctica, Bartlett's reputation was
afforded the same type of support from those that knew him. Just like the colleagues of
Collins and Cassin, pilots of the Erebus tragedy, when Gordon Vette and the New Zealand
Airline Pilots Association (NZALPA) came to examine the allegations of Chippindale
CIAA in 1979.

It took years of painstaking and costly research by the friends of Bartlett to identify metal fatigue as being the sole cause of the wing separation. A prominent campaigner for Bartlett's exoneration was Mount Cook ski-plane pilot, John Stokes. Stokes was also one of many who searched for Chadwick, see chapter 3. Even to this day, aviation historian Richard Waugh and others are still campaigning for the full exoneration for Alf Bartlett.

Professors Les Erasmus and Neil Mowbray were able to show that Bartlett should not have been held to blame, and so the original report dated 14th February 1962 needed to be withdrawn. It was withdrawn by another draft report prepared by Ted Harvie this time on 11th April 1972. Eventually on 16th January 1984 it was the chief inspector of air accidents of that time, Ron Chippindale, more about him later, who formally replaced the report which he dated 14th February 1961 (sic). Such typos abound with Chippindale. The date of the first report was actually later - 14th February 1962. Sometimes this chief inspector of air accident's name was spelled Chippendale and Chippindale especially in official documents. emails to me from his contemporaries have his name mainly spelled with an "e" and thus I sometimes continue with their choice of spelling.

This was another example of blame the pilot by so-called expert inspectors of aircraft accidents. The pilot was an experienced aviator running a small airline providing the community an important pioneering service so required by New Zealand in late 1961. In brief, the aircraft for its time was a modern all weather IFR approved design providing speed and comfort. Unfortunately, there was a construction/design fault and weakness in the main wing-spar of this aircraft genre. This design fault was not recognised or admitted for years by the manufacturers – Rockwell.

As misfortune would have it, this accident was the first of many to the Aero Commander genre, which were all subject to this same design weakness. Personally, I believe that it was a construction mistake. The main wing spar with its caps was cold-bent by five degrees both sides of the fuselage to produce a dihedral and then again bent forward by another five degrees. Any bending of metal involves initiating a degree of weakness at the bend site. This bending took place at wing station 24, or 39 on the longer wing version, and all the hairline fractures commenced at that point. The New Zealand accident inspectors did not realised how bad the fracture was in the spar caps of this Aero Commander due to inexperience of metal fatigue in 1961. Instead, the captain, Alf Bartlett, was initially accused of Pilot Error allowing the propellers to hit Mount Ruapehu, by flying too low and colliding with the volcano.

This alleged collision was the cause of the wing detachment, according to the 1962 official NZ air accident report. Paddy O'Brien, who was then CIAA. O'Brien had not recognised the design weakness and metal fatigue as being the fundamental cause of the wing detachment at that time. He, like his successor, was fixated with the blame the pilot philosophy. All five passengers and Bartlett were killed outright.

Paddy O'Brien was also to become involved just a short time later with the Dragonfly incident when ZK-AFB went missing on 12th February 1962. O'Brien concluded that the stresses over rough usage and then the actual, alleged, contact with the volcano caused the wing-spars to fail on ZK-BWA.

This was totally wrong and was the onset of many subsequent New Zealand air accident reports that were questionable for the next 37 years. Even now, TAIC has yet to acknowledge this scandalous blame the pilot mantra.

Some 10 years later, E.F. (Ted) Harvie became the CIAA. He was the same Inspector who so unwisely in 1967/8 tried to blame Brian Waugh's flying when the latter ditched into the Shotover (Chapter 5) and followed poor practice in the subsequent investigation. Waugh was alive and well capable of demonstrating Harvie's mistakes. On 11th April 1972, Harvie re-wrote the Aero Commander accident report 1192(P) after the 1962 version was supposed to have been declared a nullity by the then Minister of Transport, George Gair.

It has to be conceded that the reports from both O'Brien (1962) and Harvie (1972) may not have recognised how bad the catastrophic design flaw was in the Aero Commander genre. Even now, the weakness caused to the wing spars by the cold bending of five degrees twice, whilst being noted, still has not been recognised as the fundamental initial cause of the weakening of the Aero Commander wing. Prof Les Erasmus believed that fatigue damage started to accumulate in the lower spar cap with the first flight of each aircraft. An early hard landing by Bartlett at Oklahoma did not initiate the metal fatigue. It was already inherent in the design, it just speeded up the process for ZK-BWA.

Steve Swift was one of the world's foremost fatigue evaluation engineers. He presented the definitive study of the Aero Commander saga and its wing failures. I know from personal experience that current wing-stress consultants working with BAe Systems and most other aircraft manufacturers learnt much of their expertise from Swift's lectures, books and papers during their training.

Steve Swift wrote a paper presented at the 18th Symposium of the International Committee on Aeronautical Fatigue in May 1995 at Melbourne. He said that the Aero Commander's main wing spar was an aluminium alloy I-section made up of tee extrusions known as caps joined by a sheet web. An unusual feature was that the main spar was continuous from wing tip to wing tip. On each side of the fuselage the main spar was bent up five degrees for dihedral and five degrees forward for sweep. The 2014-T6 alloy caps were bent cold in the fully heat-treated condition.

Comparison of the way the 1977 case of Boeing 707/300 freighter G-BEBP was handled in the UK illustrated the shortcomings of O'Brien, Harvie and Chippindale. Both these cases, ZK-BWA and G-BEBP, involved metal fatigue showing up for the first time due to a design fault. Bill Tench recognised the seriousness on the first occasion that the 707 may have had a possible metal fatigue problem that could be present in other 707s. An investigating team was swiftly put together and sent to Zambia. The end result was that timely early airworthiness directives (ADs) were issued so that the other 521 airborne/airworthy 707s were inspected immediately. It was discovered that a large proportion of those aircraft had the same metal fatigue problem as G-BEBP. Lives were saved by Tench's skill and real expertise in recognising a problem. Yet another spar cap, but this time a stabiliser spar cap suffering metal fatigue.

This was not to be for the Aero Commander and its main wing spar design/construction fault, metal fatigue was not accepted by the New Zealand "experts" to have been the prime cause of ZK-BWA Bay of Plenty Airways accident at Mount Ruapehu in November 1961. Again, it was a combination of inexperience, incompetence and intransigence by the New Zealand inspectors of air accidents that failed to recognise that the problem was not pilot error. Be that as it may, when another Aero Commander crashed in April 1964 in Canada (CF-JOK), which was clearly due to a wing spar failure at exactly the same wing station (WS24) as that of ZK-BWA, the writing was on the wall. Thereafter there was no excuse for O'Brien, Harvie or any of their successors.

Perhaps a brief more detailed explanation of what these wing spars and their "caps" are. They are the skeleton inside an aircraft's wing providing the strength in the same way that an RSJ metal beam provides strength in building construction, except that wing spars are mainly high-grade aircraft aluminium alloy – being so much lighter than steel. I can do no better than to quote from Les Erasmus' author's note in "Taking Off" p.214.

> The front spar is the main load-carrying element in the wing, and can be considered as an "**I**" beam with the upper and lower flanges representing the upper and lower spar caps. These spar caps are critical elements in providing wing strength and such a large crack in the lower spar cap would seriously reduce the strength of the wing.

A little bird whispers in my ear that if the process of cold bending during manufacture is not done exactly right, a weakness is left in the crystalline structure of the metal at the focal point of bending. The degree of such a weakness may be classified and so I cannot explain further.

The Canadian Aero Commander CF-JOK wing spar failure did not appear to have been accompanied by failure of the rear spar cap as was ZK-BWA. But the rear spar was not cold bent. There had been a heavy landing by ZK-BWA at Oklahoma on 26 September 1958 when Alf Bartlett first flew ZK-BWA. That caused substantial damage to the starboard wing. It was the failure to observe that metal fatigue had been present in both the main and rear spar caps only to be exacerbated by the heavy landing. Post-crash inspection revealed that the fatigue had been advancing for a long time, in both front and rear spars.

In Harvie's 1972 draft report at section 2.1.3, he made one of his biggest errors. I quote:

> In the absence of evidence to the contrary, it is concluded that the total failure
> of the rear spar lower cap and partial failure of the rear upper cap probably took
> place when the aircraft made a hard landing at Oklahoma City.

There was plenty of evidence. The evidence staring O'Brien and Harvie in the face was the need for the addition of 105 pounds of lead in ZK-BWA. This was added in June 1961 to the tail to keep the aircraft in balance. If there had been total failure just of the rear spar lower cap caused by the Oklahoma 1958 heavy landing, then the lead weight would have been considered much earlier than 1961. It was this initial total rear spar failure on the day of the crash at Ruapehu, that permitted the starboard wing to "hinge" or pivot forward. The propeller cut into the fuselage and caused the insulation to flow out looking like a fuel spillage. The wing and starboard engine then finally separated completely (at wing station 24) coming to rest well clear of the remaining fuselage. The normal clearance of the tip of the propeller and the fuselage was only about 105-115mm. Another observation is that the propellers did not extend below the bottom of the fuselage. Little chance that the propellers could have contacted the ground without fuselage damage at the same time.

At this point, it was the famous George Bolt, then in charge of TEAL Engineering, who was responsible for overseeing the maintenance of ZK-BWA. He must have discussed the reported nose-heaviness with everyone involved. We know that Denis Little designed the shape and the positioning of the lead weights and Denis' contribution to the debate was recorded in Pacific Wings years later in 2002. But George Bolt and Ted Harvie were close colleagues. Bolt had even written the foreword to Harvie's book about the latter's pioneering 1933 flight. The Aero Commander was a very advanced aircraft, perhaps the most modern, swift and efficient aircraft serving internal flights for New Zealand in 1961. It is impossible to think that Bolt did not discuss this with one of the most knowledgeable, by repute, aviation expert of that time, who was Ted Harvie. Denis Little was equally as puzzled at the time as Harvie.

When it came to investigating the November 1961 wing failure, Harvie and George Bolt, who only died in 1963 shortly after the first accident report by O'Brien, will have thought they knew it all. Rob Hoover, the famous US display and aerobatics pilot, was the demonstration pilot for the Aero Commander. His displays of flying the Aero Commander showed how rugged the aircraft appeared. Chief Inspector Paddy O'Brien could have been forgiven for his dismissal of lack of structural integrity as being a possible cause of the wing detachment as per original report 1192 para.102 (k).I quote:

> As a result of this investigation the structural integrity of the Aero Commander
> 680S aircraft as a type is unquestioned.

One can see this report was so wrong with the benefit of hindsight. Instead, he again latched on to the blame the pilot scenario. This is exactly the same as his successor Chippindale would do when blaming the pilots in the Erebus tragedy.

This claim of absence of evidence regarding the complete failure of the lower rear wing spar cap in 2.1.3 is so similar to Chippindale's Erebus report at 2.5 when he wrote:

> No evidence was found to suggest that they [the TE901 pilots Jim Collins and Greg Cassin] had been misled by this error in the flight plan, centre of McMurdo Sound flight path, shown to them at the briefing.

Ted Harvie had been a good teacher to Chippindale who remembered how not to find evidence as a face-saving excuse. Whenever I see that "I can find no evidence" the cynic in me always thinks that the person saying that or declaring it did not look carefully enough, if at all. Just like Nelson at the battle of Copenhagen in 1801 when he could not see the flag signal to withdraw – as he used his telescope with his blind eye! Such an easy way to hide a lie, so commonly used in all government circles.

The truth was that far from flying too close to the crater of Ruapehu, Bartlett had kept 500 feet above and well clear of that mountain, although he was probably providing a memorable view of the volcano. A notable part of the flight! Harvie's conclusion about low flying at 2.2.1 (21) was due to his mistake in interpreting the passenger's photo No.4 that proved that Bartlett did not fly within 500 feet of Ruapehu. Bartlett did not contravene reg. 38 of the Civil Aviation Regulations of 1953.

Harvie's mistaken opinion of photo no.4 was debunked in Erasmus' report of 19th March 1981. Harvie had suggested in his own 1972 report (para 1.15.28), that Irvine Down's camera was aimed more or less directly ahead. Erasmus, after practical experiments was able to show that for photo number 4, the camera was in fact pointing down about 17.5 degrees, if not more. Harvie's claim that Bartlett was diving into the crater lake, based on this misreading of photo no.4, was untrue. (2.2.2.1 findings item (9)):

> The pilot altered course appreciably to starboard and initiated a dive towards the crater lake area on the summit of the mountain.

That finding was complete nonsense!

Harvie was particularly vociferous regarding the alleged breach of Reg. 38, the 500 feet clearance rule. At para 1.15.39 he stated:

> It was learned that low-level passages across the summit area and dives towards and across the crater lake had indeed occurred on other flights and one former passenger mentioned, inter alia, 'a dive under power towards the crater lake … till the aircraft was below the level of the ice cliffs surrounding it.'

I was astounded to see such hearsay being given this weight as evidence by Harvie. It is becoming ever more apparent who had trained Chippindale to gather hearsay evidence. Who was this former passenger? How qualified were they to comment on altitude etc.? Earlier, Harvie had identified the witnesses on Ruapehu as A, B, X and Y. Then he later debunked the evidence of witness Y regarding the estimate of the length of time witness Y had ZK-BWA in sight, as it did not fit into his theory of the cause of the crash. Was this also a lesson taught to Chippindale, how to disregard inconvenient evidence?

I had always wondered how Ted Harvie had made so many errors of judgment or displayed such a lack of common-sense.

Fast forward to 1967. His handling of Brian Waugh's accident at Queenstown just five years later was appalling. He allowed Waugh's aircraft Dominie ZK-AKT to be burnt after the engines had been recovered. This prevented investigation into the failure of the pilot's seat harness which resulted in significant injuries to the pilot (Brian Waugh) and the end of his career as a pilot. Harvie's mishandling of that 1967 investigation of the failure of both port and starboard engines of ZK-AKT was equally plainly incompetent. He had allowed the engineering company responsible for the maintenance of the Gipsy Six engines to volunteer any failure of correct maintenance on those same engines. Such a lack of common-sense. It was not until I got to page 158 of the final chapter 7 "North Cape to Bluff" of Ted Harvie's own book "Venture the far Horizon" that the penny dropped. Enter Mrs James Colway (nee Trevor Hunter) and her common sense.

Edgar F. (Ted) Harvie needed Mrs Colway's assistance. She was one of the most extraordinary young female aviators in New Zealand's history without whom Harvie probably could not have completed his epic 1933 flight in one day from North Cape to Bluff. A pity she was not on hand to help Harvie recognise his Aero Commander problem.

Having been in an aircraft flying through the Southern Alps myself in 1962, admittedly on a sightseeing trip with Brian Chadwick in a Dominie, I know it is very difficult to estimate exact height without some ground object to give the required perspective. However, my 8mm cine film provided much detail to help confirm height and if those films were to be examined forensically to the standards of Professors Mowbray and Erasmus, a reasonable estimate of our heights could be ascertained. If Harvie was willing to accept an anonymous witness report of "dive under power straight towards the lake" and that this was one of many times Bartlett flew low illegally, then there should have been photographic evidence available, if it was true. As it was, it was useful hearsay evidence for the likes of Harvie to rely on for his "Pilot Error" proposition. This similar method was copied by Chippindale during the investigation of the Erebus tragedy when he blamed the pilots for that tragedy.

I contacted Bartlett's son, Russell, who during an exchange of emails provided the following comments:

> The pattern of Aero Commander wing failures we now see so clearly was not as

clear in 1961, but even back then we were supported by a number of engineers, including the late Professor Neil Mowbray, who took a more analytical approach than did O'Brien and Chippendale.

Subsequently, Russell was kind enough to provide further notes about his father's aircraft, ZK-BWA:

> The handling consequences of the wing flexing in flight were called an unexpected centre of gravity problem – so 105lbs of lead were put on the tail. [See Ed. comment below.] On one occasion the plane fell back on its tail while parked." [Aero Commander ZK-BWA had a tricycle undercarriage.]

> My father had some association with de Havilland, having learned to fly in a Tiger Moth, and later, with first baby and wife aboard down under, flying from Auckland to Dunedin in a Fox Moth. The airline once chartered a Dove (Mark 8 I think) which by 1961 standards was a bit slow, but still quiet and stately.

Russell Bartlett is now one of the most experienced KCs (Kings Counsel, that is, a senior barrister) in New Zealand. If he was unable to persuade the New Zealand authorities to correct the injustice of the Chippindale report of 1984, then who can. The most significant comment by Russell is of course the addition of 105lbs of lead to the tail of ZK-BWA.

In the magazine "Pacific Wings" there were some remarkable exchanges between December 2001 and July 2002. Denis Little, the engineer who was entrusted to design and fit this volume of lead into the aircraft commented that the wing was twisting due to the fracture wrote:

> I did not immediately see the significance of the nose-heaviness and the installation of ballast weights to correct it…The effect of this twisting would have been to reduce the angle of attack of the starboard wing and, to compensate, the angle of attack of the port wing would have increased. …earlier causing movement in aircraft centre of lift.

Any properly trained aircraft accident inspector knowing of these massive ballast weights should have realised there was a big problem with that aircraft. Wings twisting due to partial failure of the wing spars and the adjustments with ballast should have been notice that there was a serious problem. But this was ignored in the reports of O'Brien (in 1962) and Harvie's 1972 draft report - later released by Chippindale (in 1984). Surprisingly, neither Harvie nor Chippindale completely cleared Bartlett saying,

> The available evidence does not prove conclusively that … the propeller blades came into contact with mountain terrain before wing separation occurred, neither does it prove conclusively that they did not.

The photographic and witness evidence did prove conclusively that ZK-BWA did not hit the crater of Mt Ruapehu. It proved that Harvie/Chippindale's official statements were wrong and that they were incompetent to assess good evidence. Disregarding the additional expert witness reports of Professors Erasmus and Mowbray, Chippindale could not bring himself to give the total clearance that Bartlett deserved. Chippindale also never understood what was evidence in the Erebus Saga. His cross-examination during the Mahon Royal Commission of Inquiry demonstrated a number of these shortcomings.

Effectively, Chippindale was covering up in 1984 for the incompetence and failure of his predecessors to realise that the addition of this massive ballast was evidence and in fact was absolute proof of structural failure of the rear wing spar and the weakening of the main spar lower cap. This addition of lead ballast was tried months before the final flight over Mount Ruapehu. In 1980, during the Erebus investigation, Chippindale had become a part of the cover-up of incompetence within Air New Zealand and the New Zealand Civil Aviation Department, but I deal with that in chapter 6.

Tragically, there were many subsequent Aero Commander wing separation in-flight accidents, another 23 aircraft, according to Steve Swift's later reports. Plainly many additional deaths were caused by the failure of the New Zealand Inspectorate to recognise how serious was the design weakness in the wing spars of Aero Commanders in 1961. Chippindale had the opportunity to correct this by 1984. I have prepared further comments about the standards that ICAO expect from the Air Accident Inspectors of the various participating countries.

As I write, I have come across another likely case of wing failure when Horace R 'Slim' Byrd, a Ferry Pilot, went missing in 1984 (Aviation World – Autumn 2023). He was moving an Aero Commander 690B (ZS-JRF s/n 11491) back to the United States from South Africa. On 5th December 1984, en-route from Windhoek to Abidjan, over the Gulf of Guinea, his aircraft disappeared without warning. How many other instances of "missing without trace" were there of Aero Commanders?

Chippendale's Erebus accident report issued in June 1980 is referred to in chapter 6, that was some four years before his Intransigent Aero Commander report of 1984. I have made comparison with the investigations of ZK-BWA by the New Zealand Inspectorate with that of G-BEBP of 14th May 1977, carried out swiftly and competently by international air accident inspectors like Bill Tench.

It is difficult to see whether Chippindale made any alterations to Harvie's written report of 1972. Why did it take 12 years before the revised report was released? Harvie was a pioneer in New Zealand aviation. But was he trained appropriately to become an inspector of air accidents and then in turn complete Chippindale's training? Possibly Harvie's behaviour and actions were evidence of Chippindale's lack of appropriate training and was the true cause of his subsequent questionable behaviour.

As stated earlier, Harvie was the first to fly in one day from the far north tip, North Cape, to the southernmost point of the South Island of New Zealand, Bluff, way back in 1933. This was in a Gipsy Moth but he had a passenger mentioned earlier, Miss Trevor Hunter.

Later during the second world war, Trevor Hunter paid her own way to get to England with three other Kiwi ladies, enlisted in the ATA and was part of the delivery squadron of pilots delivering and flying Spitfires, Wellington Bombers etc in aid of the war effort. In all, she flew about 42 different types of aircraft and built up over 1,200 hours solo in those aircraft. How much or how little did she contribute to Ted Harvie's feat? We will never really know. She most certainly was more than capable of adapting to most of the aircraft used by the RAF during the war. Assisting with a little Gipsy Moth would have been no problem for her. Being pedantic, if she was in the front cockpit, she would have been the first aviator to have crossed the line of the first flight the length and breadth of New Zealand. Food for thought! Should the record books be rewritten?

There was a lot more to Miss Hunter than the brief mentions much later in the book written by Harvie of the exploit. Doubtless she often took over when Harvie had navigation problems. She did not get the acknowledgement or praise for her part in the exploit. She eventually married James Colway, a journalist from Wanganui, and was much revered by the New Zealand aviation world.

She obtained her forename as a result of her mother's insistence when pregnant that she was carrying a boy and so the name Trevor stuck.

Ted Harvie had flown sometimes as a pilot, sometimes as a passenger, and briefly with Kingsford Smith and notables like Francis Chichester and George Bolt. However, it is not clear that he had much, if any training in metal fatigue. That was the chief requirement for the investigation and review of the Aero Commander wing spar fractures. Ten years had passed after ZK-BWAs accident when Harvie prepared his 1972 report. Chippindale took over from Harvie as chief inspector in 1975 after having retired from the RNZAF in 1974. In 1979/80, there was his notorious accident report on the Erebus tragedy of TE901. That Erebus accident report was finalised in May 1980, but then the Mahon report emerged in April 1981, contradicting many of Chippindale's opinions.

Chippindale had clearly kept Harvie's draft report on ZK-BWA under wraps until early January 1984, possibly due to the Erebus debacle that concluded with the final judicial review by the Privy Council in late 1983 concerning Mahon's perceived lack of natural justice not given to the liars of Air New Zealand. Chippindale had plenty of time, 1972 to 1984, to study the many reports on Aero Commander wing fractures that Harvie did not have. It is even more astounding that Chippindale had not realised the significance of the under engineered wing spar caps and the relevance of the cold bending by five degrees of the spars. But then his 2002 letter to Pacific Wings magazine demonstrated how ignorant he had been and still continued to be up to that time when he tangled with aviation historian Richard Waugh. It was apparent that Chippindale had not bothered to read up about the 24 wing failures of Aero Commanders, or the 35 inspections that found catastrophic fatigue. But this is the requirement of a Chief Inspector of Air Accidents. He did not do his job. The critical exchanges through the aviation magazine Pacific Wings are dealt with in some detail in the appendix.

APPENDIX TO Chapter 2 ZK-BWA re 1984 Accident Report of November 1961 Bay of Plenty Airways 1192(P)

Aero Commander Wing Fracture.

I have made a brief reference to correspondence that was published in a reputable aviation magazine "Pacific Wings" during the period December 2001 to July 2002. The title of the article and subsequent correspondence related to a feature paper entitled "Air Crash Injustice" by Richard Waugh about the whole Bay of Plenty Airways Aero Commander accident. The subsequent exchanges published within "Pacific Wings" magazine shows so clearly the incompetence of the New Zealand air accident authorities including TAIC's ignorant CEO and his former chief air accidents inspector.

The names in date order of their exchanges through Pacific Wings Magazine are as follows:

P.32 of the Dec/Jan 2002 edition of Pacific Wings.

Feature article by Aviation Historian Reverend Dr Richard Waugh.

Dr Waugh's article, Air Crash Injustice, was written over six years after the award-winning paper had been presented by S.J. Swift at the 18th Symposium of the International Committee on Aeronautical Fatigue at Melbourne (May 1995) with the approval of the Civil Aviation Authority of Australia. That date was before 1999 when Maurice Williamson became New Zealand's transport minister. Williamson curtailed Chippindale's many free air trips courtesy of Air New Zealand. Had Chippindale attended the Melbourne Symposium or read Swift's 1995 paper, Chippindale's comments in the March 2002 Pacific Wings would have plainly been untruthful.

In some considerable detail, Swift's 1995 paper listed in Appendix B the 24 incidents of total in flight failures as well as the massive metal fatigue fractures found in 35 ground inspections of the wing spars. Appendix C summarised those in-flight failures as well as the ground inspection discoveries for each model. As Chippindale was still the TAIC Chief (CIAA) between 1995 and 1998, it was his job to have studied these results, even if he did not attend the 18th symposium on Aeronautical Fatigue at Melbourne in May 1995. As stated earlier, it was before Chippindale's free flights with Air New Zealand had been stopped, so he could have attended.

P. 9 of the March 2002 edition of Pacific Wings. Response to Waugh's article above by Ex Chief Inspector of Air Accidents Ron Chippindale.

Chippindale defended his predecessors, O'Brien and Harvie, saying they were well qualified and experienced. He also wrongly stated that the experiment with the propellers had failed. He said that bending just 20mm did not produce the same resulting extreme bend displayed by the ZK-BWA propellers. He took no account that the propellers used in Professor Erasmus' experiment were 4.5 times stronger, probably for safety during the experiment than on ZK-BWA. This difference was completely lost on Chippindale.

However, the most remarkable comment within Chippindale's response was his following absurd statement:

> I cannot recall anyone producing evidence that there were 24 Aero Commander accidents that resulted from the separation of a wing in flight after the ZK-BWA accident. However astounding though this statement is. Should the assertion of an author who is an 'Aviation Historian' and Reverent [sic] be dismissed lightly?

It is accepted that the S.J. Swift paper was issued in 1995, but in the period 1962-1984, before Chippindale refused to exonerate the pilot, Alf Bartlett, there were a large number of incidents indicating that there were problems, and law suits from airlines owning Aero Commanders, with those suspect wings. His refusal to acknowledge that there was a serious defect, when the lead ballast was used for a period, is unforgiveable within the Harvie 1972 draft report. Chippindale was responsible for releasing the report no.1192(P) in January 1984. Doubtless the timing of the Erebus Privy Council judgment in late 1983 triggered the January 1984 release by Chippindale.

Chippindale's method of criticising Waugh by labelling the latter throughout as "Reverent" and likewise using the inverted commas to the title of "historian" was rude and childish. His ignorance, whether in 1984 of some problems and most definitely by 2002 his ignorance of the 24 in-flight wing separations that were so clearly listed and tabulated by Swift is, using Chippindale's own word, "astounding". He had to have been the most intransigent inspector of air accidents ever, but such was his overconfidence and self-pride that he felt from being the chief inspector of air accidents in 1979/80 at the Erebus disaster. He obtained a reputation within the NZ aviation industry that no other inspector could have acquired, all for the wrong reasons, constantly adding the blame the pilot mantra, which he got away with during his lifetime.

P.31 of the April 2002 edition of Pacific Wings. Response from – 1. Professor Les Erasmus and 2. John Britton, at the time the chief executive officer of TAIC, on Chippindale's March 2002 comment.

Professor Erasmus stated:

> Mr Chippindale is correct in that both air accident reports record the existence of the fatigue crack in the main spar of the starboard wing [of ZK-BWA]. However, the report authors [Harvie and Chippindale] did not concede that the starboard wing was in imminent danger of failing before the accident [at Mt Ruapehu].

Even worse, John Britton as chief executive officer of TAIC joined in by aiding and abetting Chippindale, as did so many. I quote from Britton:

> Aviation safety is better served by using TAICs limited resources to investigate accidents and incidents which are more relevant to today's aircraft, systems and organisations. The lack of relevance to modern air safety and accident investigation and the unsuccessful appeal to the Ombudsman indicates that attempts to remedy any perceived injustice may need to be addressed through other means – perhaps the justice system. *[Ed. Comment - I have not been able to find any reference about this appeal to the Ombudsman mentioned by Britton]*,

> Before taking up the cause advocated by Rev Waugh 'for the good of the aviation industry', readers may wish to draw their own conclusions by reading the second [Harvie] report [that report released in 1984 containing erroneous date etc. on page 3]. A photocopy of the complete 87 page report can be purchased from the Commission for $15.00 including GST.

This latter response is hardly in accordance with the first TAIC principle of accessibility. But this was 2002 before the internet was so widely considered. TAIC was always behind in the technological stakes. $15 was far too much to pay for Chippindale's fiction.

P.35 of the June 2002 edition of Pacific Wings. Correspondent, William H Allen of Auckland, a teacher at the NTSB FAA Accident Investigation School at Oklahoma.

William Allen drew attention to the four photographs in a camera which had been found in the wreckage belonging to a passenger, Mr Irvine Down. He was in the front seat next to Alf Bartlett the Pilot. These showed the approach to Mt Ruapehu. Mr Allen was annoyed that TAIC neglected to consider all the facts when trying to establish causes of the accident.

These were the photographs Professors Neil Mowbray and Les Erasmus produced for the consideration of Chippindale's 1984 report. Eventually it was conceded that all four photographs showed that ZK-BWA did not fly below the top of the crater of Ruapehu at any time and that the wing separation was in clear air. But Harvie had still accused Bartlett of flying well below the 500 ft minimum, to the extent that it included an infamous "does not prove or disprove" comment about the propellor hitting the ground and causing the wing separation. See Para 2.2.1. (19) of the 1984 report.

P.32/3 of the July 2002 edition of Pacific Wings. Correspondent, Denis Little, was TEAL's assistant development engineer at the time. (TEAL - Tasman Empire Airlines was the forerunner of Air New Zealand with the merger of TEAL with NAC)

Denis Little's boss was the late great George Bolt OBE, a legend in New Zealand aviation history. Bolt asked Little to design and fit 105lbs of lead ballast in the tail of ZK-BWA between June and September 1961 that Barlett's son, Russell, referred to in our exchange of emails. This lead weight was a major issue in 1961 and everyone was aware of it. Any child with a balsa wood glider would be aware of the principles of centre of balance adjustments with coins for adjusting weights in their models. But it contained no warning bells for the NZ inspectors of air accidents, whether they were O'Brien, Harvie, or Chippindale.

Denis Little described his experiences and the sign that the wings were twisting for some reason. We now know with the benefit of hindsight that the fracture of the rear lower spar cap was by then extremely advanced sufficient to have allowed the wing to flex to such a degree.

Professor Erasmus reported on the camera experiments used from cockpits of other Aero Commanders to verify that the passenger's photographs showed that ZK-BWA was always flying above the highest part of Ruapehu's crater. I will let him have the final word:

> There is no doubt at all that the wing on ZK-BWA failed by metal fatigue. The subsequent separation of 23 Aero Commander wings in flight and discovery of major fatigue cracks in the main lower spar caps of a further 35 aircraft is surely proof of a serious design fault.

T.A.I.C a Sideways Look

According to the Annual Reports of the New Zealand Transport Accident Investigation Commission (TAIC), the words of its fundamental principles include the following:

1. Accessible

2. Trustworthy

3. Fair-Minded

4. Open-Minded

5. Reliable

6. Credible

There have been a number of criticisms of TAIC and the New Zealand CAA within the New Zealand aviation circles. However, understandably, current pilot licence holders are reluctant to be openly critical of those officials and CAA colleagues who could so easily suspend or withhold pilot licences. In one case, I have detailed knowledge of a pilot's New Zealand CAA record which is endorsed with unfounded complaints from another country. Every year the pilot complained that he had to explain the origins of the black mark on his record. The complaint related to the fact that he was unwilling to release certain information as it was not permitted under New Zealand aviation laws.

Nevertheless, the power that can be exercised by New Zealand CAA officials is difficult to appeal against. Pilots are intimidated and reluctant to complain. I am not so constrained. I cannot resist commenting on these fundamental principles. Rod Lovell, an Australian Pilot was treated even worse by his Australian CAA after the DC-3 ditching in 1994. That still persists to this day. Perhaps the civil servants in other countries are as difficult to their own pilots. Doubtless, useful in possible future official cover-ups. It is well known that the Official Secrets Acts are to keep government Official's Acts of Blunder Secret!

TAIC and its forerunners failed to achieve all these six principles repeated within its annual reports. At one stage in writing my manuscript, I detailed all the events showing that these fundamental principles were a fictional presentation from public relations officers who were totally ignorant of what really had happened over the years. I have cut these detailed examples out from my book as it took far too much space and began to bore.

But I will comment briefly:

Accessible.- Only if you are happy to pay for fiction.

Trustworthy.- I suggest you read Paul Holmes 2011 book "Daughters of Erebus" and his list of Chippindale's lack of trust.

Fair-minded, open-minded, reliable, credible.- Again, Paul Holmes book "Daughters of Erebus" debunks all these as do the S.J. Swift 1995 report and the writings of experienced professors Mowbray and Erasmus.

IN SUMMARY

It is important that accident reports filed under ICAO annex 13 are accurate so that lessons are learnt. Compare the cases of the Lusaka 707 stabiliser detachment G-BEBP with that of the Aero Commander wing detachment ZK-BWA reports of 1962 (O'Brien) and 1972 (Harvie) as checked and released by Chippindale in 1984.

These show a massive difference in past standards of the UK/US Inspectorates with that of New Zealand. In one case despite it being the first of a design problem weakness, it was identified. Immediate swift remedial action was taken – thus preventing further loss of life. So unlike the New Zealand inspectorate which even after 62 years plus, ZK-BWAs metal fatigue at WS24 was never recognised as being the prime cause of the wing separation. Therefore 23 more cases, and lives were needlessly lost over many subsequent years. Fractures from the faulty spar cap design were also diagnosed in ground inspections of another 35 cases.

Increased standards may be imposed by ICAO on nation states themselves. The privilege for any individual regulatory state's CAA or equivalent FAA to oversee safety standards of its airlines may need to be reviewed and replaced by an internationally funded regulatory body. Aircraft now weighing 500 tons or more are risking flight over another country's territory. To grant this privilege there have to be appropriate standards with airlines suitably overseen under ICAO recommendations and standards. All State authorities must demonstrate that they have these adequate technical and financial resources. So often the New Zealand Inspectorate have claimed limited resources when carrying out investigations. The 1967/8 incident between Waugh and Harvie when the latter left the investigation of the engine failures to the maintenance staff of the airline was typical of those times. Then there was the Fletcher parachutists take off crash at Fox Glacier, inadequately investigated initially.

When with hindsight earlier ICAO annex 13 reports are found to be lacking or some new evidence comes to light showing a report is wrong, the ability to file an attachment is built in to Annex 13. See G-BDAN the Dan Air 1008 report that was changed as the original Spanish report was wrong. With respect to non-international reports, a formal attachment may not be necessary. Just a memorandum would probably suffice.

Richard Waugh writes that the Bay of Plenty Airways injustice must be second only to the Erebus tragedy as being the most controversial accident report in New Zealand. I would tend to disagree. Admittedly there were 257 lives lost at Mt Erebus and only 6 lives lost at Mt Ruapehu. But the former involved a combination of simple human mistakes subject to a cover up by incompetent management, aided and abetted by the dishonest state shareholder prime minister Muldoon, not a design flaw in the DC-10. The latter Bay of Plenty injustice was the inability to recognise an aircraft design that was inherently dangerous and likely to disintegrate in flight after a time. This had world-wide implications for aircraft design faults and the continued intransigence of the New Zealand Inspectorate and its successors was the worst type of failing in the aviation world. Something ICAO Annex 13 was designed to eliminate.

How do we know whether there were many other incorrect air accident reports by New Zealand inspectors? In Richard Waugh's 2018 book "Shot Over into the Shotover", (on page 61) there was a note of a complaint about Chippindale's conduct of another later investigation. I followed up those comments with the contributors. It seems that despite Chippindale tape recording interviews with witnesses, his reports of those interviews were sometimes totally different. It seems that Chippindale did not always write fairly or accurately what these witnesses actually said. That was so dangerous. His blunders in other cases were not isolated incidences. Perhaps in many cases, his reports and subsequent conclusions were equally just as wrong.

The International credibility of TAIC has been at stake for a long time. Knowledge of metal fatigue is still a current main requirement. In fact, it is the main requirement in most accident investigations, whether it was an accident in 1961 or last week. Despite Britton's last famous plea which I repeat: "Aviation safety is better served by using (TAIC) resources more relevant to today's aircraft". How wrong can one be? The display of incompetence shown throughout all the investigations into the Bay of Plenty Airways accident and others will not disappear until recognition is acknowledged by the current incumbents of TAIC.

If not acknowledged, how can the international authorities have any confidence that New Zealand's TAIC and CAA are able to recognise the simplest case of the difference between pilot error and a whole series of wings detaching due to metal fatigue? Are New Zealand's aviation authorities competent to carry out air accident investigations under annex 13? Or that their Airlines have been suitably regulated? They are so slow in acknowledging past errors. Bay of Plenty Airways tragedy with ZK-BWA is sadly typical.

It was at the 28th November 2019 gathering of the Erebus victims' families that the then New Zealand Prime Minister Jacinda Ardern offered a "whole hearted" and "wide-ranging" apology to the surviving family members of the Erebus disaster victims. "After 40 long years … setting down grief will only be made harder if we don't accept our part in these wrongs". This was followed by an equally sincere apology from Air New Zealand's Dame Therese Walsh. In the light of all the subsequent wing failures of the Aero Commander designs after that of 21st November 1961, TAIC being the successors to the Inspectors of Air Accidents, O'Brien, Harvie and Chippindale – with Government support should do the same for the families of Alf Bartlett and his passengers and apologize whole heartedly. If a Prime Minister can apologize after 40 years, so can the current executive staff of TAIC do likewise for Captain Bartlett, his family and his passengers more than 60 years later.

A sideways look at the UK

Before I leave this chapter, the involvement at the highest judicial level of the judges in the Privy Council, two names stand out having been involved in one of the most disturbing miscarriages of justice in the twentieth century. I am referring to the conviction of the Birmingham Six and to Lord (Nigel) Bridge. He failed to recognise that the six had been tortured by the West Midlands Serious Crime Squad until they "confessed". The supposed expert in explosives was the incompetent Dr Skuse, who was no better than Chippindale as an investigator. The privy councillor Lord (Leslie) Scarman was successful in unravelling the errors of his fellow judge Nigel Bridge with the truth eventually being revealed but that took 16 years.

Time after time, appeals were made by and on behalf of the Birmingham Six, who were totally innocent. These appeals were rejected so many times by 18 judges over a period, included Lord Denning, such was the weight given by Dr Skuse to his expert evidence. The convictions were only unravelled by the work of Lord Scarman and new evidence uncovered by Devon and Cornwall police of the falsification of police note books and discovery of Dr Skuse's incompetence. Those innocent men were only released after a total of 100 years had been served in jail by the six. So much for reputations.

The comparison of the Birmingham Six injustice and the Bay of Plenty Airways case come down to similar incompetents, who were Dr Skuse and Ron Chippindale. After a certain time, more evidence became available. TAIC continues to this day to support the 1984 report due to Chippindale's reputation. Time and again, the Birmingham Six defence has been used subsequently by defence barristers with some success. The current commissioner and chief executive officer of TAIC will doubtless continue to defend their erstwhile error prone, intransigent former colleague Chippindale, as did the 18 judges defend Lord Bridge and Dr Skuse. Why? They believe that as the Bay of Plenty Airways accident and their subsequent revised investigation was reviewed as satisfactory by an ombudsman, who could find no failing within TAIC, that would be enough. Perhaps the competence of that ombudsman should be questioned. Was John Britton correct in saying that an Ombudsman had been appointed? This requires re-examination, in the light of so many cover-ups within the legal system and other authorities in New Zealand. I am reminded of the 2021 book - "The Justice Mirage" - by Rob Moodie in which he names and shames so many.

UK Summary

The revised report released by Chippindale in 1984 on the Aero Commander accident was basically wrong, no matter how many Ombudsman reviews, or other judges' opinions, like the innocence of the Birmingham six and that 18 judges were wrong until Scarman. Alf Bartlett was not a cowboy pilot, nor did he not hit the crater of Ruapehu. He was a victim of metal fatigue in a Wing Spar Cap that was going to fracture at any time due to the normal stresses on a wing during flight, as it did in 23 subsequent cases, Possibly more if Slim Byrd's disappearance was caused by the metal fatigue in the wings. TAIC can never run away from these facts and the sooner they acknowledge that, the better.

Same comment applies to Boeing 737 Max and the pilots of Lion Air 610 (29/10/2018) and Ethiopian Airlines flight 302 (10/3/2019), pilot error was first claimed there!

Main sources of information –

Priceless file of original documents, correspondence, reports and original photographs from the Reverend Dr Richard Waugh's 2003 "Taking Off" book archive with Bruce Gavin Chapter 9 Aero Commander and Appendix 3

Air Crash Injustice – Les Erasmus, Neil Mowbray et al

Les Erasmus report 19th March 1981.

Steve Swift – Aero Commander Chronicle May 1995

Pacific Wings magazine and its contributors:-
Richard Waugh, Ron Chippindale, Les Erasmus, John Britton, William Allen, Denis Little. TAIC annual reports

Supplementary information directly from Alf Bartlett's son.

CHAPTER 3

THE DRAGONFLY

Details for chapter 3 - Brian Chadwick with his Air Charter aircraft ZK-BCP and ZK-AFB DH89B and DH90A – (8 passengers plus Chadwick on board BCP Dominie) and (4 passengers plus Chadwick on board the Dragonfly). Flights on 19th January and 12th February 1962.

Background and 8mm Film

Chadwick flew his DH89 and DH90 Biplanes from his base at Christchurch on sightseeing trips to Milford Sound. Maximum fuel loads were required to give the necessary range for both aircraft. About 150 such trips were made by Chadwick. His last was that with the DH90 Dragonfly on the 12th February 1962.

I was a passenger on board the flight in the Dominie ZK-BCP some two or three weeks before the Dragonfly went missing. My parents filmed, comprehensively for those times, the whole of the Dominie flight using rare precious standard 8mm cine film. This showed the flight path and demonstrated the skill of this pilot in his own backyard.

The search for the de Havilland Dragonfly DH90 which disappeared on 12th February 1962 was the largest missing aircraft search in New Zealand unless you count the accident on 5th November 2005 when a helicopter ZK-HTF went missing, eventually found by Darryl (Dazza) Sherwin just 14 days later on 19th November on the sides of Mt Karioi.

Brian Chadwick had emigrated to New Zealand from England in 1951. He had been a colleague of Brian Waugh [Chapters 1 and 5] from the time when they were both flying together in the North of England. They had both served in the RAF during World War Two.

Chadwick had a number of positions as a pilot and manager for various small companies post-war providing much needed transport around New Zealand until he started his own business in the late 1950s - Air Charter.

Chadwick was among the most experienced light aircraft pilots in New Zealand in 1960-62. He had a sense of adventure and was a pioneer in the truest sense of the word. New Zealand as a whole was and still is full of pioneers, probably the best known may have been Sir Edmund Hillary. Sir Edmund had been scheduled to fly as commentator on the fateful 28th November 1979 DC-10 trip to Antarctica and he just escaped from the Erebus disaster by chance. Later, he married the widow of Peter Mulgrew, the man who took his place. (See Chapter 6).

Chadwick obtained the DH 89B Rapide/Dominie ZK-BCP and later in 1961 added the well-known and historic DH90 Dragonfly ZK-AFB to his fleet known as "Air Charter". The DH90 was smaller than the DH89B Dominie. Both these aircraft were biplanes designed in the 1930s and in their time, they were very economic and able aircraft. However, by 1961/2, they were well past their prime but with Chadwick's careful maintenance, they could do the job required – in normal circumstances. The Dragonfly was one of the first regular scheduled airliners in the South Island. It was flown and so loved by Captain J.C. (Bert) Mercer, the earlier pioneer who died in a 1944 accident.

Mercer had pioneered so much of South Island passenger flying, Chadwick took on Mercer's role, including the acquisition of the Dragonfly which Mercer had imported new from the UK. W H Tench, the famous UK accident inspector has written about the essential lessons always learnt from every accident. In his book, "Safety is no Accident", he describes how a relatively insignificant accident study produced results which were relevant to the safety of many subsequent aircraft. Hence the importance in NZ history of Chadwick's Dragonfly named **Kiwi Rover.** It still must be found.

The Southern Alps of New Zealand are not normal. They contain some of the most accessible scenic and spectacular vistas in the world, provided that you can travel by air. Equally these mountains can be the most dangerous. They are equivalent of the spectacle of Antarctica which Air New Zealand tried to exploit in the late 1970s, albeit with DC-10s, with disastrous results. Both Air Charter and Air New Zealand were in fact trying to achieve much the same goals. The first was a one-man tourist operator in 1962 and the latter, a vast corporation with over 8,000 employees in 1979. The ice, snow and glaciers of the Southern Alps are considerably easier and quicker to access than Antarctica, hence the greater sudden danger to the unwary and unprepared.

The flight planned for 12th February 1962 would normally have taken place in the larger Dominie ZK-BCP. Unfortunately, there was a landing accident to the Dominie 12 days earlier on 31st January at Queenstown. In those days Queenstown's runway was not the clean asphalt it is today. It was untarmacked and unpredictable. The undercarriage of ZK-BCP was damaged on that landing by an assistant pilot of Chadwick. Therefore Chadwick had no alternative but to use the smaller Dragonfly ZK-AFB until repairs had been made to the Dominie aircraft.

The Dragonfly could only take four passengers, whereas the Dominie accommodated eight, as on my flight about three weeks earlier with keen amateur 8mm cine cameramen Albert and Daisy Fautley, with me in tow. However, my parents were not inexperienced in filming and they had made a number of historic films from 1957 onwards across Canada and the United States as well as on the continent and UK. Some seven minutes of their film have been posted on YouTube but some more out-takes have come to light which helps identify most of the exact route flown. Those out-takes included the spectacular low-level entry to Milford Sound which is no longer permitted following accidents in the Sound.

My parents filmed the flight of ZK-BCP comprehensively and in such detail that it is now possible to identify the flight path through the mountains to the coast then into Milford Sound. We refuelled at Queenstown, returning to Christchurch that evening. Exactly as planned for 12th February 1962 for the Dragonfly flight.

This film was effectively the dress rehearsal for the 12th February flight for Dragonfly ZK-AFB. The date of our "Fautley" flight cannot be identified exactly, but following articles in the weekly Salvation Army newspaper "War Cry", I have identified 19th January 1962 as being the most likely date. That newspaper also acknowledged that my parents were presenting earlier 8mm cine films from the UK and confirmed the connection with Brigadier and Mrs Albert Bartlett, the parents of the Bay of Plenty Airways pilot.

I am sure that our return flight from Queenstown to Christchurch was the exact reverse of the flight path intended by Chadwick in the Dragonfly on 12th February 1962, due to the weather and clouds covering the Divide on that day. (i.e. the much talked about Mackenzie Route) It was that route which Chadwick indicated he would take whilst in conversation with the weather forecaster.

The amount of cloud, wind strength and direction can be assessed from forensic viewing of the film. As far as is known, this is the only complete film of Chadwick's flying.

This rare film indicated the route to the Glaciers, at least it was thought to be so. The film had been heavily edited by my father to eliminate poor quality film. He was overcritical as some out-takes were spliced together by myself as a lad, not good splicing, but at least they were saved for posterity. In places, these outtakes were better in the identification of our flight path than the spectacular YouTube posting.

One YouTube clip was thought to be "out of sequence". It related to the first entry to the High Southern Alps. That sequence could have been near Mount Hutt on the eastern side of the divide or the entry to Whataroa from the west. It was the most critical part of the film in assisting with the location of the subsequent flight of the Dragonfly.

In Richard Waugh's book "Lost without Trace", many eye-witness reports were examined. One example was that the aircraft was flying in circles to gain height. The theory being it may have been indicative that Chadwick was attempting to gain height to cross the Divide there, and not flying via the Mackenzie country, much further South. I suggest that it was far too difficult to see or identify what a small aircraft several thousand feet above is doing, especially when there is nothing to indicate how important such an observation may have been later. So many similar reports must have suffered from these types of inaccuracies.

This debate continues even after 60 or more years between the different search groups.

I compare those reports with an incident on the day of the disappearance of another light aircraft in the region. I am referring to the loss of ZK-EBU on 29th December 1978 when a Cherokee Six, with seven persons on board, went missing on the West Coast after emerging from Milford Sound. Communications and organisation of searches were not as good then as today with Sat Navs, I-phones and the like. But there was one report which was ignored at the time by the official SAR organisers as the sighting was several hours after ZK-EBU should have run out of fuel.

Search And Rescue did not take into account that there was a disused mining airstrip which a pilot as experienced as Edward (Ned) Morrison could have used to land to wait for the weather to clear. That would have been the Nickelspoon Mining Company airstrip near Gorge River which was relatively close. Gavin Grimmer, another experienced pilot, thought that Ned may have landed there to await the passing of the weather front in the hope that better weather in the lee of the front would allow the flight to recontinue. Not to be discounted would have been a landing on a beach. Nominally the west coast beaches can be useable two hours either side of low water. In an emergency, depending on the firmness of the sand, this four-hour window may have been greater on the day depending on so many variables. Then under pressure of oncoming dusk, Morrisson may have taken off again with his 6 passengers on a get-home-at-any-cost attempt.

Instead, he may have become unaware of his exact position and ended up flying down and up the (Blue) Moeraki River as was observed by Jenny Barratt. Her report, admittedly a few days later, was discarded by the authorities since her sighting was well after the time the fuel should have run out. This ignored the possible use of the mining company airstrip, but this is what an efficient, professional SAR organisation should consider. Namely local knowledge. Grimmer was described as an amateur in a television programme about this but it was the amateurish SAR organisation that ignored good witness reports. Probably the same happened with the Dragonfly.

It is easy to see with hindsight, that the organisers of Land SAR should have been aware of this possibility. Perhaps these "professionals" should learn from this lack of foresight of possibilities. Jenny had observed an aircraft looking like EBU at the mouth of the Moeraki River just under the cloud base of about 100 feet. Unfortunately, her report was not made for several days as Jenny was unaware of ZK-EBU being missing. Communications in those days were so different to that of the present. Jenny Barratt was a qualified glider pilot and in New Zealand, that means a lot. If she had observed something in the air, albeit for just a few seconds, that was a reliable report. To have been ignored by the official search party organisers is evidence of the intransigent attitude so often encountered with officials, not just in New Zealand. I note that Jenny Barratt was one of many attendees at the 61st reunion at Christchurch Airport on 12th February 2023. Her continued interest in the Dragonfly and other missing aircraft confirms to me that she was an experienced observer that to have been ignored by SAR shows a rather unfortunate low standard of that organisation of that time.

The filmed flight in ZK-BCP. The first sector, Christchurch to Milford through the mountains was spectacular. The film is available on YouTube. There is no complete unanimity of opinion as to the exact route we took through the Divide but it appears that we would have crossed a number of "saddles" at the top of the Godley Glacier to emerge at the head of the Tasman Glacier and then proceed down the western side of Mounts Tasman and Cook. I swear that at one stage we were so close to the mountains that the snow was disturbed and a small avalanche or flurry of snow was thrown up as we passed. Could the Dragonfly have crashed in the snow only to be covered immediately by the resulting avalanche? Perhaps similar to the loss of our family's friend in the helicopter at Routeburn in 2004 (see Chapter 8). Was that crash immediately covered over by snow? Currently Lew Bone is investigating possible sites around Mt. Aspiring but access to the likely areas is so costly and physically difficult in the high country his research indicates is a likely place. His leads come from sightings of oddities by helicopter pilots such as Alan Duncan, a legend in NZ history.

Disappearance

The Official "Missing Aircraft" Report of Civil Aircraft Accident No. 25/3/1214 had to be inconclusive for the obvious reason that the aircraft had not been found. The Inspector noted a number of irregularities relating to the paperwork that recorded the servicing and maintenance of both the Dragonfly ZK-AFB and Dominie ZK-BCP. Brian Chadwick was one of the more experienced Licenced Engineers capable of maintaining both de Havilland aircraft in the peak of condition. He had been the squadron leader of a maintenance and service unit in World War II and had been an aircraft engineer before he learnt to fly (like Brian Waugh).

Knowledgeable aviators believe that Chadwick's aircraft were well maintained. Technically an independent aircraft maintenance company, Airwork in Christchurch, was supposed to carry out the 50 and 100 hour licenced checks as required for Air Charter's operator's licence by the NZ CAA. Paddy O'Brien's main criticisms were concerning incomplete record keeping of aircraft Log Books – for both the Dominie and Dragonfly. It did not prove that ZK-BCP and ZK-AFB were badly maintained, just that Chadwick omitted many flight hours in the log books reducing the frequency and cost for these External independent 50 hour and 100 hour checks. ZK-BCP and ZK-AFB were better maintained by its pilot – Chadwick - than employees of Airwork. Chadwick had everything to lose including his life – if the necessary maintenance and checks were not carried out meticulously. I recollect that Chadwick's parents told us that their son pampered his aircraft and disliked other hands interfering with his babies, when we visited them later in 1962.

I was told one tale by an experienced pilot. A top-dressing pilot was always suffering engine failures after careless maintenance and servicing. This engine failure problem ceased when the pilot made the engineer concerned accompany the pilot on the first flight in that aircraft after that servicing and overhaul. Thereafter never again did the pilot have a problem with the aircraft! I leave this thought with you but I am of the view that Chadwick's aircraft were better maintained without outside interference from CAA or Airwork.

The search for Chadwick and his Dragonfly had been the largest in aviation history of New Zealand. It may be difficult to understand why this aircraft deserved such a massive search undertaking. But in 1962, New Zealand had a population of about 3 million. A famous historic twin-engine biplane with five persons missing was big news.

Chadwick was one well-known innovative pioneers at that time. He had helped open up New Zealand's economy for tourism as opposed to pure transport across the NZ nation's natural Divide – the Southern Alps. Long distance jet engine air travel was still in its infancy. To put this in perspective, 1962 is closer in time to the first flight 120 years ago than the Wright Brothers at Kittyhawk and Richard Pearce at Timaru in 1903, than 2024. Even more poignant is that both aircraft were designed just 30 years after the Wright brothers with little modification. It was Moncrief and Hood who just a few years before, in 1928, were the first "to go missing" in G-AUNZ while attempting to cross the Tasman Sea. G-AUNZ is another of Gavin Grimmer's list of missing clients. At the time of writing, only ZK-HNW with our family friend on board has been found from his list of missing clients.

Weather issues and the Search:

Regrettably, with hindsight, it is clear that the search was not comprehensive. Due to poor weather, only the western side of the mountains were able to be searched by appropriate aviators such as Brian Waugh. He knew Chadwick's flying style inside out. I continue to be puzzled that the weather was reported to be so bad that nobody could fly through the Divide. Only in more recent times has it been confirmed that there were other flights in the area on that day.

On page 129 of "Lost without Trace", the co-ordinator of the official search parties - the experienced Stan Quill – ex squadron leader - sent out a RNZAF Harvard aircraft to try to fly the flight plan (of the Dragonfly) from base (Wigram) to Franz Josef. The Harvard made it through "although the weather was not good". [Comment: It could not have been that bad either!] In the same area, a Piper Super Cub was flown by Ken Eden from Rangiora to Arawhata (this had to be the same route as Chadwick intended!). Then Ian Ritchie flew from Milford to Te Anau. When I look at my cine film of our flight in January 1962, there were considerable cloud banks shown everywhere especially that to the east of Milford Sound. Chadwick still found a route through to Queenstown, albeit we almost crashed due to a severe downdraft. Parts of my film are poor quality not because of poor camera work but poor visibility in mist and clouds reducing the sunlight.

It was highly unlikely that the Harvard pilots were as experienced or able as Chadwick – so I believe that Chadwick was capable to have crossed the Divide to Franz Josef or Fox Glaciers. Then he may have flown down the West Coast in better weather than anyone believed. However I have since changed my mind about the Harvard pilots. They were highly skilled albeit less experienced than Chadwick. Later, these same pilots were central to the Erebus saga – (see chapter 6) – I have been able to maintain direct contact, learning so much about the Dragonfly but also the inside story of the Erebus accident report and the Mahon Inquiry. But that is another case. I still question the efficiency of the organisation of the official search. In Brian Waugh's book in the chapter "Chadwick is missing", he describes how the young RNZAF pilots were not properly briefed as to colour of the Dragonfly or that Chadwick was a highly skilled and experienced IFR pilot. There was also the incident when two searching aircraft flew towards each other one having misread the air charts and been in the "wrong" valley. Probably one valley was missed at that crucial time!

One of these young RNZAF pilots was Peter Rhodes. He very kindly gave me much information on the search techniques they had to learn very quickly, to be able to survive in the Southern Alps. Many of the charts were simply wrong. So many dead-end valleys ready to catch out the unwary. It is quite possible that this is what happened to Chadwick when the crash site was then covered up either by snow and ice or some other avalanche which is a common feature in the area. The Homer road tunnel to Milford is constantly monitored and often closed due to the hazard of avalanches. Perhaps Chadwick's crash site could have been covered by an avalanche, hence the difficulty of finding them even today.

When the weather improved on the Eastern side of the Southern Alps, the officially funded search had ceased. Therefore parts of the Eastern Side of the Divide and other previously heavily clouded areas may not have been searched well in February 1962, if at all before the jungle enveloped the crash site. Certainly not as thoroughly as on the Western side under the watchful eye of Brian Waugh. However, Chadwick may still have crossed the Divide and then flown as far as Mt Aspiring where there were a number of likely sightings. But it keeps coming back to coordination of searches. The SAR chief around Aspiring was Paul Powell, a well-respected experienced SAR chief. I have little doubt that his organisational skills would have covered all reasonable possibilities in that area. Currently even after 60 plus years, the inaccessible eastern side of Rainbow Valley, part of Paul Powell's patch, is still considered a "hot-spot" deserving of more attention. Memories of finding the missing helicopter ZK-HNW in 2012 (see chapter 8) indicate that if ZK-AFB was covered by snow and ice on first crashing in Rainbow Valley, with climate change, it may well re-appear as have aircraft in the European Alps in more recent times.

Local pilots diligently continued to look out for Chadwick, this without official funding for years when flying over the bush. There is nothing so dense as the New Zealand bush. The official February 1962 searches based from Wigram did not appear to have the young RNZAF pilots briefed to know what to look for. If Brian Waugh's remarks were true, the lack of knowledge of the colour scheme by the young RNZAF pilots was a big mistake.

ZK-HNW was a green helicopter that was eventually found on grassy green slopes. Likewise what sort of impact would the Dragonfly have had in the type of terrain it may have crashed into? See chapter 8.

Radio calls?

These SAR search parties may not have known about a young Ross Jamie McDermott and his mother. They had heard a distinct but soft "Mayday" call in a television break that evening of 12th February 1962 in their Epsom, Auckland home. In "Lost …without Trace?" and repeated in "Traced but still missing" this 16-year-old boy was quoted as having contacted CAA, NAC and Radio Auckland but no one had heard a thing.

This intrigued me. In 1959, I had been shown by a Dutch Phillips radio expert how and why the old valve radio sets antennae could work. After using Google street map view for the former McDermott home, it was possible to see that with all the wires in that road and the various signal boosters attached by McDermott Senior, who was another radio expert, to the TV set, VHF radio signals 600 miles from Fiordland were not so remarkable under certain conditions. In effect, the electricity and telephone wires in the street may have been forming a linear radio telescope.

In order to satisfy my curiosity, I contacted Jamie McDermott. His experience and knowledge with communications and radio had been passed on to him from his father. The incident on 12 February 1962 also acted as a career spur. He went into the telecommunications industry. He was one of the experts who connected New Zealand with the rest of the modern world. He was just 16 when he heard that mayday call. He was 75 when I had a long zoom meeting with him on 22nd August 2021. Eventually it became quite an emotional meeting for me as both of us recognised the mutual deep-rooted feelings that had been pent up for years. With respect to his comments in Lost and Traced, he said:

> "Nope I know exactly what I did. I called Mangere Airport (Now Auckland civil airport) and got air traffic control. To us it was just the Control Tower. They heard nothing. I then called RNZAF Whenuapai. Same result. I did the same with Hobsonville. Same result. Finally I called Mosick Point Radio. They had also heard nothing and I was getting pretty upset because someone had to have heard it. But they did not. After a number of long and challenging conversations years later with Murray (a colleague in telecommunications), we came to the conclusion that (my mother and I) were the only ones to have heard from that aircraft after it had crashed. I have carried that for all my life".

He felt that nobody had fully believed him. That was until Gavin Grimmer and more recently by me. It was an emotional contact and I had not realised how deeply I had been affected, albeit subconsciously, by this near miss that almost ended my life in 1962. Something he and I shared, his reactions and mine, albeit 13,000 miles apart. More recently, I filmed a presentation for the Dragonfly reunion for the meeting on 12th February 2023 at Christchurch airport. At the end of that presentation, a man stood up and recounted his own experience having flown with Chadwick as a lad about 10 days before the flight that went missing. The film had a considerable effect on him and they reminded him of our mutual close shaves with destiny. His name was Peter Graham.

It was both an emotional and stressful day for some attendees and bearing in mind that it was 61 years after the aircraft went missing, for over 100 people to attend, some from afar, indicates the continued interest in the Dragonfly accident. I was able to watch the Reunion on a live Vimeo link and I believe that the TV cameras recording the meeting provided much of the headline news that evening on terrestrial TV.

What was the significance of the McDermott Mayday?

If it was a radio call from the Dragonfly that evening, the aircraft may not have been smashed to pieces. Then again, I have heard of doubts whether, except for Chadwick, any of the passengers would have known how to make "mayday calls" or was able to operate somehow a radio albeit rather broken. Dare I introduce sub carrier harmonics. I contacted the brother of one of the passengers, John Rowan, Louis Rowan's brother. He was adamant that Louis was well versed in all such radio calls with his adventures in Papua New Guinea etc. I have no idea about the Savilles or Darrell (Stan) Shiels. But if someone did survive, there were at least two persons capable of making such a call, if the equipment and atmospheric conditions allowed. John Rowan and a large number of his siblings and relatives attended the reunion from Australia. I am sure that if it were possible, Louis Rowan would have been involved in any attempt to send out a mayday call, and try to affect a rescue for all on board. It was not just members of the Rowan family that attended the reunion. A New Zealand relative of Valerie Saville (nee Bignell) was also present. Such is the continued interest in this Kiwi Rover.

Assuming the Mayday was from the Dragonfly, then it may have been a controlled crash into bush, ice, snow, even on the side of one of the many lakes. John King's book on aviation tragedies relate accidents whereby pilots and passengers had survived the initial impact of the crash but left the crash site for the bodies to be found months or even years later nearby.

As for radio signals and distance, even in the Erebus saga, there was a report about a radio ham in Wellington with Bernard Lagan, who was a famous US radio Reporter of that era, due to atmospherics on 28/29 November 1979, Lagan was able to listen in on the US Navy helicopters flying in Antarctica searching for the missing DC-10. He heard that very first awful call reporting the finding of the crashed DC-10. (See website: erebus. co.nz, guestbook p.4)

What would be left at the crash site after 60 years?

The Dragonfly was a wood and fabric covered aircraft so apart from engines propellers landing gear and some main structural parts, nothing is likely to have lasted more than a few weeks so I am told. I disagree. A family of Dragonfly searchers, the Reeves, have collected debris from other old crash sites of similarly constructed aircraft. Surprisingly much of the wood and fabric has survived well due to the protection of aircraft dope. The Bert Mercer 1944 DH84 Dragon crash site is still littered with debris – it has not rotted away hardly at all.

Despite the passage of years, occasional evidence comes to the surface which may have originated from the Dragonfly, a lady's shoe and most recently an old aircraft harness have been found. Admittedly there is much debate about the provenance of the shoe and harness but a lot of money and expert resources would have to be spent without much likelihood of usefulness. Surprisingly, shortly after the reunion on 12th February 2023 and with all the publicity that it generated, there was another SAR exercise by the NZ police involving over 100 officers for three days in the bush on the western side of the lower South Island. There had been a previous exercise in 2021 in the Huxley Valley but that was just an exercise to bond the various amateur search party members in co-ordination of the various teams and helicopter protocols. Had they consulted more widely and really searched higher up or within the deep jungles of the Huxley, they may have had more luck.

The NZ Police exercise was carried out after the discovery of the harness on the west coast. It seems that an expert on Dragonfly aircraft believed it was a possible item from Kiwi Rover. I did make contact with this pilot who was fortunate enough to have flown the only other airworthy Dragonfly in the world – G-AEDU – the Duchess, in her bright red livery, as she is affectionately called. I am also aware that this aircraft has also had a few modifications enabling modern flight safety to 2023 standards than applying in 1938. This would include aircraft harnesses. I have examined as far as a photograph can allow, the buckles on the end of the harness. I am told that de Havilland would not manufacture such items themselves but subcontract the manufacturer. So the end buckles by themselves are no proof of coming from de Havilland. A multitude of users would have manufactured the harness. One school of thought after circulation through the internet of the photographs was that the harness came from a ships life boat.

As it was, the final presentation at the reunion was made by Bobbie Reeve. He and his family have always believed that Brian Waugh was right when he opined that Chadwick did not cross the Main Divide in the Hokitika/Haast area and that he must have followed the Mackenzie route, as Chadwick had told the controller prior to take-off. This was supported by a number of "quality" visual reports of the Dragonfly. A John Patrick (Paddy) Gordon had been interviewed and filmed by the Reeves who recounted his experiences of the 12th February 1962. Paddy Gordon had been a member of a Deer Culling team with an Evan Blanch but earlier in that week he had been a very sick man with wisdom teeth problems. After treatment, he returned to the Hopkins valley to meet up with his team on the 12th. He was on his own that morning at the Red Hut DoC (Dept. of Conservation) at the confluence of the Hopkins/Huxley rivers when an aircraft flew over the valley entering the Huxley valley. The timing was possible, fitting in with all the previous witness reports on the eastern side, that is, the Mackenzie route. Paddy Gordon had not provided any report earlier but the previous witnesses of the sightings around Lake Ohau all fit in and provide credence to the report, albeit as late as was my contribution to the knowledge of the Chadwick saga, so it should not be ignored.

But then there is the complication of Ken Eden and his Super Cub. Richard Waugh mentions this on page 121. I quote:

> Eden flew from Rangiora to Arawata in a Piper Cub and in later years remarked to

the author (Richard Waugh) – "It was difficult on the Canterbury side and stinking weather over the Alps.

This flight path could have been the same as Chadwick's "Mackenzie Country" route. Eden was trying to get to Haast on the west coast. Could it have been Eden's aircraft (a Piper Super Cub) that was the shadow of the aircraft observed by Paddy Gordon making the trip up the Hopkins/Huxley rivers to get through to Haast via the Brodrick Pass into the Landsborough valley and hence on to Haast? It is a very commonly used passage through the Southern Alps for light aircraft to get through to Haast. Paddy Gordon was unsure of what type of aircraft he saw (bi-plane or single wing) as the visibility was so bad. Could he have been mistaken and heard the Piper Cub. How good was the identification of the sound between a Piper Cub with one engine and a Dragonfly with two engines? Did Ken Eden provide SAR with details of his flight path to help eliminate sightings of his aircraft with that of the Dragonfly? What was Eden's exact flight path? This should have been investigated by SAR organisers at the time so that sightings of his flight were not mistaken for the Dragonfly. Lack of commonsense by professionals?

The Reeve family have been searching for a number of years but it is clear from the films they have made, that the likely country in which they believe ZK-AFB may still be resting, is as impenetrable as that which hid the Taylorcraft ZK-ATY for two years, ZK-MBI for six years and helicopter ZK-HNW for nine years.

My eldest nephew is conversant with de Havilland Aircraft construction and has considerable knowledge of metal fatigue in aircraft. Much of the details of metal fatigue in chapter 2 with the Aero Commander prime material were used for his early training. He has since been employed as a wing stress consultant for major aircraft constructors. He believes that if the DH90 smashed into 100-foot tall beech trees, the wings would be broken off and the remains of the fuselage stuck between the trees or eventually fall to the ground, completely engulfed by the thick bush, never to be found again, except by chance. But if the bush was that thick, it is unlikely to be found by chance. The jungle in which the Taylorcraft and Piper Cherokee could not have been so thick. Alternatively, it may be buried under a snow or rock avalanche higher up a mountainside (compare ZK-HNW 2004-2012) only to re-appear if or when the permanent snow melts.

Having been with Chadwick, albeit years ago, I recollect that he did fly very low on occasions. Would he have attempted the Gates of Haast low level flight path from Wanaka to Haast? I think that highly possible. It all depended on the cloud cover. He may have tried for the Brodrick Pass, discounted that as Kiwi Rover did not have the performance of a Piper Super Cub and elected to try the Gates of Haast route. With the problems with the radio compass, could he have turned left too soon and found himself tracking up the Albert Stream. Nearby is the Dragonfly peak as named by Paul Powell. If anyone had a good idea of the location, it would be Powell, head of that SAR region. Lew Bone believes it was to the west of Dragonfly peak and my guess is that it may be to the east of Dragonfly peak. It is one recurring dream I keep having but there is no scientific evidence for this theory, except that it is a possible scenario which one knowledgeable pilot of the area says it is distinctly possible. My dream of Mt Albert is probably due to my father's name, and that of Albert Bartlett, also my shirts were from Prince Albert. I leave it there.

Later in 1962, on returning to the UK, my father searched through the telephone directory to find Chadwick's parents who, we were told by Chadwick himself whilst at Milford, lived in Rochford near to Southend. The 8 mm Cine Film was then shown to the parents. William and Clara Chadwick had never seen their son flying before and it was a sad evening. I do believe that they were grateful to see the film which was a type of closure for them. That was when my parents provided Chadwick's parents with the famous Queenstown Photograph of Chadwick and seven passengers. I recollect accompanying my father to deliver an envelope to the Chadwicks' home a few days later, probably the blown-up print specially for William and Clara. There may be other photographs still about. There was no subsequent trace of that photograph until it was borrowed from the Chadwick family by Richard Waugh to be published in Brian Waugh's "Turbulent Years".

APPENDIX – The 8mm Cine Film as posted on YouTube

The importance of the rare film.

Much confusion was originally caused by my film on the assumption that only one cine camera had been used. It was some time before I rediscovered that my parents had used two cine cameras. The editing of the sequences and splicing the scenes in the right order, which was done some six months later back in the UK in late 1962, was always challenging. It was even more confusing for forensic analysis by aviation experts until the two-camera issue was resolved.

At one stage during the forensic review of the film in New Zealand in particular by Gavin Grimmer, the order of the scanned clips had been changed from the order of the original edited 8mm celluloid to make the film appear in sequence. Clearly the editing by my father in joining the film clips from both cameras was inexact but until that issue was resolved, I was not a popular boy with the experts who were trying to extract the maximum information as to Chadwicks' flying habits. Even worse was the editing of the discarded bad and spoilt film from the out-takes found many months later. As a 13-year-old, I had just stuck the outtakes together on one reel as discarded by my father without a thought as to order. Surprisingly, with a few exceptions, they were in some order as I stuck the pieces together as my father discarded them. As it is, these outtakes display more forensic information than much of the main film as posted on YouTube. They even show where Ken Eden and Brian Chadwick may have flown on the same exact flight-paths near to and at the west coast at Okuru and where some of the airstrips have been subsequently carved out of the jungle.

The film still deserves more careful re-analysis if it becomes necessary to determine the routes and flying styles of Chadwick in this light biplane when carrying a full load of passengers at the extreme end of its range.

Whilst at Milford Sound, the film showed dense cloud banks to the east with no apparent way through to Queenstown. I regret that Brian Waugh never had the opportunity to view our film for comparison with the weather further up the coast he experienced on the 12th February 1962. On our flight, Chadwick chose to fly up the Arthur River towards the Sutherland Falls, eventually appearing over Wakatipu from the south via the Von River. I am still debating with other pilots what was the exact route followed from Lake Quill to the Von River on our flight including Kynan Yu.

There had been a discussion between Paul Beauchamp Legg, who was an experienced DH90 pilot, often flying Kiwi Rover before Chadwick bought her. Chadwick told Beauchamp-Legg of the occasion he had been stuck above clouds on this same Milford to Queenstown sector. I speculate that Chadwick may have discovered an alternative route for our trip. Hence the unexpected downdraft. He obviously had not flown that exact route before with the wind direction persisting on our day. The cloud density may have been similar on our trip with ZK-BCP.

We will never be sure of the comparisons with the weather between the two flights of ZK-BCP and ZK-AFB. As it was, on our day Chadwick flew under the clouds but very close to the ground where we encountered the severe downdraft possibly at Eglinton when crossing a saddle. There had been a discussion whether Wakatipu or Te Anau was prettiest. My father had been advised by his friends in Lower Hutt near Wellington (Eric and Joan Howse) to see Te Anau. Normally the flight sector, from Milford to Queenstown, would not skirt Te Anau. There was the incentive for Chadwick to add Te Anau to our trip as fuel levels were good, to settle which lake was the prettiest.

The film shows the take-off at Milford on what is now runway 29. There was a strong northerly crosswind as indicated by the windsock being blown hard. ZK-BCP flew up to Harrison Cove where there was just enough room to do a 180 degree turn to track back overhead the Milford Sound Airstrip. Thereafter a right turn above the airstrip to enter the Arthur River and Lake Ada. Lake Quill and Sutherland Falls come into view.

The next original filmed sequence was above the Von River where it entered Wakatipu. However, there was a short two second clip from the outtakes that indicated we entered Wakatipu well from the south above the Von River. It was where we hit the massive downdraft. I know I was extremely scared and we all thought that was it, final. We were weightless for a considerable time.

It was this sub-conscious recollection that may have caused me when learning to fly to experience spinning training some 26 years later in Essex. So many things happened to me whilst learning to fly that I had flashbacks in my mind about that flight through the Southern Alps with Chadwick. When we landed at Queenstown, Brian Chadwick said words to the effect "You thought we had bought it there!" Clearly Chadwick had not anticipated that downdraft and I believe strongly that a similar situation could have arisen on 12th February, but not necessarily between Milford and Queenstown. Possibly in the opposite direction?

It was at Queenstown that my father took the famous photograph shown reproduced on the back cover of Richard Waugh's 2005 book "Lost without Trace?" which had been incorrectly labelled "Brian Chadwick with seven tourist passengers and Air Charter's Dominie ZK-BCP at Queenstown, August 1961." (Chadwick Collection) which had previously been reproduced 14 years earlier in "Turbulent Years" albeit in black and white, Brian Waugh's autobiography in chapter 10, "Chadwick is Missing" on page 131.

I remember my father taking that photograph very well. Chadwick had just made his comment about the downdraft. We had all calmed down and father wanted to get a good photo to share with Chadwick's parents. The laughter was about the dark glasses Chadwick wore all the time. Father insisted that he took them off so that Chadwick's parents would recognise him later back in the UK. The young lad standing centre stage, in the photograph next to Chadwick in 1962, was me. That photograph has subsequently opened so many doors for me. So much has come my way because everyone trusts that young boy with information, anecdotes and secrets normally only disclosed on death beds!

At Queenstown, a float plane landed and taxied alongside Chadwick's Dominie. There is a lovely sequence of Chadwick obtaining the fresh Rainbow Trout from the float-plane pilot. I have recently been advised that was Don Nairn and his Outrigger Dick Hutchison. I have even been given the name of the refuelling engineer – Owen Aitken. A few days later, I have more film of that float plane landing on Wakatipu. It made a big splash and I have always wondered whether that was the occasion it was damaged due to the wheels not having been retracted for a landing on the lake.

Don Nairn wrote a book about his sea plane and float plane experiences – "Gold Wings and Webbed Feet" 1996. Published and Printed appropriately by Craig Printing Co of Invercargill

The parallels with Erebus

The last words between Maria and Jim Collins – the Erebus pilot - concerned a reminder to him to pick up blue cod on the way back from Antarctica at the refuelling stopover at Christchurch (on 28th November 1979) Apparently Christchurch was then the only place where this rare Blue Cod could be obtained. Such a delicacy was not available in

Auckland at the time. Chadwick likewise was lucky to pick up a fresh Rainbow Trout for his wife Sylvia at the Queenstown refuelling courtesy of Don Nairn. I understand that Pippa Collins did eventually complete her mother's blue cod order some 30 years later after the Erebus accident. That memorable and noteworthy event was on Pippa's 2009 return from Antarctica at the Christchurch stopover.

Encounter with John King aviator extraordinaire.

I was going to leave this puzzle there until I obtained the book by the monarch of New Zealand Aviation journalism, the appropriately named John King [now editor of "The Aero Historian" for the Aviation Historical Society of New Zealand]. His 1995 book, New Zealand tragedies – Aviation Accidents and Disasters - a most respected book and ahead of its time,showed photographs of a number of downed aircraft, not least on p.125 of a Taylorcraft ZK-ATY. That aircraft went missing in 1956 but was found 30 months later in bush country near Lake Waikaremoana. Not that far from Gavin Grimmer's home of findlostaircraft.co.nz fame in the North Island. The Taylorcraft pilot's body was found 50 metres away, 30 months after his disappearance.

There were complaints of the organisation for the search for ZK-ATY by the pilot's aviation friends. The RNZAF wanted to avoid a lot of light aircraft flying over impenetrable jungle country and it was some time before those aviation colleagues were able to join in the search. By which time, after seeing the photograph of the crashed aircraft, the jungle had already "absorbed" the small plane. The chance of observing damaged flora was lost unlike that of the search for ZK-HTF in chapter 8. It was only by chance that a timber mill manager on a recce for suitable trees stumbled on the wreck of ZK-ATY, but that was 30 months later. More sadly, it was clear that the pilot, Alex Clark, had survived the initial crash but the final cause of death was not determined.

An even more remarkable case was that of a Piper Cherokee ZK-MBI. That disappeared on 21st May 1995 but was not found until 8th April 2001 by a hunter stumbling across the wreckage. The pilot was a student pilot under supervision and training. The radio calls were made, the last being at 3.30pm with a position report that was clearly wrong. The wreckage was again completely absorbed in the dense Huiarau Range jungle to the west of Gisborne and it must have been impossible for the crash site to have been seen from the air.

Could something similar have happened to the Dragonfly in the South Island? The search area for the Dragonfly was and still is so much greater than that which hid ATY, MBI or HNW for so many years. Lessons for the search for ZK-AFB as expounded by Gavin Grimmer and Chris Rudge in their books.

Many years later, I learnt to fly. Flying in a light aircraft subject to some turbulence as a norm, brought back subconscious memories of the incident in the Southern Alps with Chadwick. One part of training for the PPL is stall recovery. Some years earlier, recovery from spinning had been included in the syllabus. One can rapidly lose several thousands of feet when spinning. Stalling and its recovery can be achieved in less than 100 feet – no comparison with the loss of height when spinning. I requested one of my Seawing Flying Club instructors to demonstrate spinning and recovery and one day, a suitable aircraft was available. I was able to measure the height at commencement of the spin and then record the height on recovery. The difference was 2,000 feet but it felt less than the weightless time in ZK-BCP between Milford and Queenstown. I can only estimate that we lost about 3,000 feet in that flight in 1962. At the age of 13, I had used one of my nine lives!

I found the 1995 book by John King very helpful as an introduction to the details of the Erebus affair (see chapter 6). When my film was first scanned and sent to New Zealand, I was asked to provide an article for Aviation News New Zealand. The editor was this same John King whose book I had so admired.

I sent my brief notes outlining events that I was going to include for that article expecting to relate just a few topics say, 3-5 out of 20 parts of the whole story. One note I made was about an encounter with A10s I had whilst learning to fly. Immediately John King asked what happened, ditched everything else he wanted me to write about my flight with Brian Chadwick, and suggested that I wrote about these A10s as he had an unnerving experience in the US with one. He had written an article ready for publication and he needed something to go with it, to fill the space I expect. I was so surprised that the chief editor of New Zealand's respected aviation magazine wanted my anecdote of a highlight of my days as a student pilot.

I am delighted that I have had special permission to reproduce the whole of the jointly written article originally published in 2021. I apologize for departing from the main theme of air accident investigators but in a way, the experiences that both John King, Brian Andrews and myself went through could have gone badly wrong and we might have been subjects of an air accident report ourselves.

The Article was entitled "Up Close and Ugly"

John King:

The Fairchild Republic A-10 Thunderbolt II could never be described as an elegant aeroplane. Designed for close air support of ground troops, with a secondary mission as forward air controller-airborne support, it's built around the VW Beetle-size GAU-8 30mm rotary cannon with seven barrels on the Gatling principle, firing 3,900 rounds per minute.

Powered by twin GE TF34-GE-100A turbofans mounted high on either side of the rear fuselage, the A-10 has straight wings with numerous hard points and is heavily armoured to protect pilot, engines, fuel tanks and systems. The prototype first flew in May 1972 and production ended in 1984 with 715 examples built, but after some dithering about being replaced by the F-35, vastly more expensive to operate, the A-10 is still in service with upgraded avionics and new wings for fatigue life extension.

Republic's military jets have enjoyed "Hog" nicknames, starting with the 1946 straight-wing F-84 Thunderjet "Hog", followed in 1950 by the swept-wing F-84F Thunderstreak "Superhog" and the mid-1950s Mach 2 F-105 Thunderchief "Ultra Hog". While the A-10 was officially named the Thunderbolt II after the company's WWII-era P-47, its pilots and crews of the USAF attack squadrons who flew and maintained it gave it the rather fitting "Warthog" nickname.

At 16.26m long and 17.53m wingspan the A-10 is a large aircraft, bigger for example than the DH98 Mosquito, and when it suddenly looms alongside an unsuspecting civilian aeroplane, big, grey and far from prepossessing, it tends to catch a pilot's attention …

In the USA …

Nearing the end of an epic transcontinental July 1984 flight with Nick Oppegard in his Cessna 195 floatplane N3877Y from upstate New York, I was chief co-pilot/navigator/float pumper-out/crawler across oily spreader bars (don't ask), flying westwards from Moses Lake, Washington, towards a gap in the Cascade Range.

By this stage I was reasonably comfortable with the American aeronautical charts, having successfully navigated a lowish-level and meandering route through the Rockies. Although there was still a bewildering amount of fine detail on the 1:1,000,000 CF-16 on my lap, the Jacobs radial blocking the forward view was making reassuring rumbling noises, the weather was fine and all seemed right with the world.

Until a great big ugly grey thing suddenly materialised off the port wing, blocking a fair bit of the view southwards. A startled look at CF-16 revealed an inconspicuous hatched area marked R-6714A, otherwise known as the Yakima Firing Center and probably not a good place to be flying in an unarmed floatplane. Oops!

Fortunately an immediate right turn towards the nearest boundary caused the Warthog to go away and stop molesting us. The whole episode probably took less than a minute.

I Wrote:

… and in the UK

My PPL navigation flight test (NFT) was conducted by Brian Andrews, CFI at Seawing Flying Club, in Cessna 152 G-BNJE. My logbook says 20 March 1989: 1.45hr Southend to Halesworth and back to SND, with a practice divert to Earls Colne.

Halesworth was a Suffolk WWII airfield where in 1943 there was the most famous Glenn Miller concert held in the hangars. I had been reading masses about the 8th Army Air Force bases in the UK in WWII before my NFT. I had remembered the positions of many of those massive bomber airfields, so as I flew over these sites, even where the runways, which were laid during the war by Ove Arup, had been dug up and returned to agriculture, all were easily recognised.

Most had runway alignments southwest/northeast and so these were like arrows (signposts) on the ground. As for finding Halesworth, I knew it was no problem, even in IMC (poor weather), with all the ground pointers as the runways there are now occupied by Bernard Matthews' turkey farmhouses.

I was talking to my examiner, as you do on the test, but then we started chatting about Glen Miller and the American airmen who lost their lives in the fields below and the concerts they held.

At that point an A-10 Warthog appeared on my side (port side of course). Then another buzzed Brian on his side, followed by a few more above and below. I couldn't see exactly how many and at first, I was rather scared.

My examiner went bright scarlet and was immediately on the radio to AFIS as we were outside controlled airspace, albeit the whole area had US bases. We had not breached any zones. AFIS was asked by Brian whether the A-10s knew we were there, but on my side I could see the pilot of the Warthog very clearly and in fact we waved to each other.

Thereafter I thoroughly enjoyed a treat of a lifetime, never to be forgotten. The film *Top Gun* was a box office hit in 1986, some three years earlier, but this was much better than Tom Cruise's experience. We were surrounded by these Warthogs, flying in formation with a Cessna 152 "just not possible" I hear you say.

Brian was extremely cut up about it because it was breaking all the rules and he felt in great danger. The normal cruising speed of a C152 is much lower of course than an A-10's, but they kept with us for some time. The angle at which they flew alongside was like a Concorde taking off with its nose high in the air. They eventually pulled away after I reduced speed and to annoy them put on two notches of flaps, and then it was impossible for them to remain in formation.

Then it was back to the NFT, but I didn't like Brian's colour. He gave me the standard test to see whether I could find a diversion airfield, saying "Earls Colne". I was somewhat concerned at Brian's health and suggested that we divert immediately to Cambridge where medical assistance was available quickly.

He calmed down after a few expletives and I did the necessary to demonstrate that I could find the divert, after all, it was another WWII airfield, then back to Southend without getting in the way of the Viscounts, B707s, and Vulcan.

Brian said that he never wanted to go through all that again, so he passed me.

Thirty years later I found myself in a jeweller's shop with my wife and met Brian's son. His father had retired for some years as both pilot and jeweller, but he was there helping out during the pandemic.

Brian came out of the back of the shop, not looking at me but the jewel he had in his hand. I asked him whether he remembered any of his students' flight tests.

"Just the one," he said. "This awful student had arranged with some American pals to buzz the aircraft with their A-10s."

He took off his jeweller's glasses and put on his everyday glasses, and then the recognition came through. Such occasions can never be arranged.

One of my wife's close friends married a former US flyer. I told him about the A-10s and he burst out laughing. He said he had flown A-10s and that they sometimes flew alongside a lone aircraft for the practice, although it was frowned upon and he would deny admitting this.

Was it was possible that he was in the squadron that buzzed us, now living just 400m from my former examiner's shop in Shoeburyness, having caused such unforgettable mayhem in our lives?

As printed in Aviation News October 2021 page 28

The story was in one of the last printed editions of Aviation News as it went online-digital the next month and is now no longer a printed magazine. May be someone thought it better not to print such a story again in fear of retribution by the Americans.

Main source of information

"Turbulent Years" - Brian Waugh.

"Lost without Trace?" – Richard Waugh

"Traced but still Missing" – Gavin Grimmer

"Missing" – Chris Rudge

"Gold Wings and Webbed Feet" – Don Nairn

"New Zealand Tragedies - Aviation – Accidents and Disasters" – John King

"Tunnel Vision Refocused" – Martin Butler

Subsequent email exchanges with the two Waugh brothers, Gavin Grimmer, Lew Bone,

Skype calls with the Reeve family and their tiger. Numerous other correspondents wishing to remain anonymous.

www.dh90.info

findlostaircraft.co.nz

whitebusfamily.co.nz

CHAPTER 4

CRASH NEAR THE KAIMAI RANGE!

Details for chapter 4 -ZK-AYZ 03/07/1963 Kaimai – DC-3 flight 441 – Chief Air Accident Inspector, Paddy O'Brien

Synopsis

The background theme so far has been the mantra - blame the pilot. This is the one case that after due research and investigation, the pilots were almost exonerated. Within a few weeks of this accident, improvements were made to systems and weather forecasting. More radio beacons and distance measuring equipment (DMEs) etc were rapidly installed. DME equipment on aircraft was also improved or maintained with some alacrity. ZK-AYZs DME was often unserviceable. In brief, the unexpected wind strength from the East was not forecast and so during flight-planning, allowance for the extra wind strength had not been made for the IMC conditions that prevailed. Likewise, the lack of radio navigation aids, DMEs etc. all conspired to place the DC-3, a relatively low speed aircraft, well to the west of its estimated position.

The DC-3's approach to Tauranga was subsequently totally wrong being further to the west. The aircraft encountered a severe downdraft near the summit of the Kaimai range. The pilots thought they were obeying the Minimum Safe Altitude (MSA) for the approach to the airfield. Surprisingly enough, the pilots were not blamed in any way, at least not officially.

As usual, there were a number of "wise after the event" pilots who criticised the dead pilots' navigation technique, not unlike Erebus critics of Collins and Cassin to this day. As it was, DMEs and other navigational equipment and instrument radio beacons were installed as quickly as possible. Still today, the Kaimai Crash was the worst aircraft accident in terms of the number of fatalities on New Zealand soil "and may it remain so!" to quote the Reverend Dr Richard Waugh. He devoted a book to this disaster with good reason as it shows how lessons learned can be used for the improvement of safety and future good of all aviators and their passengers.

That Inquiry did not try to allocate blame but in the very best traditions of ICAO annex 13, the New Zealand aviation accident inspector tried to ascertain the true facts and then learn from the mistakes, and not blame the hapless pilots. At least this is what I first thought. This was the first aviation tragedy in New Zealand that demonstrated the usefulness of helicopters with Mike Alexander and his Hillier UH-12E ZK-HAN, later Jan Beijen with a Bell 47D1 ZK-HAJ. That help, first offered by the pilots of the helicopters, was initially rejected by the search organisers. This was the first occasion that helicopters took such a prominent part in an air accident investigation and recovery.

It has been noted that ZK-AYZ was so very close to escaping from the clutches of the mountain, by just a couple of hundred feet. The parallels with Erebus and the few seconds of hesitancy in applying "go-around power please" by the Erebus pilot Collins are so clear. But one group of pilots are cleared and the Erebus pilots blamed. "Probable cause" being used by Chippendale to blame those pilots. Something was not right from the start for the Erebus pilots Jim Collins and Greg Cassin. But what might have happened in that case had those involved in Erebus been threatened with the New Zealand Official Secrets Act, loss of jobs?

It is interesting to note that when Baragwanath was cross examining Captain John Spence of CAD during the Mahon Inquiry at Erebus, the Minimum Safe Altitude of 16,000 feet over Mt Erebus was compared with the Kaimai tragedy. Spence had to admit that the DC-10 AINS could have been directed down the middle of McMurdo Sound and not over an active volcano. Enchmarch had likewise been led over the Kaimai range due to insufficient NDBs and VORs. The lessons were not learnt to pass on to avoid subsequent events like Erebus. Then there were threats to the ATC officer not to disclose the truth ie a possible cause with the overpowering Auckland radio beacon typical of the cover-up philosophy endemic to this day in some New Zealand and UK establishment figures. I am thinking of the Post Office Horizon scandal in the UK currently being examined by a Commission of Inquiry. Could this issue regarding the treatment of Richardson and Christophersen have contributed to the ignorance of CAD when authorising flight paths over mountains and volcanos. Now read on with this thought in mind.

Radio Beacons

I was going to leave this as a very short commentary on the worst land based New Zealand Air Disaster. However, recently my inquiries reveal improvements were provided by all the new radio lighthouses. That refers to the very high frequency omni-directional range radios (VORs) and non-directional beacons (NDBs). It can sometimes lead to unforeseen consequences. In the UK, it is quite normal for Private Pilot License holders (PPLs) to continue their training to be able to fly safely on instruments when caught out unexpectedly in bad weather. This is a safety measure so they can complete the flight or make an instrument landing at the nearest available airport. This IMC rating is not intended to be a replacement for a full instrument rating. IFR in IMC – cloudy and poor visibility using the aviation instruments currently available as standard in modern aircraft. I am grateful that I went on to obtain this extra rating.

There was an NDB installed at Whanganui. That may have been installed or refurbished after the Newlands incident. It was at this NDB serving Whanganui when there was a controversial accident report of a Piper Seneca that crashed into the Ahuahu valley just a few miles north of the town, ZK-EQA. The pilot was a local businessman and philanthropist of Foxton. He had been approached by Stevens Bremner, a large NZ nationwide carpet business with its major plant in Foxton, to create a runway for small aircraft to fly managers from Auckland to their carpet factory in Foxton. After buying his own aircraft, Noel Oxnam obtained his pilot's licence. Although his latest acquisition was purchased initially for air ambulance work, he also operated a small airline on a shoestring. Noel Oxnam was the pilot on a flight from Hamilton to Whanganui when the weather changed and became extremely challenging and he crashed.

The first accident report was succeeded by an inquiry as there was much controversial comment by the official accident inspectors. John King in his NZ Aviation Tragedies book refers to Dmitri Zotov the Air Accident Inspector in charge of that case. Zotov would not discount the fact that Oxnam, who had run out of daylight hours to legally fly VFR in the worsening weather, may have been attempting to fly a teardrop pattern using the NDB of Whanganui for an instrument approach to that airfield. The problem was that the NDB may not have been giving a good radio signal from the ground station on which to base an NDB instrument approach. There was poor radio transmission due to the high ground to the immediate north of the airfield, but was on part of the NDB flight path.

As it was, Oxnam was out of time on his IMC ratings, the aircraft was only licensed for VFR daylight flying, and the aircraft was overloaded with 9 on board when only 6/7 seats were available.

Shades of the Fox Glacier sky dive accident to ZK-EUF where imbalance of load was alleged to be the cause of the accident by the TAIC inspector in charge. That aircraft was a Fletcher which had been built in New Zealand and then modified after use as an aerial crop duster. There was some suspicion that the control stick may have broken but ZK-EUF was buried before a full inspection had taken place.

Oxnam's Seneca ZK-EQA was alleged to have been loaded just outside of its weight and balance limits and that may have made the aircraft difficult to control in the turbulent conditions described by another nearby pilot, Doug McKnight.

It is hard to find out who was the chief accident inspector in charge but Zotov was criticised in the report by senior barrister and later judge Sir David Carruthers who dismissed the NDB theory. It is not clear why Sir David could have been so certain of his opinion. The acting chief inspector of air accidents was Milton Wylie. He was the Erebus air accident inspector who was in charge of the team that went to America to transcribe the Cockpit Voice Recorder of TE901. He had Barney Wyatt, Don Olliff, and Arthur Cooper in that first team. Later Chippindale replaced their report with his own transcription. But this was a time when Ron Chippindale was nominally the chief inspector. This accident to ZK-EQA was on 12th May 1988.

I was informed that the nose-wheel assembly of the Seneca was found sometime later by the mayor's husband who was also a pilot. It was found in another ravine some distance from the crash site. Noel Oxnam's son confirmed it was the missing wheel. If it was true and the nose wheel and assembly came off the badly loaded Seneca during normal flight, it could then have become totally out of balance. Once that nose-wheel assembly had come off the aircraft, subsequently nobody could have piloted the aircraft safely. Nevertheless, Oxnam will always be remembered as one of the town's most generous characters. When a cavalcade of five hearses spanned out in arrow formation across the wide main street of Foxton, all the shops were closed out of respect for the Oxnam family.

ATC Officers Richardson and Christophersen

However, my attention has further been drawn to an essay in a New Zealand aviation magazine that was written by George Richardson the Air Traffic Control officer based in Auckland. He was monitoring ZK-AYZ and in radio contact with that aircraft from Whenuapai ATC until he passed on the ATC control and radio communications to Tauranga tower's controller, Murray Christophersen. All of a sudden, everything I had previously read about the pilots not being automatically blamed by astute air accident inspectors was questionable. However there seemed to have been parallels with the Erebus events and Air New Zealand some 16 years later. Yet another cover-up?

The important fact related to the flight was the weather. Clearly the wind was the proximate cause of ZK-AYZ being blown off course and caught in a downdraft in the lee of the Kaimai mountains. During the official Inquiry, glider pilots and others testified as to how the air billowed in the lee of those mountains and that there were waves of both up and downdrafts. What was not addressed in too great a detail? Why had the radio compass and beacons allowed Flight 441 to stray so far off course onto the wrong side of Kaimai in the first place? Richardson reported that the Auckland Whenuapai NDB's frequency was

336KHz – (WP). The Tauranga NDBs frequency at that time was 340KHz – (TG).

The Auckland WP NDB was a very powerful transmitter. It was well able to overpower the much weaker signal on that very close frequency then of 340KHz at Tauranga. Flight 441 was doubtless tuned to TG on 340KHz (Tauranga's Radio Beacon) at one time prior to the crash. ATC at Tauranga had passed the various clearances for the IFR approach to ZK-AYZ. The aircraft's radio compass should have been tuned into 340KHz. But was it? Could it have been overwhelmed by Whenuapai's 336KHz transmissions? With this in mind, I would like to quote an extract from Richardson's essay:

> During one of the recesses of the hearing at Hamilton, I voiced the opinion
> of several controllers as well as my own about the real possibility of radio
> interference between the two radio stations WP Range and TG NDB [due to the
> 336 and 340 close frequencies]. I was advised in no uncertain terms that I was
> prohibited from offering this information to the court [of Inquiry] and the Official
> Information Act [New Zealand's Official Secrets Act] bound me, and if I chose
> to ignore this warning, dire consequences were imminent. Reference was made
> to my new and young wife and was of exceptional severity. This may sound
> dramatic, but it was what actually happened.

Such were the alleged threats at Kaimai. There were threats to the executive pilots at the Mahon Erebus Inquiry, namely the risk of them being sacked or losing seniority if they did not toe the Air NZ line.

The closeness of radio frequencies in the 1960s had a greater significance than we can appreciate today with our digital radios and direction finders. Richardson felt threatened by someone from suggesting that the true cause of the aircraft's flight path had been due to the transmitters overlapping frequencies. The inquiry was charged with the following:

> Establish the time and place of the accident, and the circumstances in which it
> arose [i.e. why was it on that flight path] and any facts which in the interests of
> public safety, should be known to the authorities charged with the administration
> of civil aviation …

It was reported that ZK-AYZ was seen at Kerepehi and then abeam Paeroa. Clearly AYZ was already somewhat off track to the west of Kaimai. The radio call was at 9.04am ETA two minutes, i.e. indicating that the pilots thought that they were just four miles away. Were the radio compasses tuned to Tauranga TG 340KHz? Or had the more powerful Whenuapai WP signal of 336KHz beacon interfered? That radio call at 9.04am indicates that 336WP could have been overpowering 340TG and hiding the fact that AYZ was more than the estimated four miles from Tauranga.

George Richardson may well have been right but Richard Wild QC and company managed to smother that theory. Tauranga's Tower ATC officer Murray Christophersen gave the clearance to descend from 5500 feet to 4100 feet. It was approved and read back. Murray had no idea that AYZ was 20 plus miles away and not just the four miles indicated by the call at 9.04am. The cloud cover was 5/8ths at 1200 feet and 8/8ths at 2000 feet so AYZ was flying blind relying on the radio beacon and radio compass, without a DME (Distance Measuring Equipment). A DME was installed at Tauranga very soon after the accident to AYZ. In comparison TE901 in Antarctica was 27 miles off course despite AINS.

Court of Inquiry

This may be similar to the Erebus cover-up 16 years later by Air NZ. The lead barrister for the Minister for Civil Aviation at the Kaimai Inquiry was the legendary Richard Wild QC. His son was John Wild, who, as a judge, crossed swords with Rob Moodie [the author of The Justice Mirage] in the case of the Berryman Bridge Saga. Then again the case of Anne Hunt author of "Broken Silence" when Wild issued an ex-parte injunction in collusion with David Collins, a former Solicitor-General.

Richard Wild QC was in a prime position to smother unwanted inconvenient secrets by the use of the Official Information Act. It is so clear that the air traffic controllers were extremely worried that the pilots Enchmarch and Kissel may have been misled by such close radio frequencies. In times of severe weather conditions, those overlapping frequencies of the radio beacons could lure the pilots on to the cliffs of Kaimai.

It was the forerunner of TAIC that resulted in the Newlands incident where another NDB was sending out misleading signals but CAD and NZCAA were unable to recognise that fact until NZALPA's expertise became involved. It seemed that there were electricity transmission cables interfering with the Wellington NDB's signal at Newlands. New Zealand's past and present TAIC did not then have the resources required for any truly independent incident inquiry. Is this still a problem today?

These radio directional beacons with their close proximity (336KHz and 340 KHz) that caused such concern to Richardson and other Air Traffic Controllers was clearly being hidden from the public in the normal Kiwi authority way. Perhaps that was why Chippindale became involved in the commission of inquiry into the accident that led to the death of President Machel of Mozambique on 19th October 1986, some 23 years later. Machel was being returned to Maputo after an African conference in a Soviet TU134A. The pilots were as usual blamed, but over the years, some unpleasant truths seem to have leaked out. The Doppler VOR at Maputo that the pilots were trying to use had a frequency of 112.7. Not long before the crash, another Doppler VOR had been installed at nearby Matsapa with the frequency 112.3.

Chippindale's brief was this. He was instructed by the South African Commission of

Inquiry to review the conspiracy theory that the VORs were being tampered with. The object of this being an assassination attempt on Machel. I believe that Chippindale may have had access to secret files connected with the Kaimai radio frequency interference and word gets round in aviation circles of those types of information. Chippindale went to RACAL the VOR manufacturers in Raynes Park London. This was before his free flights ban with Air New Zealand. The manufacturer's experts were very surprised at the closeness of the VOR frequencies allocated of Maputo and Matsapa, but unless the Maputo VOR was switched off or interfered with, they did not think the Soviet pilots were misled.

Chippindale relayed this opinion to the South African Margo Commission of Inquiry. Unsurprisingly the Soviets disagreed with this opinion. Years later, after Mandela married Machel's widow, Mandela set up a review of the events surrounding Machel's death but no further conclusions were reported. Understandably, there were considerable political side effects of Machel's untimely death, but had the lessons been learnt from the proximity of the radio beacon frequencies in New Zealand being a factor in the crash at Kaimai, subsequent allocation of frequencies of VORs in Africa, albeit 23 years later, would have been very different.

Chippindale's other foray into world politics was his assignment to join the investigation team for flight KAL 007 which was shot down by the Soviets on 1st September 1983. Some four years earlier, the Russians had assisted Chippindale's inquiry in the Erebus disaster when he suggested that Rhodes obtain photographs of McMurdo station and the accident site in Antarctica taken on 28th November 1979 by their surveillance satellites. Rhodes was successful in that mission (see chapter 6). Probably Majors Osipovich and Kasmin were the Russian pilots ferrying those photos from Arctic station Vostock to Scott Base. Stranger connections have been known.

But I conclude with this thought - Sub carrier harmonics can affect radio signals that have such close frequencies. These possibilities have been investigated in "Traced but still Missing" by Gavin Grimmer when reviewing the Mayday call heard by Ross Jamie McDermott on 12th February 1962 that may have originated from the Dragonfly of Brian Chadwick.

Main sources of Information

"Kaimai Crash" by Dr Richard Waugh.

"New Zealand Tragedies Aviation Accidents and Disasters" by John King.

"Traced but still Missing" by Gavin Grimmer

"The Justice Mirage" by Dr. Rob Moodie

"The Erebus Papers" by Stuart Macfarlane (report of the transcript of Captain Spence cross examination per page 124 EP)

South African Board of Inquiry Report C9-CAA#

Private emails from anonymous contributors fearful of NZ authorities.

George Richardson's Essay

CHAPTER 5

FORCED LANDING OR DITCHING AT QUEENSTOWN

Details for chapter 5 - Forced Landing/Ditching? at Queenstown
ZK-AKT 15/04/1967 Shot Over into the Shotover River – DH89B.
Brian Waugh's last flight as Pilot in Charge.

Background

This accident was the final straw for Brian Waugh as it ended his career as a pilot. This was the same pilot who had crashed in the north of England in 1954 [See chapter 1.] He was the first to be prosecuted in a UK civil court for careless flying. Richard Waugh's latest aviation book, at the time of writing, was based on this accident. In my opinion it was his best technical book so far. He was particularly well placed to write with considerable accuracy and authority as to the events. He had access to his father's papers, letters and some official records etc. that most authors would die for! There were a number of fine contributions by knowledgeable aviators and a respected and well experienced former TAIC Chief Air Accident Inspector, Tim Burfoot. Hidden within those other contributions were even more leads for me to unearth some remarkable stories - so easily missed if not read carefully. Well worth further research which unearthed the stories of Chippindale away from his expertise with the Erebus investigation.

Synopsis

Brian Waugh had a charter to collect two Americans from Te Anau to Queenstown. The aircraft was the ubiquitous de Havilland Dominie/Rapide which Waugh was so familiar with that like the Spitfire Pilots, it is said that the aircraft fitted Waugh more like a suit. Whilst the weather was not ideal, it was of little consequence in the short 30-minute trip. ZK-AKT was like Brian Chadwick's ZK-BCP the Air Charter Dominie aircraft. The engines were pre-war Gipsy Six and the ideal fuel had been Octane level 73. This octane level was crucial. At the centre of the subsequent engine failures this knowledge was only ascertained after some struggles obtaining the true facts from the engineering company that was maintaining the aircraft.

Between 1962, and the loss of the Dragonfly, and 1967, the fuel octane rating had been increased from 73 to 80/87 "leaded" fuel. It was 73 octane that Owen Aitken supplied to Chadwick on our trip at Queenstown in 1962. Due to this octane change, the exhaust valve guides had a nasty habit of coming loose with valves sticking, then the inevitable consequence was loss of engine power, if not total failure.

As it was, Brian Waugh's port engine failed shortly after take-off from Te Anau. The aircraft was lightly loaded and so there should have been no problems continuing safely on the starboard engine to Queenstown. Waugh was used to dealing with a single engine failure, whereas the smaller Dragonfly of Brian Chadwick could not cope with the loss of an engine and maintain height.

But then Waugh's starboard engine also lost power over Queenstown at a crucial time in the single engine approach to landing. A total power-off emergency landing was then required. Despite all Waugh's experience and skills, he was not able to reach the Frankton runway but had to ditch in the Shotover River just short of the runway. Lovell's DC-3 ditching at Sydney had 46 seconds warning, Waugh must have had even less but still Harvie was ready to criticise Waugh. A pity really because Harvie had been a knowledgeable and respected aviator. He let himself down badly as an accident investigator in this case. Likewise with the investigation of the Aero Commander of Alf Bartlett at Ruapehu.(Chapter 2).

The Shotover River was once the centre of the gold mining area of New Zealand. In the mountains above that river there remains more gold awaiting landslides to expose the mother lodes than has ever been extracted. Brian Waugh claimed that he was the first person to go panning for gold in an aeroplane, as said in his "Turbulent Years" p177. But did it provide entry to the Goldfish Club?

The 1967 accident investigation system in New Zealand was still very primitive. Richard Waugh's book "Shot over into the Shotover" describes clearly the arguments Brian Waugh had with Ted Harvie who became the NZCAA chief accident inspector just prior to Chippindale. Waugh had to fight to get the authorities to carry out a useful investigation. Harvie had been O'Brien's assistant at Kaimai. - On 16th June 1968 Brian Waugh wrote to Harvie:

> "I may seem awkward and I apologize for being alive, but I am standing up for the rights of all pilots to be able to rely on a thorough investigation of any accident".

Compare this with Collins inability to argue his case with Chippindale on Erebus 12 years later. Had Collins survived, no doubt he would have been just as angry with Chippindale as Brian Waugh was with Ted Harvie.

At one stage, Harvie was reluctant to exclude "Errors of Judgement" by Waugh for not making a safe landing on the runway at Queenstown. Harvie had completely ignored the fact that the critical loss of engine was not that of the port engine which had already stopped early on the flight back from Te Anau but it was the starboard engine that let him down at the crucial stage during the approach to landing. Waugh fought his corner fiercely with Harvie when the former realised that Harvie had not secured an investigation into the untimely demise of the starboard engine that had up to that time continued to provide power.

Initially, Harvie relied on the engineering employees of Tourist Air Travel to volunteer information relating to the condition of their engines and then report to him, in his role as the NZ CAA chief inspector of accidents as they thought appropriate. Investigation into the starboard engine was not at first carried out.

Notably the successor to Harvie was Ron Chippindale of Erebus infamy. Chippindale's training as a flight safety officer in the RNZAF commenced in 1962 until he joined AAIB in 1974. He became chief air accident inspector in 1975 until his retirement on 31st October 1998, when Tim Burfoot took over as chief air accident inspector within TAIC. Chippindale's experience had not extended to wide-bodied jet airliners, like the DC-10s.

The Newlands Incident

At this stage, it would be useful to understand the background to the New Zealand air accident investigators using the undoubted knowledge and experience of the airlines, pilots and engineers concerned in an incident. This practice originated from a near miss on 21st September 1975 known as "Newlands". The IFR approach to Wellington's airport was guided by a non-directional beacon (NDB) on the hilltop at Newlands just six miles north of Wellington airport. It was an essential part of the Instrument let-down procedure for aircraft in poor weather or for those flying IFR.

Despite the procedure as to height at each stage of completing a circuit based on the locator of the NDB, aircraft were flying far too close to the ground on many occasions. One pilot, Don Nichols, was close to crashing on 21st September 1975 and the air accidents inspectors cited pilot error. The New Zealand Airline Pilots Association (NZALPA) investigated the incident and they found that the signal from the NDB was being interfered with by electricity power cables.

It was clear that the NZCAA air accident inspectors did not have the depth of technical knowledge required to understand what was happening at the Newlands NDB and so thereafter, due to limited resources of the air accident investigation department and for other financial resource funding, it became acceptable that the department could be assisted by appropriately knowledgeable pilots and from representatives such as engineers from the airlines to assist in accident investigations. However, 1975 was some time after the 1967 ditching of ZK-AKT and the final flight of Brian Waugh as pilot in charge.

Fast forward to the effect of this case in the conduct of the Erebus Inquiry. It was to be one of the most remarkable decisions taken by the air accident inspectorate but that was the legacy of Newlands. Ian Gemmell for Air New Zealand was appointed by Chippindale and likewise the outranked, Peter Rhodes on behalf of NZALPA. Gemmell was ever present at the interviews by Chippindale of the Air New Zealand pilots. This was intimidatory and some evidence obtained by Chippindale may have been biased in the presence of Gemmell, their big boss! Rhodes was better trained and more up to date than Gemmell or Chippindale with international air accident investigations, having had his promotion to full DC-10 captain delayed whilst he completed the latest accident investigation course in Australia. Unfortunately, Rhodes was still technically only a first officer and so was outranked at every stage by Gemmell. This despite Rhodes having more modern investigatory training. Rhodes did not have the advantage of "in camera" hearings and so he may have maintained a more circumspect relationship with Mahon.

Lessons

There is an excellent chapter (5) "Resolutions and Lessons" in the "Shotover" book. It is not my purpose to go through the detail in this case study, except to note that the conduct of the Erebus investigation, which was some 12 years after Shotover and Brian Waugh's experience, disregarded so many of those lessons experienced between Brian Waugh and Ted Harvie. Richard Waugh's book, in effect, illustrates what went wrong with Harvie and the CAA inspector of accidents similar to the 1979 investigation by Chippindale.

What would the New Zealand public have thought if the official Erebus accident report had been prepared by Air New Zealand staff? Some think a lot was prepared by Gemmell, particularly the amendments to the CVR transcripts, and that Gemmell greatly influenced what went into the rest of Ron Chippindale's report.

Pause for thought. Chippindale's early career was based on the same training as Ted Harvie. In fact, Harvie mentored Chippindale. W H (Bill) Tench in the UK was involved in the evolution of the ICAO annex 13 reporting standards. Clearly Ted Harvie's investigations into the Shotover ditching of Brian Waugh was primitive. It is possible that Waugh was the first pilot to formally complain about the NZ Civil Aviation accident inspector's methods.

Peter Mahon in his book "Verdict on Erebus" on page 62 refers to the established procedures in New Zealand "contrary though they may have been to the policy of Annex

13" of ICAO. Basically, New Zealand accident inspectors did not take signed and written statements from witnesses so that there is a danger that conclusions reached may have left on one side verbal statements which do not coincide with the view of the investigator". Completely contrary to police practice of taking signed statements.

I have heard even more disturbing comments directly from witnesses involved in air accidents that Chippindale's normal practice would be to tape record interviews. But when transcribed later in the official reports, those transcriptions bore little resemblance to what the witnesses actually said, but rather supported Chippindale's theories of accident causation.

Those antiquated methods included inspectors relying on engineering employees of the companies being investigated to confess to any shoddy work carried out by them. A reminder this was 1967. Fast forward to 1979 (Erebus tragedy) and Chippindale's invitation to Gemmell and Rhodes which was due to the Newlands incident. Otherwise, nothing had changed for 12 years in New Zealand air accident investigation.

Appendix to Chapter 5
Forced Landing or was it Ditching? With the Dominie ZK-AKT– DH89B into the Shotover.

I have briefly mentioned the Goldfish Club in connection with Brian Waugh's claim that he was the first person to go panning for gold in an aeroplane. Whilst this may have been a tongue-in-cheek comment, I know from personal experience that there were new gold bearing lodes being exposed in 1962 and for just 10 minutes panning, I panned about £10 worth of gold dust in one secret location on that river using the technique I had been taught at Knotts Berry Farm, Los Angeles in 1957. I had been advised of this location by a former miner friend of our hosts. The Shotover River was once one of the main gold-mining rivers in New Zealand.

The Goldfish Club is a worldwide association of people who have survived an aircraft accident by parachuting into the water or whose aircraft crashed into the water, and whose lives were saved by a life-jacket, inflatable dinghy or similar device. When Brian Waugh ditched his aircraft into that river, somewhat short of the Queenstown runway, it must count as his admission ticket into the Goldfish Club. It was late autumn and there was a fair amount of water. Without the rapid action of engineer John Muir of Tourist Air Travel who happened to be at the nearby Lower Shotover Hotel, Waugh may well have drowned. That must qualify Waugh as a "gold-dust" member of the Goldfish Club. Most pilots would have qualified in a more conventional way after parachuting from a stricken aircraft perhaps after an aerial dog-fight in battle. But not Waugh with his panning for real gold claim.

Ditching – Lovell DC-3 – Sullenberger A320

Two pilots with more conventional claims to join The Goldfish Club on ditching their aircraft were Rod Lovell in a DC-3 on 24th April 1994 and Chesley Sullenberger in an Airbus A320 on 15th January 2009. Most people will be familiar with the latter case as this was the ditching of the jetliner in the Hudson River, New York in the middle of winter and all 155 on board were saved by the prompt action of Sully Sullenberger, his co-pilot FO Jeffrey Skiles and in fact the whole crew.

After initial criticisms that the perceived need to ditch was found to be unreasonably based, Sully and Skiles were treated as the heroes they indeed always were. Their aircraft had suffered from a bird strike shortly after take-off and they had just 208 seconds to consider their subsequent action. By comparison, Rod Lovell had just 46 seconds to decide to ditch after the port engine failed on take-off and a sick starboard engine not producing enough power to stay aloft. Lovell had to use his experience as a military pilot with the Australian Air Force including supersonic fighter jets but managed to set down in Botany Bay having taken off from Mascot Airport just 46 seconds previously. Doubtless Sully's past experience also helped in his higher profile case.

The title of Lovell's new book tells the tale in a nutshell "From Hero to Zero". He had been castigated by certain Australian authorities of the time, namely by BASI (Bureau of Air Safety Investigation) and by CAA (Civil Aviation Authority – of Australia).

With hindsight, it is clear that the Australian CAA employees were at fault in the supervision of the maintenance of the DC-3 and were covering up their failure by blaming Lovell. In brief, Lovell saved the lives of all 25 persons on board the DC-3 by a perfect ditching in the sea. This was 1994 and the officials at that time of BASI and CAA were critical of the unfortunate pilot who should have been treated as much of a hero as Sully and Skiles were some years later. They took Lovell's flying licence away and it was not until well after the ditching in the Hudson River that questions began to be asked about the investigations by the Australian authorities.

Later in the year 2009, after the Hudson River ditching episode of Sully and Skiles, there was another ditching on 18th November when a Pel Air Westwind jet came to grief at Norfolk Island, that was VH-NGA. There was an Australian Senate Enquiry into the Pel Air accident report by the successors to BASI (ATSB) and CAA (CASA), who had once again plainly criticised the pilots. Whilst the Senate Enquiry took some time, the truth in the Pel Air Westwind case gradually emerged that the original BASI investigations and criticisms were as flawed as those criticisms of the 1994 DC-3 ditching by Rod Lovell in Botany Bay.

The Senate Enquiry allowed some parts of the hearing to be held secretly "in camera" to prevent retribution by ATSB and CASA of some of the witnesses. [Comment: See chapter 6 and the Mahon Report where Peter Rhodes was called by both ALPA and Air New Zealand. Rhodes was thereafter the target of both sides in the Erebus debacle but was likely privately briefing Mahon who referred namelessly to some of these matters in his book Verdict on Erebus. Even more noticeable were the photographs opposite page 89 in Mahon's book "Verdict on Erebus" with the label "Three men whose evidence about flying hazards had a significant effect at the inquiry". On the left was Gordon Vette, on the right was Antarctic expert Bob Thomson, but centre stage was Peter M Rhodes.]

There had been a subsequent fatal disaster with a DC-3 in the Netherlands on 25th September 1996, PH-DDA. That was of an aircraft owned and run by their Dakota Club. The Dutch were therefore inspired to build the first full simulator for the DC-3. Eventually Lovell was able to experience that simulator and all the readings, engine performances, propeller feathering angles were fed into the Dutch simulator. Lovell was now in a position to start to recover his reputation that had been so tarnished by a certain part of Australian Officialdom. In 2019 he published his own book, From Hero to Zero, describing the trials and tribulations these accident investigators caused with the ever present blame the pilots' mantra.

As I write, efforts are now being made to re-open the Australian files attached to the ditching of his DC-3 VH-EDC. It is clear that the stewardship of the Australian CAA into the surveillance of the aircraft owners and their maintenance and the falsification by BASI of parts of the original accident reports is now being revealed. It is possible that type of documentation which may be still available would have pleased His Honour Justice Peter Mahon, if he had been able to obtain the same during the Erebus Inquiry (See Case Study 6). I wish Rod Lovell all the success in unravelling a saga equally as important to the future safety of air travel in Australia as well as with ICAO and annex 13 progress.

Just a passing thought. Next time the cabin staff demonstrate as part of the safety briefing to air passengers "how to put on a life jacket" would it be in order to ask whether the captain has practiced or had any training ditching the aircraft? Whether this training was in a simulator or not may not matter, provided it was to the safety standards demonstrated by Lovell in 1994 and Sullenberger in 2009. If not, then the life jacket drill may be a waste of time!

Main sources of Information.

"Shot Over into the Shotover" – Rev Dr Richard Waugh (from personal and some official correspondence maintained by his late father pilot Brian Waugh.)
"Turbulent Years" - Brian Waugh
"From Hero to Zero" – Rod Lovell
"Kiwis Can Fly" – Jeremy Burfoot
Additional information from contributors to Richard Waugh's book.

CHAPTER 6

THE EREBUS DISASTER

Details for chapter 6 - ZK-NZP 28/11/1979 – DC-10 Flight TE901
The Erebus disaster with 237 passengers and 20 Crew lost.

INTRODUCTION

State Fraud using the Warsaw convention.

Apart from being a review of Air Accident investigations, this case is more notable for having become one of the largest Corporate and State Frauds successfully perpetrated. It includes the failure of the international Legal Justice System between the United Kingdom and New Zealand in the nineteen eighties.

In view of this observation of what happened in New Zealand following the tragedy at Mount Erebus on 28th November 1979, I recount the law relating to UK Royal Commissions of Inquiry as well as other such investigations set up under the Companies Acts, similar in both the UK and New Zealand at the relevant times. The powers were said to be denied to Mr Justice Peter Mahon to express his opinion in his unique way of the veracity of those who gave evidence under oath in the Royal Commission of Inquiry. This followed the spotlight of the disaster in Antarctica when a DC-10 Airliner crashed causing the deaths of 257 innocent passengers and crew. The fraud was perpetrated against those 257 lost souls' families by Air New Zealand, the State Airline and Civil Aviation Department of New Zealand

The law relating to the conduct of Commissioners with regard to Inquiry Reporting:

Extracts from Maxwellisation report 2016 Blackstone Chambers and Natural Justice

It was this 2016 report that clarified the law of Natural Justice which should have been recognised by the relevant authorities, including New Zealand's High Court, Appeal Court in the nineteen eighties together with the judgments of the Privy Council.

Lord Denning re Maxwellisation

Quote:- "It was suggested before us that whenever the inspectors thought of deciding a conflict of evidence or of making adverse criticism of someone, they should draft the proposed passage of their report and put it before the party for his comments before including it. But I think this also is going too far. This sort of thing should be left to the discretion of the inspectors. They must be masters of their own procedure. They should be subject to no rules save this: they must be fair. **This being done, they should make their report with courage and frankness, keeping nothing back. The public interest demands it.** (My emphasis)

The public interest demands that, so long as he acts honestly and does what is fair to the best of his ability, his report is not to be impugned in the courts of law."

Maxwell v D.T.I. [1974] QB523.

Lord Denning was supported by Law Lords Orr and Lawton who gave concurring judgments.

Less than seven months after that Court of Appeal's decision in *Maxwell re Pergamon Press*, these central legal principles as set out were approved by Lord Diplock himself during his judgment into the Hoffmann La Roche inquiry. The final court in which he was presiding being that of the House of Lords.

Lord Diplock stated:

"…I would accept that it is the duty of the commissioners to observe the rules of natural justice in the course of their investigation – which means no more than that they must act fairly by giving to the person whose activities are being investigated a reasonable opportunity to put forward facts and arguments in justification of his conduct of these activities before they reach a conclusion which may adversely affect him."

F Hoffmann La Roche & Co AG v Secretary of State for Trade and Industry [1975] AC 295, 368D-E and 369D-F.

A brief extract of part of paragraph 377 of His Hon. Peter Mahon's words when he made his report **with courage and frankness** (my emphasis) in using the following words to fit the occasion –

"I am forced reluctantly to say that I had to listen to an orchestrated litany of lies,"

In the Privy Council's judgment, Lord Diplock said "the judge (Mahon) failed by inadvertence to observe the rules of natural justice". If anyone failed by inadvertence, it was Diplock whose memory failed to remind him of his own 1975 judgment when he agreed with Denning in the Maxwell case. Why did Diplock and his fellow judges make such a blunder?

This can be answered very simply. The Privy Councillors had been lobbied by the two New Zealand Judges, Sir Owen Woodhouse and Duncan McMullin. In a bid to keep their attendance quiet, these two judges secretly flew separately to the UK in 1983 specifically to lobby the members of the Privy Council. They were the ones who suggested the words "Manifestly wrong" which the New Zealand attorney general's counsel repeated in his final submission. I believe that this lobbying was technically an attempt to "pervert the course of justice" by two members of the judiciary. This perversion was successful to the extent that Diplock and his fellow judges, including the later red-faced Lord Bridge (judge in the Guildford Six scandal), who ignored their own previous House of Lords judgment in the Maxwell case.

This is the most disgraceful episode of the tragedy at Mount Erebus when the relatives of 257 souls were denied the compassion as well as the financial compensation that they deserved. It was a corporate fraud by the state of New Zealand on those relatives. It has never been rectified.

Is there a statute of limitations for Corporate Fraud in New Zealand?

Instead the 1971 High Court Judgement was quoted. This was overturned by Dennings 1974 appeal court judgement. Supported by Diplock's 1975 Hoffman La Roche case in the House of Lords.

There can however be no Statute of Limitations on THE TRUTH.

Part 1

Bare bones

Air New Zealand's Flight TE901 on 28th November 1979 was a sightseeing excursion trip from New Zealand to Antarctica. This fourteenth trip crashed. This was caused when Air New Zealand changed the co-ordinates fed into the navigation computer a few hours before the flight, and never told the pilots that those co-ordinates had been changed on which they had been briefed. The first accident inquiry was carried out by air accident investigators led by Ron Chippindale. It blamed the pilots for disobeying what he wrongly claimed was the minimum safety altitude of 16,000 feet.

The second inquiry was a Royal Commission of Inquiry with just one Commissioner, Justice Peter Mahon, a High Court Judge. He found that the pilots were not at fault. He said they had been misled by slipshod Air New Zealand management in changing the navigational co-ordinates by 27 miles. That change led the flight path towards the 12,500-foot-high active volcano, Mount Erebus. The reports from these two inquiries directly contradicted each other. Is there controversy as to which report was correct, even today?.

Air New Zealand took much trouble to hide and destroy as much as they could of the documentary evidence that, had it been produced to the commission, the evidence would have proved their slipshod management and would also have proved that the pilots were not at fault. Such destruction and document shredding were much in evidence. Air New Zealand's defensive actions were simple and plain evidence that its executives and its directors themselves knew that their management was the basic cause of the crash.

The most important pieces of documentary evidence were the notes from Air New Zealand's briefing of the pilots made by the captain, Jim Collins, in his ring-binder note book. It is also clear that he made a note of the critical McMurdo Sound waypoint near the Dailey Islands on his New Zealand Atlas and on the two charts on which he had worked. He probably drew in the flight lines from the Cape Hallett waypoint to the McMurdo Sound waypoint. One chart had been lent to him by co-pilot Graham Lucas's friend at Nelson, and the other had been bought by Collins. The other important documentary evidence which Air New Zealand made to disappear were the notes of the briefing made by co-pilot Greg Cassin. He had left them at home on the day of the accident. Cassin's wife was a qualified pilot and had seen the notes.

Paragraph 377 of the Mahon Report in full reads

> No judicial officer ever wishes to be compelled to say that he has listened
> to evidence which is false. He always prefers to say, as I hope hundreds of

judgments which I have written will illustrate, that he cannot accept the relevant explanation, or that he prefers a contrary version set out in the evidence. But in this case, the palpably false sections of evidence which I heard could not have been the result of mistake, or faulty recollection. They originated, I am compelled to say, in a pre-determined plan of deception. They were very clearly part of an attempt to conceal a series of disastrous administrative blunders and so, in regard to the particular items of evidence to which I have referred, I am forced reluctantly to say that I had to listen to an orchestrated litany of lies.

Comment

What Mahon said is pure Shakespeare with the perfect iambic pentameter as used in three of his most famous tragedies, Macbeth, Hamlet, and Lear. Mahon has been criticised by lesser mortals for the dramatic use of the rhythm of Shakespeare as it attracted the legal attention that otherwise it would have received in the subsequent court cases in both the New Zealand Court of Appeal and the Privy Council in London.

Dramatis Personae

I am providing pen descriptions of the individuals who participated in the cover-up, as well as the lawyers for Air New Zealand, the management pilots, the Airline Pilots Association of New Zealand, the line pilots, and the Civil Aviation Department (CAD) government officers who were supposed to regulate and oversee standards within Air New Zealand. The Ministry of Transport includes accident investigators and CAD was part of that. To get a better understanding of the facts, it is important to realise what were the motives of the various individuals who were giving evidence to the inquiries.

It may be unusual but appropriate in the circumstances to commence this chapter in the style of a Shakespearian play, but the accident to a DC-10 on a sightseeing trip to Antarctica in 1979 with the loss of all 257 souls on board, it may be more appropriate. The cause of the crash is now quite clear with the hindsight of more than 40 years.

Due to the complexity of the investigations and the false testimony that was given throughout, for a full understanding of the case, it is best to know the main players and the roles that they played in the DC-10 Tragedy at Mount Erebus, flight TE901, the subsequent inquiries, as well as in the court cases. Know their financial incentives.

His Honour Justice Peter Mahon

Peter Mahon was one of the most experienced judges New Zealand was fortunate to have. He was also one of the best at recognising witnesses who were lying. With the passage of more than 40 years, it is clear that he recognised those liars, and that with other private information not supplied during the public hearings, he had identified who was pulling the strings, intimidating witnesses, and what their motives were. The motive of the orchestrator was to reduce the size of the claims for negligence that could be made by passengers. Those potential claims could ultimately have fallen on the New Zealand tax-payer.

Ron Chippindale, Ian Gemmell and Peter Rhodes – The chief air accident inspector and his two special advisers selected for this one investigation. The other senior accident inspectors from the NZ Ministry of Transport were **Milton Wylie** from Auckland and **David Graham** from Christchurch.

Chippindale first acquired his knowledge and technique of air accident investigations in 1962, whilst with the RNZAF at Cranfield in the UK. After he retired from the RNZAF, he was appointed New Zealand's chief inspector of air accidents in 1975. He held that position until October 1998. He appointed Ian Gemmell, who was chief pilot for Air New Zealand, and secondly Peter Rhodes, who represented the New Zealand Air Line Pilots Association (ALPA). Rhodes and Gemmell were employees of Air New Zealand. The Antarctica sight seeing trip was Gemmell's baby. Rhodes, was only a first officer, that is he was a co-pilot. However, Rhodes was the most qualified accident investigator, because he had spent a considerable amount of time being trained in big jet accident investigation.

During witness interviews conducted by Chippindale, he was frequently accompanied by his special technical assistant Gemmell. No doubt his presence was intimidating to those company witnesses to toe the company line. Their evidence under oath at the Mahon Inquiry may have been more truthful.

Although I criticise **Ian Gemmell** for his false and misleading evidence, like Peter Mahon, I recognise his brilliance to have thought through and achieved this plan to absolve Air New Zealand, mostly thought up during his flight to Antartica on 29th November 1979. Mahon compared Gemmell with Von Manstein, the German WWII General who was way ahead of his colleagues.

In later life Gemmell's abilities were put to good use setting up the aviation world in Polynesia, very close to my heart.

Rhodes first gave evidence for ALPA on 1st October 1980 with the help of witness statements drawn up by **Paul Davison**, junior counsel for ALPA and Collins estate. Air New Zealand sacked Rhodes for doing so. Subsequently Rhodes was called as a witness by Air New Zealand. Then he was re-employed, albeit at the cost of half his pension. Such was the pressure Air New Zealand used against any vulnerable employee who gave evidence against the company or against the pilot error mantra of Chippindale.

Mahon referred to the incident in paragraph 348 of his report. So important was this observation by Mahon that much was written by their lordships at the Privy Council on the subject. After that intimidation, Rhodes was labelled as unreliable by many. Little assistance was provided by the Airline Pilots Association (ALPA) to protect their witnesses from retribution. At times, over many years, Rhodes overtly supported Chippindale's views. But since his retirement, Rhodes now fully supports the Mahon Report.

In 2012 Rhodes was again under pressure by the government as well as by the Transport Accident Investigation Commission (TAIC). This was the result of an air accident in which a sky-dive cameraman was killed when his parachutes would not open properly. Rhodes and Dave Hall, the owner of Lake Wanaka Sky Dive, were interviewed under caution by investigators for Health and Safety at Work regimes. TAIC was committed not to make inquiries with a view to prosecution. But the Health and Safety at Work agents make inquiries with a view to prosecution. Rhodes and Hall were threatened with 15 years jail for alleged safety infringements. The pressure on Hall resulted in his suicide. Such is the pressure that Government agents can place upon aviators and sky-divers. That is no different from what Air New Zealand managers exerted upon their hapless pilots in 1979-1980 during the Erebus affair. Most denied this pressure.

Les Simpson and Derek Ellis – Like Rhodes, Simpson's evidence at the Royal Commission was probably the most damaging to Air New Zealand. The airline had successfully impounded and shredded all the documentary evidence from RCU briefings, except for exhibit 164, that proved the pilots were instructed that the flight path was in middle of McMurdo Sound. Simpson left the employ of Air New Zealand and he became a pilot for other airlines. Some time later, he was unhappy with his new employers, and he wanted to return to Air New Zealand. Because he had given evidence against Air New Zealand, he needed to curry favour with its management. Ellis was a retired British Airways Concorde pilot. Simpson and Ellis claimed via an aviation magazine that the ALPA lawyers had coerced Simpson into giving false evidence about the evidence he had given to the Royal Commission about the briefing.

That claim of coercion would have been useful to enable Air New Zealand to restore faith in the Chippindale report. In the most comprehensive book of all on the subject, "Erebus Papers" author **Stuart Macfarlane** used more than 10% of the 734 pages in detailing this accusation by Ellis and Simpson. Fortunately, ALPA's lawyer, Paul Davison, had retained Simpson's hand-written draft of evidence. Absolute proof that Simpson had not been a victim of any pressure from ALPA's lawyers to give perjured evidence. In other words, that proved that the claim by Simpson and Ellis was false. Ellis had praised Chippindale's report which meant he criticised Mahon's report. He received much public acclaim for doing so.

Ellis made a number of claims about Chippindale's involvement with the South African Commission of Inquiry into the fatal accident suffered by an African political leader. Those claims were factually wrong. That shows he was unreliable.

Gordon Vette was the famous DC-10 pilot who had trained most of the Air New Zealand pilots who were involved in the Antarctica flights round Mt. Erebus, including the pilot of the fatal flight, Jim Collins. Vette could not believe that Collins was guilty of poor airmanship as had been claimed by Chippindale. At Vette's own expense, he brought an expert, Prof. Ross Day, from Monash University, Australia, to give evidence to the Royal Commission about the optical illusions that pilots can be subject to when flying in Antarctica. The white surface whiteout illusion was the ultimate cause of the crash when the whole flightdeck crew could not perceive Mt Erebus due to that type of optical illusion. His evidence about whiteout was one of the factors which destroyed Air New Zealand's case that pilot error caused the crash. Because Vette continued to give evidence that whiteout was one of the causes of the crash, Air New Zealand constructively dismissed him by having Ian Gemmell on the flight deck as check captain on Gordon's flights. In 1982, Gemmell watched each of Vette's actions in total silence, flight after flight. That became intolerable and Vette was forced to resign, and thereby suffered great financial loss. Vette went on, with the initial help of Peter Mahon, with his research into the appropriate training for pilots and into the conduct of investigations into all transport accident investigations.

Pilots Jim Collins, Greg Cassin, and Graham (Brick) Lucas; Flight Engineers Gordon Brooks and Nick Moloney – Jim Collins had the reputation throughout all of Air New Zealand aircrew and cabin staff as being one of the very best and safest of all pilots. The co-pilots of the fatal flight, Cassin and Lucas, were highly experienced with thousands of hours on DC-10s, whereas Chippindale had none. Brooks and Moloney were equally as experienced. They would not have accepted any shoddy flying practices. They were both noted to express their firm opinions whenever any of their pilots were below standard.

Arthur Cooper, Don Olliff, Barney Wyatt, and Milton Wylie — These were the team members who transcribed the cockpit voice recorder (CVR). The CVR was the continuous tape system that recorded the last half hour of the conversations carried out on the flight deck. The sound reproduction system of the DC-10s in 1979 was poor. It required as transcribers persons who could recognise the voices of the flight deck crew, so as to be able to identify what was said and who said it. Cooper, Olliff, and Wyatt regularly flew with the accident crew and were ideal to transcribe the tape. Chippindale rejected the transcription they produced. He replaced their transcript with his own version. In doing so he was assisted by Gemmell. His official accident report, using his own transcription was released in June 1980. Cooper, Olliff, and Wyatt were let down when Inspector Milton Wylie was unable or unwilling to persuade Chippindale to accept their transcript.

Hugh Logan, Keith Woodford, and John Stanton – These three mountaineers, after setting up the helicopter pad at the crash site, were part of the team that surveyed the area, and marked out the accident site for the purpose of body recovery by the Police DVI. Disaster Victim Identification (DVI) is the process of recovering and identifying the deceased in circumstances where there is a risk of misidentification either due to the state of the deceased's body or the number of deceased people.

These three mountaineers sometimes accompanied the accident investigators, in particular Gemmell, Chippindale and Rhodes. Stanton found Collins's flight bag with his atlas and one chart. These items were taken to the Scott Base store, but were never seen again. Stanton did not tell the Royal Commissioner of these finds. But, many years later, Stanton did tell fellow mountaineer John Maine about those discoveries. Maine's statement was recorded by barrister **Paul Davison.** Davison was the young 28-year-old barrister who acted for both ALPA and for the Collins Estate.

Bruce Crosbie and Anne Cassin — Arthur Cooper, on behalf of ALPA, asked Crosbie to visit the co-pilot's widow, Anne Cassin, and to act as an ALPA family liaison officer so as to help the widow. The real significance of Crosbie's contact with Anne was that Greg Cassin had left his flight briefing documents at home on the day of the flight. It was vital that these documents were recovered by Air New Zealand as they would have provided the crucial evidence that Air New Zealand had briefed the pilots that the flight path lay down the centre of McMurdo Sound. If those documents had been produced as documentary evidence to the Royal Commission, they would have destroyed the Air New Zealand "Orchestrated litany of Lies" claim that the airline was free from blame for causing the crash.

In the absence of Anne Cassin, in ignorance of the importance of Greg's documents, her sister and brother in law gave them to Crosbie. Those documents somehow mysteriously came into the hands of Air New Zealand. Anne Cassin requested Air New Zealand to return them, but the crucial papers, which would have proved that the airline briefed the pilots on a McMurdo Sound flight path were retained by Air New Zealand, never to reappear.

Police and DVI — Inspector Bob Mitchell, Sergeant Greg Gilpin, Constable Stuart Leighton — The significant part played by Gilpin and Leighton and their police colleagues was the recovery of the bodies of the victims of the crash from the crash site. During the period when he was working the area near the cockpit, Leighton found a small ring-binder notebook. At first glance it could appear to be a diary. Leighton passed this on to his sergeant, Greg Gilpin. They both looked through it. It was Jim Collins's note book. It contained map co-ordinates and radio frequencies. These were vital items. Obviously, these will have shown that the pilots were not at fault. Therefore, Air New Zealand needed them to be destroyed, so as to conceal the fact that Air New Zealand had briefed the pilots on a flight path in McMurdo Sound.

The ring-binder was handed in and it was taken, together with many other papers found on the crash site, to the Scott Base store. The store was unattended during the relevant times. It was therefore open to Gemmell to impound the ring-binder. It was not seen again until Bruce Crosbie, acting on behalf of Air New Zealand, returned the cover to Collins's widow, Maria, but it had no contents.

The ring-binder had somehow found its way back to Air New Zealand. But not through the proper standard police system to the mortuary. There Graham Lister and ex-policeman Ian Hambly were using the recoveries of items such as diaries from the crash site to help to identify the victims. This ring-binder, like the flight briefing documents of Cassin, and the missing atlas of Collins, were key items in the whole story.

Maria Collins, and her four daughters, Kathryn, Elizabeth, Philippa, and Adrienne — Maria, Kathryn, and Elizabeth were key witnesses to prove the fact that Jim Collins had been working on relevant charts. He was undoubtedly using the flight plan he took from the briefing. One chart in particular, GNC21N, was an American chart. It was not used by Air New Zealand pilots. How Collins obtained that chart is another story. That story proved Chief Inspector Chippindale lied in his press releases, where he claimed Collins did not work on charts, and in his claim that the daughters' evidence to the Royal Commission was perjury.

Libel by **Chippindale** with the issue of the press releases in 1982

There was absolute proof that Chippindale was aware of the source of the chart GNC21N from his reading transcripts of the radio messages and the police report of the conversations between Lucas and Tait at Nelson. Therefore his accusations of perjury by Maria, Kathryn and in particular Elizabeth Collins was knowingly false. Elizabeth had unmistakeably described chart GNC21N in her evidence to the Mahon Inquiry. Any Chippindale supporters still alive need to apologize for his crass behaviour.

Maynard Hawkins, Roger Hawkins and Richard McGrane

Mayne Hawkins was pilot in charge of the Antarctica flight on 18th October 1977. His co-pilots were First Officer Ken Mulgrew and Captain Lawson. The flight path for the first two flights in 1977 was a direct line from Cape Hallett to McMurdo's Williams Field waypoint. In other words, a flight path directly over Mt Erebus. The flight path for the next four flights in 1977 was a direct line from Cape Hallett to McMurdo's NDB waypoint. In practice, all those subsequent 1977 flights were conducted in VMC down the middle of McMurdo Sound under the US Navy ATC.

Mayne Hawkins was useful to spread the myth of the 16,000 and 6,000 feet MSA "rule" which Air New Zealand adopted after the crash. Hawkins was the last to be cleared of perjury during the Superintendent Brian Wilkinson sham police investigation due to alleged lack of evidence, when he claimed that he did not descend below the alleged MSA of 6,000 feet. No photographs had then been found to corroborate a reporter's story that in fact the Hawkins' flight did descend to 400 metres (1,300 feet) or that Hawkins misled the Royal Commission.

But there are now photographs showing Mt Erebus from the same angle as in Air New Zealand's publicity brochure "The Antarctic Experience". That brochure had a photograph of First Officer Ken Mulgrew in the co-pilot's seat. It was advertising low level flight in the vicinity of Mt Erebus. Ken Mulgrew was the brother of Peter who was the commentator on Hawkins's flight - on 18th October 1977 Q.E.D.

The famous New Zealand mountaineer/scientist involved with the Mt. Erebus recovery, Colin Monteath has just published a book "Erebus The Ice Dragon - a portrait of an Antarctic Volcano 2023". This is a study of that volcano with some of the clearest photographs from many angles. On page 188, it has a photograph of that mountain from sea level at Cape Evans. The position at ground level is exactly the same as that Air New Zealand photograph of Ken Mulgrew with Mt. Erebus in the cockpit window. From a comparison forensic review of the photographs, it can be seen that Mulgrew must have been just above Cape Evans where Scott's hut is located. The angle of the Mulgrew photograph looking at Erebus confirms a height of camera consistent with 1,300 feet. Hawkins's evidence on oath to the Royal Commission was that he never descended below 6,000 feet. Now disproved.

Richard McGrane, albeit junior counsel for Air New Zealand, was the technical expert barrister for the company. He flatted with Maynard Hawkins's son, Roger, and was a regular visitor to the McMullin family. He also gave driving lessons to the then young Kathryn Collins. Later he provided most of the technical data for the Court of Appeal drawing up witness statements and likewise for the Privy Council hearings.

Woodhouse and McMullin, New Zealand Court of Appeal judges — These were the two Appeal Court judges who each had children working for Air New Zealand at the time. They were duty bound under judges rules to recuse. Subsequently that became a clear case of bias. Therefore, they should not have sat as judges in the case where Air New Zealand, CEO Davis, Gemmell, and others were claiming to overturn Mahon's statement that he had been told an orchestrated litany of lies and did not have the right to tell such home truths.

Lords Diplock and Bridge — Diplock was the judge who had a memory failure when he forgot the Maxwell case. That case had decided the law of natural justice. It was this claimed right to natural justice that Robert Maxwell made in the UK. This claim of the right to natural justice could have forever held up the reports of a Commission of Inquiry. Mahon, in the Air New Zealand case, relied on the correct interpretation of the Maxwell case. Diplock had endorsed the 1974 UK Appeal Court decision that such a report could not be held up for natural justice reasons.

It was completely clarified in 2016, by a UK treasury report, that time did not need to be given for natural justice, or that Davis, Gemmell et al were entitled to natural justice. In effect, Mahon had been right all along, and ahead of his time, while the New Zealand Appeal Court judges and the members of the Privy Council were wrong.

Another case was haunting Lord Bridge. He was the judge at first instance in the scandal of the Birmingham Six where he displayed his inability to perceive that police officers were lying. Thereby he caused the infamous miscarriage of justice and the jailing of six totally innocent Irishmen for 16 years. In that case, compensation averaging £1 million each was paid to the six victims of Bridge's incompetence. Bridge had rejected good forensic evidence which proved the appalling standards of the police forensic departments, and of an expert witness, Dr Skuse, whose investigations thereafter were rejected.

MBEs and New Zealand Special Service Medals

As far as I can establish, only two MBEs were issued by the N. Z. Prime Minister in 1981 in respect of services given in the Erebus disaster. I am sure that they were both well deserved, but so too were many others.

The recipients of the MBEs were John Stanton, the mountaineer who failed to report to the Royal Commission that he had found the Collins flight bag with his atlas inside. Stanton had come to give evidence at the Royal Commission. But he was stopped before he was able to give evidence to the Royal Commission. He did not give any statement until after the Mahon Report when he gave a statement to the effect that Gemmell had removed nothing from the crash site. Probably true except for the diary of Dianne Keenan. But he helped himself at Scott Base to the ring-binder and Atlas at the unguarded fire station store. It was the only way possible for the ring-binder to have got back to Air New Zealand where Bruce Crosbie became involved.

The other recipient of the MBE was Bob Mitchell, the senior police officer on duty in command at Scott Base and the Fire Station store. There was a record of the items in custody. Significantly, they recorded the fact that two diaries of Collins were in police custody.

Collins's black ring-binder had been replaced by another diary by some person or persons unknown, but it was undoubtedly Gemmell, who was the only person in Antarctica who knew of the change of coordinates, and their significance, that led to the crash. Dianne Keenan's diary, probably pocketed by Gemmell on the ice, had her name torn off the front page, so that to all appearances, this was still one of the two diaries of Collins. In actual fact, it was Dianne's diary that was used to replace the ring-binder so that to all appearances, there were still two diary/pocket note books as per the inventory.

Crosbie mistakenly returned that diary to Maria Collins, together with the cover of the black ring-binder which was now empty. The error was discovered. Crosbie and Arthur Cooper arranged that Dianne's diary was then returned to her family. She was the only crew member whose remains were not identified, much to the distress of her family.

Had her diary been correctly dealt with on the ice, and labelled exactly in which location it was found, it may have been possible that Ian Hambly, or Graham Lister, and their team could have identified Dianne. But the opportunist clearly found, and then concealed that small black diary. He knew it could be useful to cover up his theft of the Collins ring-binder from the Scott Base store without its disappearance being noticed. That had unfortunate effects on the Keenan family. As it is, her brother Phillip still treasures that diary, even though it was at the centre of an injustice.

Much nonsense has been written about the extract from para.377 of the Mahon report. It was in fact the accuracy of Mahon's choice of words and the iambic pentameter of his words that caught public attention. This is the language and rhythm of Shakespeare. For the legal establishment of an English-speaking nation, to complain about Mahon's words, epitomises what was wrong with that society of that time. Mahon was the most experienced judge in New Zealand in his ability to identify liars and cheats. There are a number of anecdotes of Mahon's treatment of the law which identified him as being head and shoulders above his contemporaries.

What did happen?

Even before the crash site had been identified, Keith Amies, who was the navigation systems specialist, asked Alan Dorday, who was a flight despatch officer, to check the coordinates of the flight plan which had been given to the pilots. Dorday and his senior David Greenwood, were the first to discover Collins had been given final waypoint coordinates which had been altered from those he had been briefed on. Instead of leading Collins flight into McMurdo Sound, the new flight plan aimed TE901 directly at Mt. Erebus.

They concealed their discovery from the accident inspectors, Rhodes and Graham who were present. But Greenwood, years later, confessed to Davison that he had told Gemmell that the coordinates had been shifted, so that they now aimed TE901 directly at Erebus. Greenwood told Gemmell that fact during that night before Gemmell went to Antarctica with Chippindale and Rhodes. It was with this knowledge that Gemmell thought through the situation whilst on the C130 Hercules flying to McMurdo and Scott Base.

Gemmell was welcomed by the mountaineers who included Woodford, Logan, and Stanton. He was constantly accompanied by one or more of these mountaineers but mostly

Stanton, who was in charge of the safety of all the personnel at the crash site.

The publication of the Mahon report came as a surprise to some of the Air New Zealand counsel. Throughout the Royal Commission hearings, Mahon had been ultra-polite to the witnesses, even when he was being presented with evidence that was obviously false that they had never heard of low flying down the middle of McMurdo Sound at well under 16,000 and 6,000 feet.

I have copies of the original statements prepared for the Court of Appeal hearing of three of these mountaineers. The following are brief extracts from some of those statements. The reason the statements were made was that in the Mahon Report, paras 359 and 360 contained accusations against Gemmell and Air New Zealand. Air New Zealand counsel perceived the need to defend those accusations in the Court of Appeal, using the mountaineers to give alibis.

Stanton was economical with the truth. When he was on the ice, he and Gemmell did find Collins's flight bag, although Stanton described it as a satchel to his friend John Maine years later. Compare this with Gemmell's evidence under cross examination. Gemmell said the flight bag was empty. It was, but that was after Stanton emptied it. There was some talk on the ice that there was a chart as well as the Collins's atlas in the flight bag. There was the sound of rustling of paper on the CVR. That sound was probably one chart being folded and refolded in the cockpit. The other may have been stowed in the flight bag with the Atlas.

The following are extracts from those three mountaineers' statements. They relate to Gemmell's behaviour at the crash site, not back at the McMurdo fire station store.

Keith Woodford

> Captain Gemmell's actions were at all times consistent with his being an assistant to the Air Accident Investigator. His actions were also consistent with his being unaware that the computer coordinates had been changed.
>
> The search of the crash site was obviously a very painful experience for Captain Gemmell and it was a period of great stress. It was clear at this time that Captain Gemmell was completely bewildered as to the cause of the crash. To conceal the stated information about the changed coordinates would have required a masterly piece of acting which I am confident did not occur.

Comment: Woodford was no better than Logan at Gemmell's character assessment.

Hugh Logan

> I would like to support the public statement made by Keith Woodford. While

Captain Gemmell was on site, he was accompanied by Keith in identifying the bodies of the crew and in finding the 'black boxes'. I joined the search for the voice recorder. I can only repeat that Ian Gemmell's actions and mental approach at the time lead me to believe that he was incapable of apparently "tampering with evidence" as inferred in a number of news reports I have seen. Ian Gemmell was of course on the site for only a short period of the whole recovery operation.

Comment: Logan was taken in by Gemmell, as was fellow mountaineer Keith Woodford.

John Stanton

He made a statement with 15 numbered paragraphs. In para 2, he indicates that he was the leader of the mountaineer's team, despite Hugh Logan's comment that he was.

Para 3. Gemmell was on board on 29th Nov 1979 17.15 hours. [He makes no mention that Chippindale and Rhodes were also on board.]

Para 7. At 20.00 hours the voice recorder was found. I saw Captain Gemmell return from the crash site at 20.00 wearing jersey and trousers with his jacket tied around his waist and carrying only a Polaroid camera. Keith Woodford was carrying a flight recorder.

Para 8. On 3rd December, the party with police DVI arrived (including Mitchell, Gilpin and Leighton) on the Helicopter at 0800 hours. On that same helicopter Gemmell took both flight and voice recorders [back to Scott Base].

Para 11. "All other property was placed in several body bags and collected to make up the twelfth load to be taken out.

Para 12. That the police log records that First Officer Rhodes first appeared on the site on 9th Dec 1979.

Para 13. Penn's log mentions … a body was found in the cockpit area… by Rhodes and Foley.

Para 14. I visited McMurdo Base on the evening of… 5th Dec 1979 for one hour. When Captain Gemmell returned the second time to the site at 2200 hours, the whole team including myself went with the accident team to look for the voice recorder. It was found very quickly by Captain Gemmell. He dug it out of the snow.

[Comment: Stanton contradicted himself but later issued a correction. The voice recorder was found at 2000 hours. Then the DFDR was found at 2200 hours again by Gemmell digging it out of the snow.]

During that visit Bob Mitchell told me that a Policeman was coming from New Zealand to assist him in his duties and look after property. The Policeman in charge of the property store at McMurdo [Senior Sgt Mike Muddiman] told me that he left New Zealand at 1430 hours on 6th Dec.

Para 15. I was on the last flight from the crash site on 9th Dec together with Colin Monteath and Hugh Logan.

Comment

John Stanton visited his friend John Maine in Auckland. He intended to give evidence to the Mahon Royal Commission Inquiry. But Stanton never did give evidence to the Royal Commission. During his stay with John Maine, Stanton was concerned about the fact that he had found the pilot's atlas. He described it as being a book atlas. He said it was consistent with the atlas described as belonging to Jim Collins. He said that he had found the atlas and had handed it to Inspector Bob Mitchell.

Stanton was clear that he had found the atlas in what he termed a satchel, and he was concerned and surprised that the atlas was said to be lost, when it was not presented to the Mahon Inquiry.

Stanton, Woodford, and Logan were on the crash site more than most during the initial survey. They were marking out and placing warning flags over the site. Whilst there were some minor differences of evidence, it indicates a certain minor disorganisation of their stories elicited by the Air New Zealand lawyers. That is not surprising in the awful conditions. PTSD was suffered by many of those who worked at the crash site, as well as at the other places dealing with the bodies of the victims. The fact that Collins's atlas had been found by Stanton on the crash site, and that the pilot's satchel was recovered is remarkable. Stanton's claim that he passed this atlas to Bob Mitchell is most significant.

That Collins had most likely entered the McMurdo waypoint at the Dailey Islands in his atlas was significant, is proved by the fact that Chippindale asked Maria Collins and her family for that atlas. Stanton says he passed the atlas to Inspector Bob Mitchell. Thereafter it disappeared completely.

What else could have been found on the crash site, but was not recorded correctly? To me it is obviously the Diane Keenan diary. It was relatively small and could have been easily hidden in a pocket and removed from the site. At the McMurdo store, Jim Collins's ring-binder was swopped with the Keenan diary but deceptively her name was deliberately torn off. So what was left? Collins's and Keenan's diaries which fitted the inventory bill, that had two diaries listed. Whereas before, it was just the Collins diary and his ring-binder, which could pass at a glance as being a diary. There was no security at the McMurdo store at the relevant time. Only later did police security arrive.

The finder of the atlas was Stanton and the recipient of the atlas was Mitchell. Is it unreasonable to think that Des Dalgety and in turn Prime Minister Muldoon were very grateful that such a key document, that could prove the flight plan the pilots were briefed on was down the middle of McMurdo Sound, had gone missing? Why did Stanton say nothing? Why did Mitchell say nothing? There were subsequent meetings with Gilpin, Mitchell, and Leighton. Mitchell said nothing about the atlas or the ring-binder. Both Stanton and Mitchell must have known of the importance of the discovery of the atlas, but they said nothing. Both Mitchell and Stanton were awarded MBEs (effectively the gift of a grateful Prime Minister). This was in the 1981 honours list.

Brian Kynaston Waugh. Pilot of Rapide G-AFMF that crashed due to Icing on 19th February 1954 Chapter one. He was also the Pilot of Dominie ZK-AKT on 15th April 1967 Chapter 5 who had a novel method of panning for gold during his attempt to join the Goldfish Club.
CREDIT: WAUGH COLLECTION.

Newcastle airport with G-AFMF. Circa 1953.
CREDIT: WAUGH COLLECTION.

Robin and Cathryn Simpson – BK Waugh's grandchildren at Stooprigg Fell Hexham. Most of the wreckage of G-AFMF is buried in the wet ground but many components were easily identifiable including a crankshaft, propellor and fuel tanks. After 50 years, oil from the engines could still be seen seeping to the surface of the water.
CREDIT: WAUGH COLLECTION.

ZK-BWA -Pilot Alf Bartlett with wife Alison - front, Russell, Julie and Jenny.
CREDIT: RENDELLS PHOTO SERVICE VIA R WAUGH.

Aero Commander ZK-BWA on the apron at Wellington.
CREDIT: ALEX HOUSTON VIA R WAUGH.

ZK-BWA being loaded with Auckland newspapers, part owner of Bay of Plenty Airways. Via S. Lowe.

This was the starboard wing and engine from ZK-BWA having been cleanly broken off at wing station 24.
The first occasion that the Aero Commander design flaw caused an in-flight structural failure.
This was missed by the New Zealand air accident investigators reports of 1962, 1972 1984
and still denied by TAIC in 2001.
CREDIT: MORRIE PEACOCK VIA R. WAUGH.

Brian Chadwick with ZK-BCP Jan 1962 Credit Brian Purcell via R. Waugh.

Darrell Stanley Shiels, Alwyn and Valerie Saville (nee Bignell) and Louis Rowan.
Note, John Rowan, the brother of Louis has confirmed that his brother would be conversant with radios
sufficient to make any "Mayday" calls that could have been heard by Ross Jamie McDermott.
CREDITS: THE FAMILIES OF DARRELL, VALERIE AND LOUIS.

My famous photo January 1962 – With the colourful jersey knitted by my mother
first seen in 1958 on the Isles of Scilly. I am the young man standing between Brian Chadwick
and my mother Daisy Fautley.
CREDIT: ALBERT FAUTLEY.

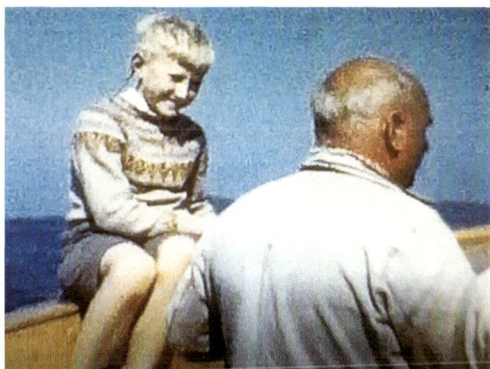

To prove it was me with the same jersey in Scilly
1958 – not long after Brian Waugh's epic break on
those islands per chapter 1.
CREDIT: ALBERT FAUTLEY.

The Dragonfly is up the Albert Stream- near
Dragonfly Peak. As a nine year old was it an omen
that the Dragonfly may be resting up the Albert
stream near to the peak that now bears its name?
DRAGONFLY PEAK. Subsequent inquiries indicate
that this location could well be a likely site for the
Kiwi Rover due to the weather on the day.
CREDIT: AUTHOR.

Brians Chadwick and Waugh on Waugh's first arrival in NZ. Chadwick and Waugh flew with the same small airlines for a time and no doubt Brian Waugh was well aware of Chadwick's flying and likely routes. Regrettably he was not used well by the official search and rescue organisation at the time or after possible sightings of wreckage in various hot-spots.
CREDIT: WAUGH COLLECTION.

Dragonfly Kiwi Rover at Milford Sound 18th Oct 1961.
CREDIT: EDNA BATES VIA RICHARD WAUGH.

February 1962 At Milford Sound Dominie ZK-BCP. Chadwick and passengers at Milford with Hotel Manager, Mac Alexander. This was thought to be the last photo of Chadwick.
CREDIT: BRIAN PURCELL VIA R WAUGH.

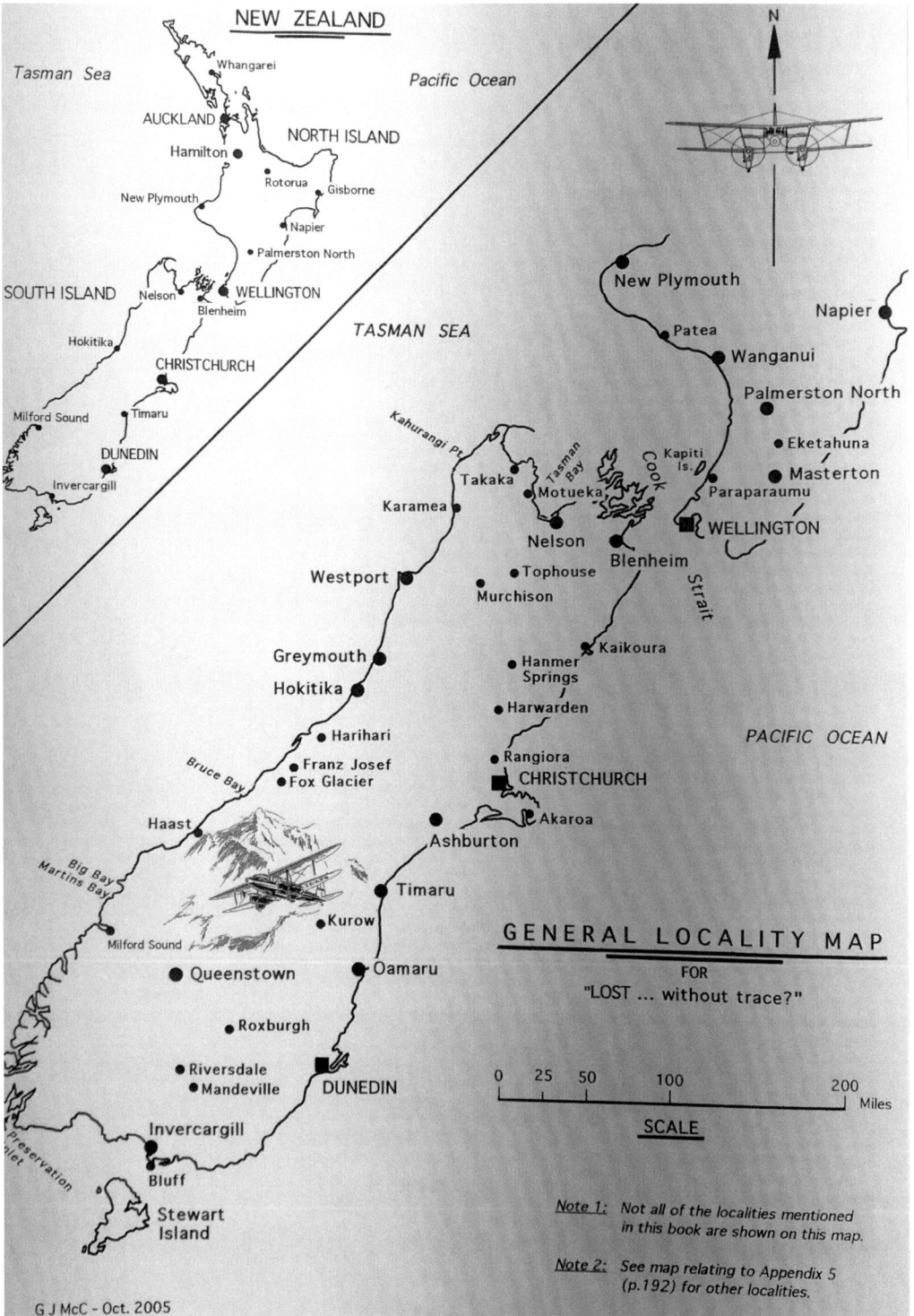

Map by Graeme McConnell.

Louis Rowan memorial.
CREDIT: JOHN ROWAN.

Brian Chadwick and Brian Waugh.
CREDIT: G C WOOD VIA R WAUGH.

Milford Sound, during the week of the Dragonfly search, February 1962 from the cockpit of RNZAF Harvard NZ1015 showing the airstrip and nearby hotel buildings. This photo was taken by flight lieutenant Peter Rhodes who became an important character in the Mount Erebus Royal Commission when TE901 crashed in Antarctica November 1979. Controversially Rhodes was the only witness for both ALPA and Air NZ.
CREDIT: PETER RHODES VIA R WAUGH.

Low level entry to Milford Sound no longer approved by Air Traffic Control.

Approaching Lake Quill and Sutherland Falls. This is the sight that the author had of the magnificent Sutherland Falls on that part of my flight from Milford airstrip to Queenstown to refuel. The weather was not so clear as shown in this photo.
CREDIT: JOHN WEGG VIA R WAUGH.

The Chadwick family at Falmouth, England in the late 1930s with their Morris Eight Roadster. From left, Brian, unidentified, William Chadwick, Clara Chadwick and Sylvia.
CREDIT: (CHADWICK COLLECTION) VIA R WAUGH.

Cessna 180 ZK-BMP (Don Noble)

Piper cherokee Six ZK-EBU (Don Noble)

Cessna 172 ZK-CSS (Don Noble)

Montage of 5 missing aircraft. [Note The Hughes Helicopter ZK-HNW lost 2004 found later in 2012 – my step-son's wedding guest – Hannah Timings].
CREDIT: ALL DON NOBLE VIA R WAUGH.

Cessna 180 ZK-FMQ (Don Noble)

Hughes 369HS ZK-HNW (Don Noble)

Earlier rare pre-war colour photograph of the Dragonfly with Bert Mercer. Had the Dragonfly crashed with this colour livery, there may have been a better chanceof being spotted against a back-ground of white green and blue. There have been some sightings in the Rainbow Valley area near Mt Aspiring of this type of colour.
CREDIT: MERCER COLLECTION VIA R WAUGH.

ZK-AFB Dragonfly over new build at Christchurch. It was later named "Kiwi Rover"
by former owner Arthur Bradshaw in 1960.
CREDIT: VC BROWNE VIA R WAUGH.

Lockheed 10A Electra Spirit of Tasman Bay, Trans Island Airways was one of the small airlines that pilots Brian Chadwick and Brian Waugh flew together. Chadwick ground looped the Lockheed ZK-BUT and thereafter TIA had problems but not before Brian Waugh obtained gold wings courtesy of grateful knowledgeable passengers from Nelson after an adventurous flight across the Cook Strait.
CREDIT: GEOFFREY C WOOD VIA R WAUGH.

Blue Cod – No Rainbow Trout. Compare with Pippa Collins in 2009 purchase of Blue Cod – her mother's order from 1979 to Jim Collins. Brian Chadwick holding the Rainbow Trout that had just been given to him from Don Nairn, at the refuelling stop at Queenstown January 1962.
FROM AUTHORS FILM.

Low flying in 1962 of Brian Chadwick.- Mount Tasman from ZK-BCP.
FROM AUTHORS FILM.

Low flying past Mount Cook from ZK-BCP. Currently the regulations are that aircraft
have to give these mountains a wider berth.
FROM AUTHORS FILM.

Rainbow Col near Mount Aspiring – A potential hot spot in the search for the Dragonfly according to research carried out by Lew Bone.
CREDIT: LEW BONE

Milford Sound – That is not a small dinghy but a large Ocean Liner – This gives perspective to the grandeur and size of the mountains around Milford Sound.
CREDIT: MATTHEW FAUTLEY.

A view of Rainbow Valley near Mt Aspiring. A hotspot for the Dragonfly searchers
CREDIT: LEW BONE.

Part of the eastern side of Rainbow Valley where there have been several reliable reports of aircraft debris near bush line.
CREDIT: LEW BONE.

Foot of Kitchener Glacier leading down to unnamed alpine lake.
CREDIT: LEW BONE.

The memorial to the pilot and passengers of the Kiwi Rover with John Rowan, brother of passenger Louis Rowan and the Rev Dr Richard Waugh QSM on the dedication of the memorial with the book, Lost without Trace? By Richard Waugh Wanaka 2006.

Kiwi Rover memorial Wanaka 1st April 2023 - Ron Cuskelly.

Paddy O'Brien Chief Air Accident Inspector
CREDIT: GARRY MILLS - VIA R WAUGH

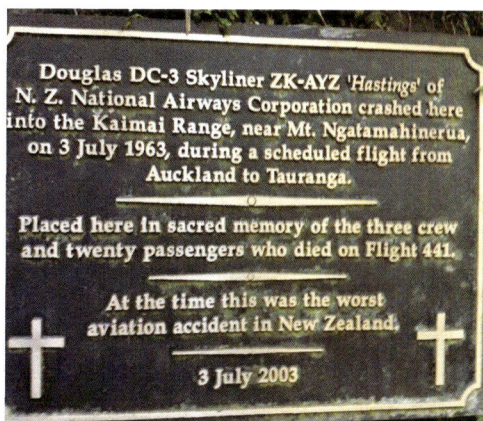

Kaimai plaque on the roadside near the quarry at Gordon 5/7/2003.
CREDIT: WAUGH COLLECTION

Kaimai memorial 3/7/2003 on crash site
CREDIT: G MCCONNELL

DC-3 Skyliner ZK-AYZ.
CREDIT: MANNERING AND ASSOCIATES VIA R WAUGH.

E. Ball (CAA) with accident inspectors Paddy O'Brien centre and Ted Harvie right.

It is to be noted that Paddy O'Brien was the Chief Air Accident Inspector who first investigated the crash of the Aero Commander ZK-BWA in 1961/2. He blamed the pilot, Alf Bartlett for flying too close to Mt Ruapehu. Ted Harvie took over as Chief Inspector from O'Brien and prepared a revised report still blaming Bartlett in 1972. That erroneous report was not issued until January 1984 by Ron Chippindale, after the Royal Commission's Privy Council judgment from 1983. Again it was O'Brien who issued the missing aircraft report on Chadwick and Kiwi Rover's disappearance on 12th February 1962. Then Ted Harvie took over the investigation into Brian Waugh's ZK-AKT had to ditch into the Shotover River in 1967. I would not describe these as the rogues gallery prior to the instigation of TAIC but I would suggest that the text is carefully read with respect to these accident investigation experts.

Mike Alexander with Father Ewen Derrick and Rev John Coveney, vicar of Matamata with Rev Roy Jamieson Methodist minister on the ground.
CREDIT: MIKE ALEXANDER VIA R WAUGH.

Mike Alexander helping Paddy O'Brien with Dr J Henderson of RNZAF.
CREDIT: GARRY MILLS VIA R WAUGH.

Jan Beijen's Bell 47 ZK-HAJ of Rudnik helicopters. This air accident was the first to be attended by helicopters in New Zealand despite the official rescue parties declining the offer of the assistance of the helicopter owners and pilots.
CREDIT: JC MCFADYEN COLLECTION – VIA R WAUGH.

Brian and Alec Waugh at Masterton race. 1964.
CREDIT: B CROPP VIA R WAUGH.

ZK-AKY Dominie 2014 Lake Manapouri.
CREDIT: JOHN KING.

ZK-AKT – being burnt at Shotover with the approval of CIAA Ted Harvie. There was some controversy about allowing the aircraft to be burnt before there had been an investigation into the cause of Brian Waugh's seat harness being broken. It was the last straw for Brian Waugh as the accident prevented any further flying as pilot in charge. Waugh had to argue with Harvie on the lack of a proper investigation into the engine failures that caused the crash.
CREDIT: M HOCKLEY VIA R WAUGH.

Allen Parker with ZK-AKT recovering the aircraft from the water. Proof as required for the Goldfish Club? Except that Waugh claimed that it was his method of panning for gold in that river.
CREDIT: M HOCKLEY VIA R WAUGH.

Brian and Jean Waugh 1968.
CREDIT WAUGH COLLECTION.

ZK-AKT
CREDIT: WAUGH COLLECTION.

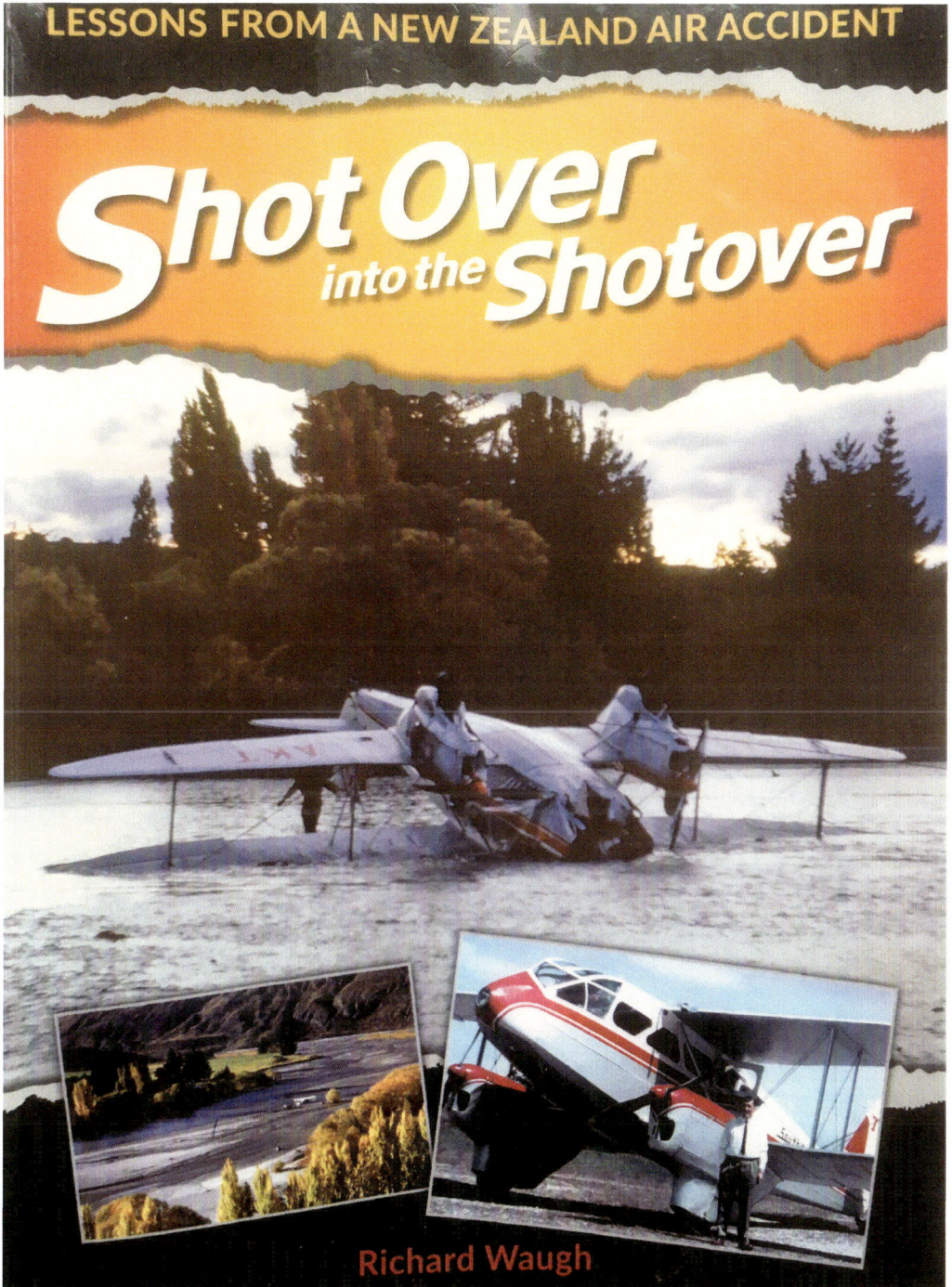

Front Cover of Shot Over into the Shotover.
CREDIT: R WAUGH.

Mount Erebus.
CREDIT: AUTHOR.

Gilpin photo of TE901 crash site.

Hon. Peter Mahon, David Baragwanath,
Sir Rochford Hughes and J Davies.

CREDIT: AIR NEW ZEALAND.

"From here everything lies to the North!"

FLOYD BENNETT

These words, shouted by Richard E. Byrd above the roar of engines of the Ford Tri Motor "Tin Goose," marked yet another milestone in aviation history. On November 28th, 1929, Byrd, with three companions, became the first to fly over the South Pole.

air new zealand

Lunch

Bay Prawns & Scallops Antarctica

Tournedos Rossini
Chicken Souvaroff

Braised Onions – Snow Peas
Spring Carrots – Parsley Potatoes

Peach Erebus

Selection of New Zealand Cheeses
Fresh Fruit Basket

Coffee – Tea

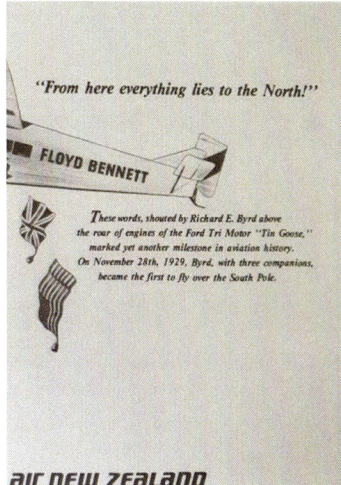

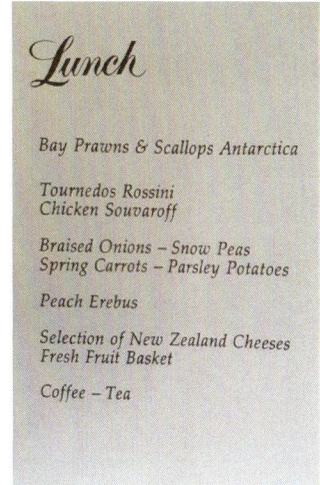

The Lunch Menu from The flight 15th November 1977 with Brizendine and Vette with Peach Erebus on the menu.
CREDIT: IAN HAMBLY.

First Officer and Co-Pilot Ken Mulgrew on the Hawkins trip on 18th October 1977 well below the alleged MSAs of 16,000 and 6,000 feet. It appears to show Mt Erebus as the DC-10 is flying directly above Cape Evans where Scott's Hut remains. Compare the angles with the photograph by Colin Monteath from the same geographical position but from sea level.
CREDIT: AIR NEW ZEALAND PUBLICITY DEPT.

Colin Monteath

Mount Erebus with Cape Evans in the foreground from the exact same spot as the famous Ken Mulgrew photograph. Ken Mulgrew was the brother of Peter Mulgrew, who was the commentator on the fatal flight on 28th November 1979.
Peter Mulgrew's widow June later married Sir Edmund Hillary.
CREDIT: COLIN MONTEATH.

Peter Mahon's acknowledgement labelling "Three men whose evidence about flying hazards had a significant effect at the (Royal Commission of) inquiry. Vette Rhodes and Thomson from his 1984 book – "Verdict on Erebus"
CREDIT: PETER MAHON.

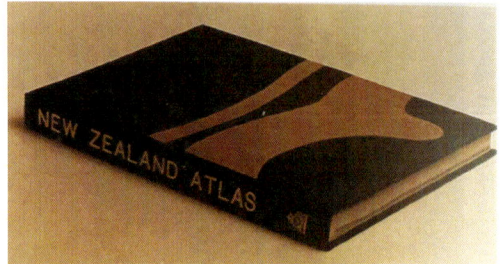

The Atlas used by many passengers with the same version of the Atlas used by Jim Collins. His copy was alleged not to have been found. Some many years later, a mountaineer, John Stanton admitted to a friend that it was found in Collins flight bag and handed in to the Scott Base store from which it disappeared.
CREDIT: A HENRY.

Comparison photo of Collins note book, ring-binder and the Dianne Keenan's diary that was used to hide the Air New Zealand confiscation of the ring-binder with the coordinates as recorded by Collins.
CREDIT: A HENRY.

CHAPTER 6

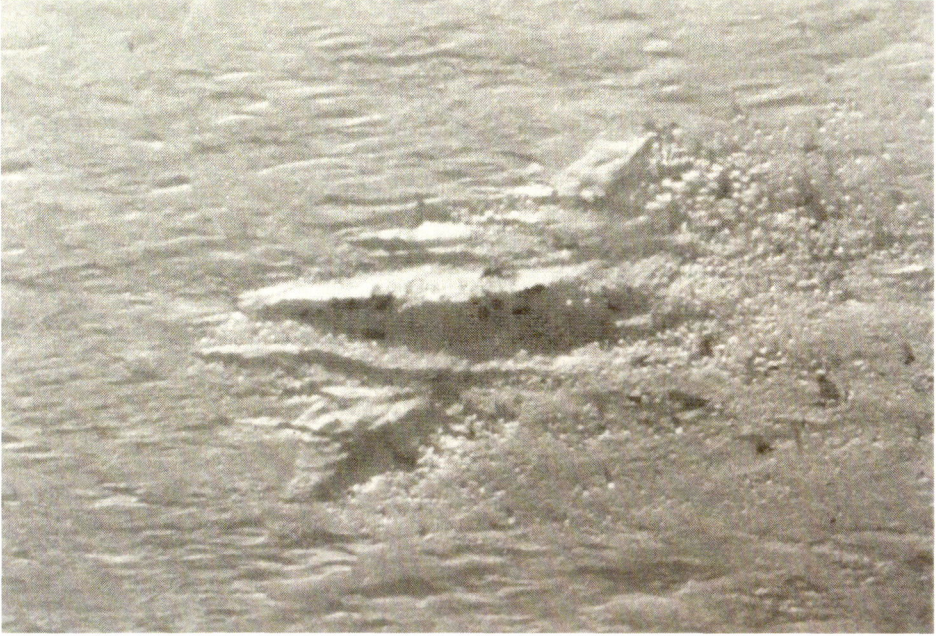

Ice Impact photo from J Kings book.
CREDIT: I GEMMELL.

CHAPTER 7

Aerial view of the Isles of Scilly – St Agnes in the foreground.
CREDIT: AUTHOR.

Sikorsky SN-61 26 seater similar to G, BEON that crashed in low sea fog on 3rd July 1983.
CREDIT: AUTHOR.

CHAPTER 8

Hannah Timings guest at the author's step son's wedding. The helicopter in which she was travelling to Milford Sound crashed in January 2004 and found November 2012 just 2 miles from the last position report, in open country.
CREDIT: TIMINGS FAMILY COLLECTION.

Bluefin via Mike Briggs.

Authors Polynesian Catamaran.

Erebus in a nutshell

The Air New Zealand McMurdo waypoint

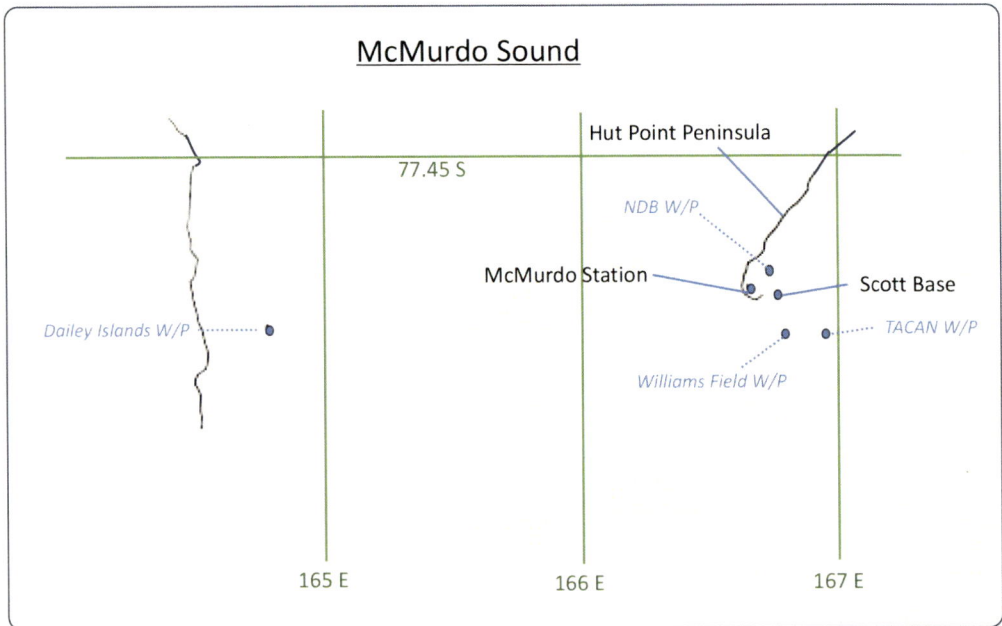

McMurdo Sound

77.45 S

Hut Point Peninsula

NDB W/P

McMurdo Station

Scott Base

Dailey Islands W/P

TACAN W/P

Williams Field W/P

165 E   166 E   167 E

Genuine scenario

1. The first Air New Zealand flight path to Antarctica was to the Williams Field waypoint. It crossed Mt Erebus, an active volcano over 12,000 ft high. That is about the height of Mt Cook.

2. The second Air New Zealand flight path was on 10 October 1977 shifted to the NDB waypoint. It also crossed Mt Erebus.

3. The third Air New Zealand flight path was in July-August 1978 shifted to the Dailey Islands waypoint in McMurdo Sound. It was 27 miles to the west of the two previous waypoints. And therefore it was far from Erebus. It remained there until the morning of the fatal flight on 28 November 1979.

At the briefing for the fatal flight the briefing officers told the pilots the flight path was to the Dailey Islands waypoint in McMurdo Sound. That was true. It was, and had been there for two years. The briefing officer, John P. Wilson handed out flight plans. Jim Collins, the pilot of the fatal flight, took one of those flight plans away from the briefing. Wilson saw Collins take the flight plan.

On the evening before his flight Collins used that flight plan to plot his flight path to the Dailey Islands waypoint in McMurdo Sound onto two maps.

The flight path which he plotted is shown by the broken line on the left to point B on the following diagram. The Dailey Islands waypoint is point B.

4. On the morning of the fatal flight Air New Zealand shifted the flight path by 27 miles to the TACAN waypoint at point A. It crossed Mt Erebus. Air New Zealand did not tell the pilots. That new flight path is shown by the solid line on the right.

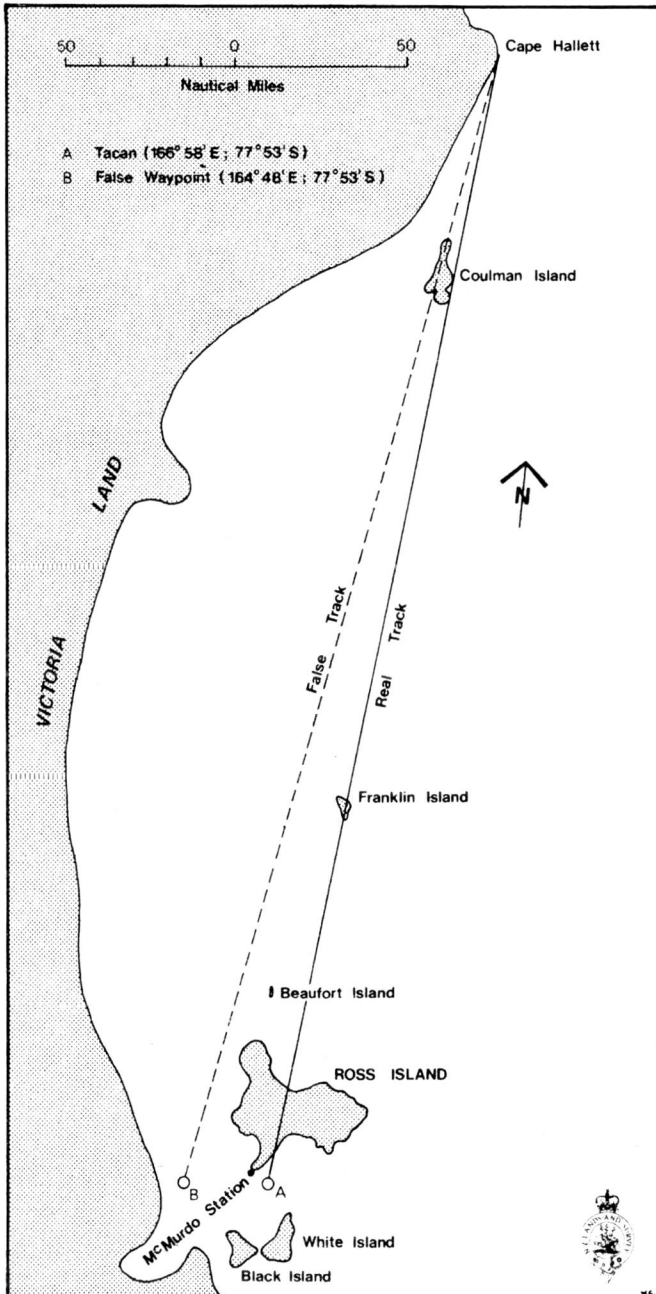

At flight despatch Air New Zealand gave the pilots that Mt Erebus flight plan to point A. The airline left blank a certain field on the flight plan. That field was there to tell pilots of any changes to the flight plan since briefing. By leaving it blank Air New Zealand told the pilots there was no change from the flight plan they had briefed the pilots on.

The following diagram shows an enlarged version of the Ross Island area.

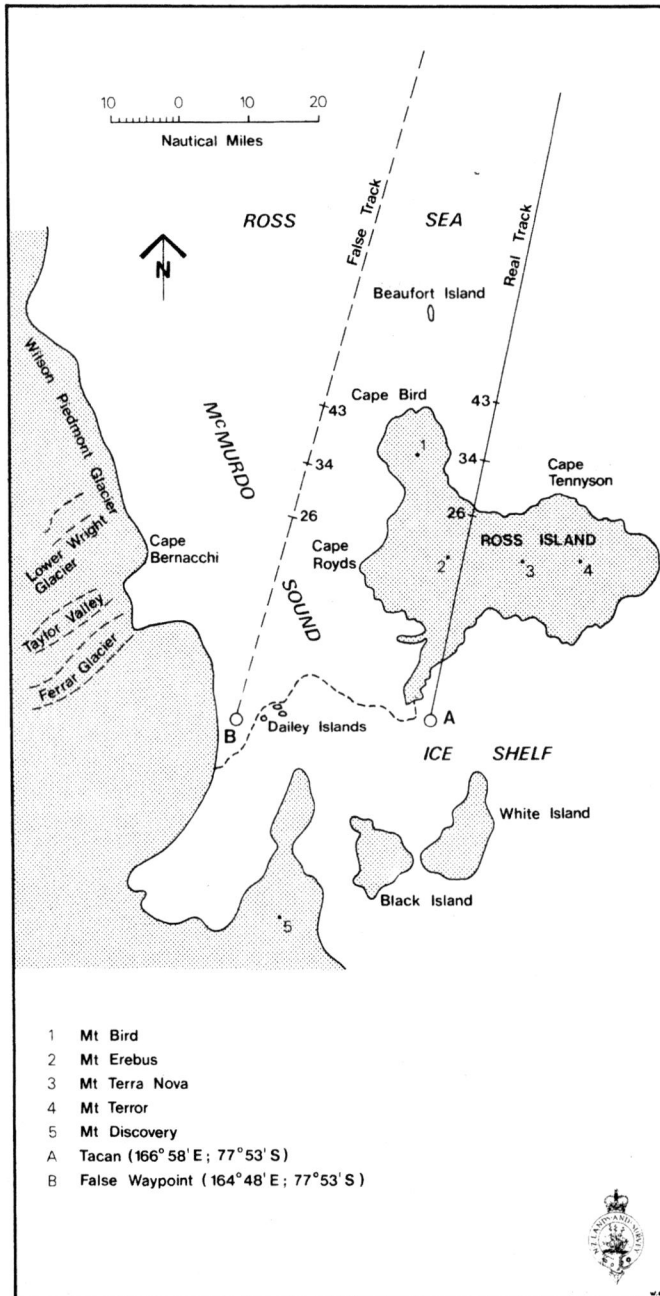

1	Mt Bird
2	Mt Erebus
3	Mt Terra Nova
4	Mt Terror
5	Mt Discovery
A	Tacan (166° 58' E ; 77° 53' S)
B	False Waypoint (164° 48' E ; 77° 53' S)

Whiteout

In a whiteout condition a dark object is visible for many miles while a snow-covered object, even a mountain, next to the observer is invisible.

— U.S. Navy Weather Research Facility

Gemmell admitted Air New Zealand deliberately concealed from pilots the existence of the Antarctic optical illusion of whiteout. It made Erebus invisible.

The pilots flew into Lewis Bay. That is the bay between Cape Bird and Cape Tennyson. They believed their flight path was taking them into the entrance to McMurdo Sound, just as the briefed flight plan showed it would.

The entrance to Lewis Bay looked exactly like the entrance to McMurdo Sound. McMurdo Sound is much wider than Lewis Bay, but the cliffs of McMurdo Sound are much higher than the cliffs of Lewis Bay, so that both entrances looked the same.

The entrance to Lewis Bay looked so alike to the entrance to McMurdo Sound, that Peter Mulgrew, the commentator on the flight deck, who knew the area well, believed he was entering McMurdo Sound when in fact he was entering Lewis Bay.

The capes on each side of Lewis Bay were not in whiteout, so the pilots had no inkling of any danger. The only sector in whiteout was immediately ahead of them. That sector in whiteout rendered Erebus and that part of Ross Island invisible. The pilots crashed as they approached Erebus. That is shown on the following diagram.

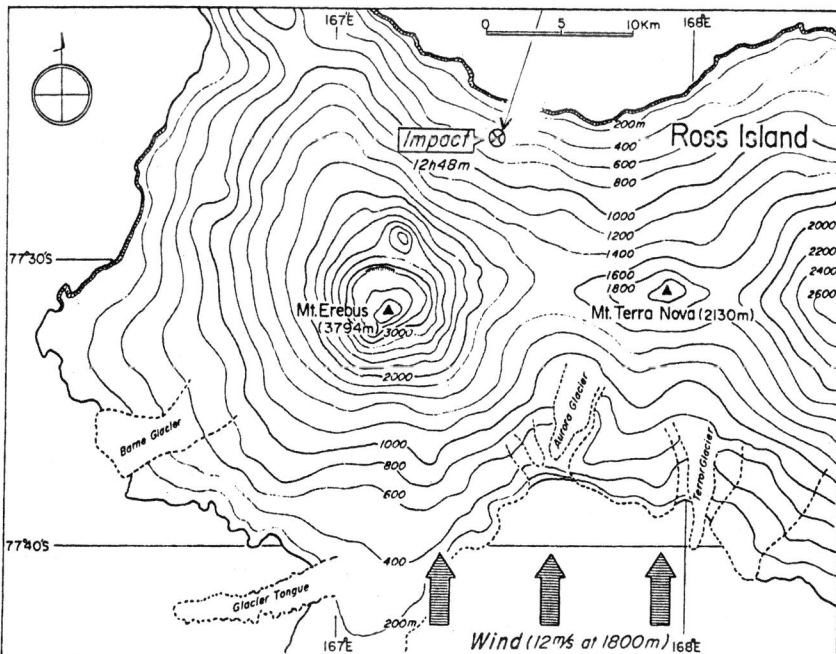

These three photographs were taken by Bob Thomson as he demonstrated to Mahon the change with the overcast cloud in the third photograph which has obliterated Mt Erebus completely by the optical illusion of whiteout. The crew of the fatal flight only saw the illusion shown by the third photograph.

There is a false horizon created, which is what the pilots would expect to see when looking into McMurdo Sound. The capes on either side (not visible in the photo) were both visible, because they are not in the sector of whiteout. They look as if they are the two capes in McMurdo Sound. Instead they are actually the capes at each side of Lewis Bay.

Mahon retraced the flight path of the fatal flight in a helicopter. He watched as Erebus ahead slowly became invisible and turned into the appearance of McMurdo Sound. It did so because of developing whiteout. Bob Thomson, the chief of the Antarctic Division took the photos.

False scenario

But that whole scenario is turned on its head by the sworn evidence of the two briefing officers, John P Wilson and Ross Johnson. They both said they had made it clear beyond doubt to the pilots that the computer flight path crossed Erebus. That means that Collins and Cassin, knowing full well that the computer flight path crossed Erebus, flew at 1,500 ft on that computer flight path. That meant it was joint suicide of those two and their murder of 255 persons.

The obvious way for the pilots to commit suicide and murder would have been to fly the plane into the Manukau Harbour. Instead, they flew all the way to Antarctica, so as to commit the most spectacular suicide and murder in history. But that scenario is so ridiculous that it cannot be true. In that case, the only answer must be that Wilson and Johnson committed perjury.

The fact must be that at briefing Wilson must have told the pilots the truth, namely that the flight path was to the Dailey Islands waypoint in the middle of McMurdo Sound. It was no business of Johnson to tell the pilots where the flight path was. He was not the route briefing officer, Wilson was. Johnson was the simulator briefing officer.

The fact is that for two years the flight path ran down McMurdo Sound to the Dailey Islands waypoint, about 27 miles away. Yet Wilson said he believed for those two years, 1978 and 1979, the flight path crossed Erebus. But it didn't. For those two years it was at the Dailey Islands waypoint in McMurdo Sound. How credible is Wilson? The answer lies in his background. Wilson used to be a navigation instructor. He had held a first-class navigator's licence, and he had logged approximately 3,000 hours as a navigator. Also, he either highlighted or underlined the Dailey Island waypoint in flight plans he handed out to pilots. He asks us to believe that for those two years he spent briefing pilots on the flight plan, he always believed it crossed Erebus, whereas in reality it was 27 miles away in the middle of McMurdo Sound. It simply is not possible for anyone with Wilson's background to be so mistaken for two years.

Conclusive proof Wilson was lying is the fact that seven pilots gave evidence that the briefing officers gave them the belief the flight path lay in McMurdo Sound, one was uncertain, none said they believed it crossed Erebus.

What motive would Wilson have had for committing perjury? The reason was that the false evidence he gave, if it had been true, would have cleared Air New Zealand of blame for the disaster, and instead would have shifted the blame onto the pilots. A brutal management no doubt threatened to sack him, if he did not say what they told him to say. My book shows that the standard practice is to wrongfully blame pilots for crashes, when it is not the pilot's fault.

What motive would Ross Johnson have had for committing perjury? Much the same reason applies to him as applies to Wilson about his threatened sacking.

As well as that, Johnson's evidence is nonsense. That is shown by the following. Captain Arthur Cooper said the following about Johnson in an email to Captain Gary Parata. Cooper wrote:

> John Gabriel, who attended the same briefing and the same simulator detail as Collins and Cassin, was sitting next to me at the Royal Commission Enquiry when Ross gave evidence.
>
> Throughout [Johnson's evidence] John kept making quiet asides to me, such as —" Bullshit! — No way! — That didn't happen! — Crap! — That's wrong! — He's joking!"
>
> At one stage Ross said that he had turned the lights on in the simulator, spread the RNC map out over the pedestal and specifically pointed out the track over Mt Erebus.
>
> As you would know Gary, that action doesn't make sense when you are only in the simulator to carry out the functions of going from magnetic to grid operation and to carry out the let-down procedure from 16,000' to 6,000', as the simulator was only set up for night operation.

Simpson said the same as Gabriel about Johnson's evidence. He said in evidence:

> In Captain Johnson's case, however, the description I heard in this court was so different to my recollection that I wondered if in fact I had attended the same briefing.

I repeat an important point. At briefing Wilson handed out to pilots four Dailey Islands flight plans. He said in evidence he took back all four, but he lied. Collins took one from the briefing, and Wilson saw him take it. We know Wilson saw him take it, because after the crash Dave Eden, Air New Zealand's director of flight operations, said one flight plan was missing, and he asked if it was at the Collins house, but he didn't ask any of the other pilots. Collins spent the evening before the flight using that flight plan to plot his entire flight to Antarctica and back.

Wilson's motive for telling the lie that he got all four flight plans back was clearly to convince Mahon that Collins had no flight plan with which to plot his entire flight from Auckland to McMurdo and back, and in that way to falsely convince Mahon that any evidence from his family that he spent the evening plotting his flight path would be perjury.

Part 2 The Crash

Background

Air New Zealand's DC-10 Flight TE901 to Antarctica on 28 November 1979 with 237 passengers and 20 crew lost was the worst aviation accident in the Southern Hemisphere and at that time was the fourth worst aviation tragedy ever. So much has been written about Erebus, podcasts recorded, television documentaries and docudramas produced. It may at first appear that I cannot add anything to some of the excellent resources so easily available. However, by chance, I have been given key new relevant information. I am also concentrating my comments on the capabilities of the air accident inspectors and their subsequent official reports. There have been political apologies and similar words from Air New Zealand in 2019. Notably both were by women, the Prime Minister and the chair-person of Air New Zealand. There was a mixed reaction to them by the public, along the lines that the apology was easy for Prime Minister of the day, Jacinda Ardern, to make as she had not even been born in 1979.

In view of the amount and quality of information I have received from many sources, both private and public, I hope that any reader will be able to follow the significance of that information which has fallen into my lap. I received it thanks to the willingness of participants to divulge their experiences to me. I was that 13 year old in the famous photograph who flew with Brian Chadwick just prior to the legendary mysterious disappearance, on one of his last sightseeing trips over the Southern Alps to Milford Sound. It was filmed on the old 8mm celluloid system That film was then shared with Chadwick's parents on our return from New Zealand. It was an epic film for those proud parents, in tragic circumstances. It was a present from their son's last passengers. This has opened so many doors for me. I became duty bound to share all this new information.

In many respects the Antarctica trips had a driving force behind it, similar to that of Brian Chadwick and his sightseeing trips to the ice, snow, and mountains of the Southern Alps. The respective ranges of the aircraft involved were the limiting factors for the DH89 and DH90 to fly to Milford Sound and Queenstown. It was the same for the DC-10s to fly to Antarctica and back, all without refuelling.

As for training the pilots for the white surface whiteout in the Antarctic, Air New Zealand trained none of the pilots for polar whiteout. Those RNZAF pilots who had been C.130 captains in the air force were now co-pilots in Air New Zealand. They had told Air New Zealand ops management that there was an offer from the US Navy to take pilots on observer flights to the Antarctic, and that it should be accepted. Management rubbished that suggestion. This refusal to accept such an important offer was one main cause of the disaster. That was because polar whiteout would have been explained. That was one example of the lack of common sense within the Air New Zealand management.

Synopsis

On 28th November 1979, flight TE901 was the 4th and final sightseeing trip to Antarctica planned for that season. The flights had commenced in 1977. In that first year, the notional final waypoint in Antarctica was the Williams Field runway at McMurdo Station on Ross Island. The flight path was from Cape Hallett, the first landfall on Antarctica, to McMurdo Station and Scott Base. It went overhead Ross Island with the only active volcano on that icebound continent. Because of the risks of flying over an ash and lava-spewing volcano, it was not a sensible course.

Even Chippindale agreed it was not sensible. He recommended in his report at 5.16: "No commercial passenger carrying flight be planned to fly over or close to an active volcano." That Antarctic volcano was Mount Erebus, which was about 12,500 feet high. Minimum Safe Altitudes (MSAs) of 16,000 feet for IFR flights were totally inappropriate for clearance above an active volcano like Mt. Erebus. Ian Gemmell in his evidence to the Royal Commission dismissed the possibility of an eruption with some disdain. He said, in effect, that if Erebus was erupting, someone would tell Air New Zealand in advance. But nobody told Vette, Potts, or Clapshaw, who were the pilots of the trip on 15th November 1977, when Erebus was erupting fiercely on that day.

The DC-10 aircraft had no navigator on the flight deck, and no chart table. They had been replaced for some years by the Area Inertial Navigation System (AINS). All that the pilots had to do was to key in the geographical coordinates from the flight plans waypoints, and the linked autopilot would unerringly guide the aircraft to each geographical position. It had been reported that the DC-10s AINS had never produced an incorrect flight path. It had always taken pilots to the waypoints keyed in. It had three separate inertial gyro systems, while most other aircraft that used AINS only had two.

The AINS had guided the 1978 flights into the Ross Island-McMurdo Sound area, and most pilots then found themselves in VMC. That means in clear air, with no clouds, and visibility of 40 plus miles. They were therefore able to avoid the mountains by eyesight. The safe passage was down the middle of McMurdo Sound, well clear of Ross Island and Mt Erebus. Radar coverage was provided for that route by the US Navy ATC at Mac Centre, which was the American Antarctic McMurdo Station. There were two pilots who did not fly down the middle of McMurdo Sound. One was Gemmell on the first charter flight in 1977, and the other was Roger Dalziell in 1979. Dalziell diverted to the South Magnetic Pole route due to bad weather.

Co-ordinates

In 1978, the flight plan coordinates were first converted and stored digitally into Air New Zealand's computer. Those computer digits had been loaded from paper files by the Air New Zealand navigation staff. Human error intervened in the same way that it did when Brian Waugh, described in chapter 1, had been misled because an extra digit, a zero, had been wrongly added to the icing level reported in the weather forecast he had been given. One of the coordinates, that for Williams Field, which should have been 166.48E, had instead been wrongly entered as 164.48E, that is a four and a six were transposed, and that mistake had never been discovered. Even by the so-called expert navigators of Air New Zealand.

Purely by chance, this mistake resulted in the ideal safe route down the middle of McMurdo Sound, well clear of Mt Erebus and its 12,500 feet peak. The new route was virtually the same as the safe military route that was used by all the Operation Deep Freeze aircraft. That McMurdo Sound route had the services of US Navy ATC ground radar, air traffic separation, and flight information services.

On the day of the Vette flight in 1977 Erebus was particularly active. It was throwing up lava bombs two kilometres into the sky. Gordon Vette had as a passenger that day no less than the president of the DC-10 manufacturers, John Brizendine. When Vette passed the penultimate waypoint at Cape Hallett, visibility was great and Erebus was completely visible. If Vette had been flying IFR with the McMurdo waypoint at 166.48, then the MSA for that day would have required a clearance of Erebus to be considerably more than FL 160. With its eruptions on that day, the MSA would need to have been closer to 22,000 feet, that is FL 220 not FL 160. Gemmell's theory did not work in practice, the volcano Mt.Erebus was erupting but no warnings had been given. According to Colin Monteath Erebus is 100 times more viscous than the Hawaiian volcanos and prone to larva bombs without warning i.e. extremely dangerous and over-flying a definite no-no.

The altered coordinates, including the Dailey Islands waypoint at 164.48 for 1978-1979, the middle of McMurdo Sound route, were ideal for everyone. The US ATC coordination was perfect for air traffic separation, radar surveillance, and the ever-busy Operation Deep Freeze traffic for Antarctica. According to Mahon, this evidence strongly supported the case that Air New Zealand had adopted this ultra-safe routing, although it may have been initially programmed into the AINS system by mistake.

In practice, the route directly over Erebus, with the nominal MSA of 16,000 feet, had become redundant. RCU briefings told pilots the flight path was down the middle of McMurdo Sound. The briefing officers later lied to the Royal Commission that it was over Erebus.

Divert to South Magnetic Pole

There was an exception to this middle of McMurdo Sound route. This was due to cloud covering much of Ross Island and hence Erebus on one day. The flight affected by poor weather was that when Roger Dalziell was the pilot in command. By chance, that was also the only flight experienced by the Route Clearance Unit (RCU) briefing officer, John P Wilson. He had pleaded to go on the Antarctic run. He never experienced a flight up McMurdo Sound to McMurdo Station or Scott Base for which he had been the briefing officer.

By chance, Roger Dalziell had been one of the young RNZAF pilots who had gained experience of flying in the white snow-covered mountains of the Southern Alps in the search for Brian Chadwick (See chapter 3 – the missing Dragonfly). John P Wilson was the briefing officer on 9th November, just two days after his own flight to Antarctica and his divert to the South Magnetic Pole.

Another noted pilot was Peter Rhodes. He had been involved to a much greater extent than Dalziell in the Erebus saga and then the Mahon Inquiry. He had also been one of the young RNZAF pilots assigned for the search for Chadwick in the Southern Alps. Roger Dalziell found that Ross Island was completely covered by cloud, and so he became the one and only pilot for Air New Zealand who diverted to the South Magnetic Pole, with the disappointed John Wilson aboard.

It was this diversion that caused the passenger disappointment with the Dalziell flight. This in turn provided pressure on subsequent flight crews, Simpson, Gabriel and Irvine as well as Collins, Cassin, and Lucas, the pilots of the fatal flight, three weeks later. Jim Collins had been under instructions from Air New Zealand to take his passengers sightseeing at McMurdo with the cloud base acceptable at 2,000 feet. Had the AINS been programmed to deliver Collins to the usual waypoint at Dailey Islands in the middle of the 40 mile wide McMurdo Sound, this low cloud base would have enabled the sightseeing trip of a lifetime as promised to its passengers by Air New Zealand. The warning issued by Ted Robinson to keep to the western coast of McMurdo Sound not to approach Ross Island would have been unnecessary with the Dailey Islands waypoint. This warning was not recorded on the CVR as it was more than 30 minutes before TE901 crashed. Collins predecessors had flown lower over Scott Base and the Operation Deep Freeze huts, and there had been no MSAs applicable then.

At the briefing by John Wilson and then Ross Johnson demonstrating in the simulator the change to grid navigation, those officers told pilots that the track was down the centre of McMurdo Sound. Hence the Minutes of a directors' meeting on 5th December 1979 which confirmed that the crash site was well left of centre. This was all before the conspiracy to blame the pilots.

It demonstrated that Air New Zealand believed the flight path lay in McMurdo Sound. The

1978-1979 ALPA pilots had all said in evidence that the briefing had told them the flight path lay in McMurdo Sound. Air New Zealand and CAD lawyers claimed that those line pilots were lying at the hearing. Of all the pilots, only Gemmell, Grundy, Ross Johnson and Mayne Hawkins claimed that the flight path was not down the middle of McMurdo Sound with MSAs of 16,000 and 6,000 feet. Ross Johnson and Mayne Hawkins both flew well below 6,000 feet. Gemmell flew down to 9,000 feet. The fiction that the MSAs of 16,000 and 6,000 feet were rigidly applied was dreamed up by Gemmell in concert with Dalgety, to benefit from the Warsaw Convention maximum compensation of NZ$42,000 per passenger.

On Les Simpson's flight he looked at his map. The converging lines of meridian misled him in his estimate of distance into thinking McMurdo Sound was 20 miles wide, when it was really 40 miles wide. When he looked at his monitor, he saw the flight path was 27 miles from the TACAN. He thought his AINS must be malfunctioning, so he over-headed the TACAN. He found his AINS was correct. When he rang Ross Johnson about other matters, he happened to mention as a subsidiary matter that the distance of the flight path from the TACAN was 27 miles.

In one of Johnson's inconsistent statements, he said Simpson had told him the McMurdo waypoint should be at the TACAN. He said Simpson included his advice in his captain's report. That was untrue, Simpson did not add that comment in his captains report. Johnson ordered that the McMurdo waypoint should be shifted to the TACAN. By doing so, he shifted the flight path inadvertently by 27 miles from McMurdo Sound to one that crossed Erebus.

If what Johnson said had been true, then Simpson, who knew the flight path was in McMurdo Sound, was going to lose the benefit of radar control and unrestricted radio communication with ATC, as well as the safety from mountainous terrain. Consequently, it was this clash of evidence with Johnson that Simpson had inadvertently started the chain of events which ultimately led to the disaster. But can one really believe that Simpson told Johnson it should be moved? Mahon did not. Mahon believed Simpson told the truth. In para.376 Mahon said he rejected the allegation by Johnson that Simpson had told him the McMurdo waypoint was incorrectly situated.

If Hewitt been told directly by Les Simpson of his surprise about the 27-mile difference between the final waypoint and the position of Scott Base and the NDB, then Hewitt would have been aware of the scale of the mistake. This was just one example of the revelation of internal disorganisation that Dalgety feared. Slipshod was the word used in the Privy Council's judgment. Catastrophic would have been more accurate.

Collins borrowed US map GNC21N and bought New Zealand NZMS135 map and marked the flight paths onto those two charts, and onto his atlas. He used the flight plan he had not returned after his RCU briefing so as to pre-flight plan for the following day's flight.

This pre-flight planning was observed by Collins's daughters and his wife Maria on the evening of before the flight.

The pilots of the fatal flight had not realised, nor had Air New Zealand told them, that the McMurdo waypoint had been shifted 27 miles, so that their AINS would now no longer take them down the middle of McMurdo Sound, but instead aimed them directly at Mt Erebus' 12,500 feet. Air New Zealand had not briefed them on other matters which were essentials for flying in Antarctica, such as the existence of the insidious optical illusion of white surface whiteout. Optical illusions are mentioned in chapter 7 and the Isles of Scilly G-BEON crash into the sea.

Two accident investigations

The first accident investigation was conducted by Ron Chippindale, who was the chief inspector of air accidents. This was a department of the Ministry of Transport. He had no experience of big jet accidents. He appointed two special assistants who had experience of flying the DC-10s. He was thereafter very influenced by his first assistant, the chief pilot of Air New Zealand, Ian Gemmell. It was he who had planned the Antarctic flights. Chippindale's other assistant was First Officer Peter Rhodes. He, like Dalziell, first experienced his mountain flying in the search for Brian Chadwick's Dragonfly (chapter 3) in 1962 when he was a pilot in a Harvard aircraft. Of the three, Rhodes was the most up to date trained air accident investigator of big jets in New Zealand at that time. That made him ultra vulnerable to pressure later from his employers, Air New Zealand. Many years later, Roger Dalziell became one of the most respected air accident consultants TAIC ever had. Rhodes likewise became a consultant beholden to TAIC.

Chippindale submitted his accident report at the end of May 1980. It was released for publication by the minister the following month, controversially before the Royal Commission began its inquiry. It had many mistakes in it that were unearthed by Mahon's Royal Commission. During the Mahon Inquiry there were many witnesses and barristers who represented the differing interests of clients. Interests were basically divided between Air New Zealand supported by the Civil Aviation Division on one side, and on the other side the crew and passengers. The result being Mahon's famous words - orchestrated litany of lies.

The author of "Erebus Papers", the most complete book on the Erebus saga, praised the advantages of the openness of the Royal Commission of Inquiry as compared with the secret gathering of evidence by Ron Chippindale. With hindsight, I have to disagree - to a certain extent. Individual witnesses, especially those employed by Air New Zealand or the Civil Aviation Division were subject to retribution by their employers, if they did not say in evidence what their employers told them to say. In a similar situation in an Australian Inquiry, where appropriate, evidence had been held in camera so as to avoid witnesses being vilified, pilot's licences being withdrawn or withheld by CASA or the other aviation authorities, or other threats. But even that does not avoid the problem completely.

Mahon's reference at paragraph 377 to an orchestrated litany of lies referred to the executive, or management pilots, and other sections of Air New Zealand claims of ignorance of low flying. It was all a lie. They had the most to lose if Air New Zealand lost the case it was putting forward. They gave sworn evidence that they had no knowledge of any flights being flown below the MSA of 16,000. Only one executive pilot, Ross Johnson, admitted breaking the alleged MSA of Air New Zealand by flying at 3,000 feet. He obviously did that because he knew that there was hard evidence available from passenger photographs and from records that showed that he did fly at 3,000 feet. (Paragraph 209 of the Mahon Report.)

Application for Judicial Review

Air New Zealand applied for a judicial review of Mahon's paragraph 377 as well as the dispute over costs he had awarded against the airline of NZ$150,000. The case was heard initially in the High Court but then transferred to the Court of Appeal. In effect, the Appeal Court was the court of first instance, an unusual situation. That means that they should have been able to hear or receive new evidence. Air New Zealand won that part of their case regarding the NZ$150K costs and that Mahon exceeded his authority in telling the truth about the organised lying. Mahon appealed against the Court of Appeal decision to the Privy Council in London. That was then the ultimate New Zealand legal appeal tribunal. Between the time of the Court of Appeal hearings (1981) and the time of the Privy Council (1983), the 1982 Falklands war took place. In that war the UK had relied upon certain indirect strategic assistance from the New Zealand armed forces. Also at that time the balance of power in the Pacific was seriously at risk. Politicians strongly feared that New Zealand could be bankrupted by massive potential claims from the passengers' families, in particular by the US citizens relatives. Politicians also feared there was a risk the Civil Aviation Division would not be not protected by the Warsaw Convention, which limited claims to just NZ$42,000.

I have received information from within the UK which may not have been recorded with respect to the Erebus saga. It has given me a different insight into the truth about Erebus. At first, I found it hard to believe that those two judges, Woodhouse and McMullin, could be so mistaken in their judgment, and yet still continue to hear the case because it involved their children's employer, Air New Zealand, while McMullin had a family friend – the junior Air New Zealand counsel – Richard McGrane.

Then I came across a book written by a retired New Zealand lawyer, Rob Moodie. He had crossed swords with the great and the good of the New Zealand legal establishment. That book was "The Justice Mirage". A number of lawyers who were involved in the

Erebus Inquiry are mentioned in it. That book contained remarks not complimentary about a number of lawyers. Some remarks were extremely critical. Once that book is taken seriously, the Criminal Cases Review Commission (CCRC) currently under Colin Carruthers should review many cases of injustice in New Zealand. It should remind all judges as to their behaviour and self-discipline, likewise barristers codes of conduct and honesty in the presentation of their clients cases in court particularly prosecutors eg PO Horizon in the UK.

Woodhouse and McMullin were not treated in the same way that Bill Wilson was in 2010, but perhaps those two were too powerful. Despite being the Court of Appeal, it was acting as a Court of First Instance. It would have been possible for Woodhouse' daughter to have been subpoenaed to give evidence about the public relations use of the Brizendine article. This is the reason why these two judges behaviour was so wrong. It was an unforgivable perversion of the course of justice far worse than Wilson's unequal loans in his joint venture with the barrister appearing before him – Alan Galbraith.

Woodhouse and McMullin were two of the Court of Appeal judges who heard the application for judicial review of the Mahon Report. It was not until after their judgments were delivered, that it was revealed to the public that these two judges' children were employees of Air New Zealand. Under strict legal protocol, they should have recused themselves but such was the power they had over the New Zealand establishment that nothing happened to them. Woodhouse and McMullin were not appointed to sit at the next Court of Appeal hearing when the Arthur Allan Thomas case judicial review appeal was being heard. Instead, Sir Ron Davison and Maurice Casey took their place. I cannot understand why Bill Wilson was sacked as a judge for hearing a case on the ground that he had close connections with counsel for one party, a relatively minor indiscretion, whereas Woodhouse and McMullin, who later had shown such bias against Peter Mahon got away with it. But then again, Rob Moodie's book, "The Justice Mirage" does explain the machinations of the New Zealand legal establishment.

Where the Chippindale Report was wrong

Chippindale's champion, Derek Ellis, who was once a pilot on the Concorde, referred to Chippindale's involvement in the crash in which a prominent Southern African politician was killed, in order to publicise Chippindale's high international reputation. Derek Ellis went further in that he thought that Chippindale had been appointed one of the Inquiry Commissioners, as he was so well respected internationally.

I fully respect Ellis for having been a Concorde pilot. However experienced aviators know that the other technical pioneer in the Concorde cockpit was the flight engineer. In fact even licenced Concorde Co-Pilots were not permitted to fly Concorde unless accompanied by a qualified Concorde flight engineer. Ellis' UK training at Filton and Brise Norton may have taught him Concorde flying but not Air New Zealand lying. This was so clearly demonstrated in the July 2000 crash of the Air France Concorde when the fuel caught fire.

Concorde's fire and subsequent crash had been caused by a number of issues, a bogie spacer had been omitted causing tyre sideways skid and drag, metal puncturing fuel tank 2. Tank 5 burst by tyre debris. Then the claim that DC-10 debris on the runway was the cause. That claim was overturned under appeal in 2012 in the courts ten years later. Parallels with Erebus cover-up – but I have no space to detail all the parallels with the mistakes of the French accident inspectorate with the mistakes of Chippindale.

Chippindale was an errand boy, for that South African Commission, and travelled to Racal in the UK with regard to the crash of President Machel of Mozambique. There was controversy with respect to the VORs (directional radio lighthouses) in the area with the signal to a Russian Tu134 in South Africa. Chippindale visited Racal the UK VOR manufacturers and after that visit he exchanged correspondence with those makers. The radio frequencies of the VORs in the area were close together, like the Auckland and Tauranga's close radio frequencies in the Kaimai tragedy.

I concentrate on five areas and references are those listed in the Chippindale Report. These I list under the following headings.

Chippindale's five wrongful claims are in regard to:

1. Radar
2. Cockpit voice recorder (CVR) transcription
3. Area Inertial Navigation System (AINS)
4. Minimum safe altitudes (MSAs).
5. Topographical charts.

1. Radar (Clause 3.36)

One only has to see that Chippindale deliberately placed this clause prominently right next to clause 3.37 (in which he said the probable cause of the crash was pilot error), to see the importance which Chippindale placed on the fact that the pilots had ignored the radar screens. I quote clause 3.36 "The aircraft's radar would have depicted the mountainous [meaning Erebus] terrain ahead."

That was a deliberate attempt by Chippindale to emphasise the alleged bad practice of Collins and Cassin by accusing them of ignoring the radar screen. But in actual fact, the Bendix radar in the DC-10s was a weather radar. It was designed to detect moisture in clouds, not to detect terrain. The New Zealand media latched on to this radar business. So much misplaced credence was given to Chippindale's pronouncements. New Zealand news media was and still is under-funded. Chippindale effectively provided news at little cost.

Chippindale also assumed that the same radar return would be shown on the DC-10's radar screen as was shown on the following US Starlifter aircraft's radar. The Starlifter followed the DC-10. But the two systems were entirely different. Captain Gumble and navigator Marlin Knock in the Starlifter C.141 had a different type of radar set. It was designed to detect terrain, and therefore, of course, it could detect Mount Erebus, in the hands of experienced navigators. Knock advised that he tried to warn TE901 just before the crash when he realised that they were not flying down McMurdo Sound. There is no record of any such communication on the CVR transcript.

Chippindale claimed that Air New Zealand pilots had told him that their DC-10 radars could see Mt. Erebus. What he said in evidence was untrue. When Chippindale had referred to his notes, he said only that First Officer Eaton "discovered that the definition of coastlines was poor owing to the sea ice being adjacent to those coastlines in his opinion." Eaton did not say their DC-10 radars could see Mt. Erebus despite Chippindale's claims.

Chippindale's tape-recorded notes of his interview with Simpson confirmed that Simpson did not use radar. They read:

> Simpson: We didn't specifically use the radar for the run into McMurdo.
>
> Chippindale: Though you didn't use it, did you do a visual comparison at all between what you could see and what was presented on the radar, around Ross Island?
>
> Simpson: No, we were just flying visually round Ross Island.

No DC-10 pilots could see Erebus on their radar sets because Antarctica is totally dry. Only moisture in clouds would be visible on the DC-10 radar. Mahon was probably advised by Rhodes to consult the Bendix manufacturer experts at Fort Lauderdale, USA. There, Mahon, in the presence of Baragwanath, interviewed Wayne Shear and Daryal Kuntman. They were the top radar experts. It then became clear that Chippindale had received no evidence about the DC-10 radar from Bendix. This single factor on which Chippindale based part of his claim of pilot error, was totally wrong.

2. Cockpit voice recorder (CVR) transcription (Clause 3.35)

The CVR, known as the black box, albeit actually red-orange, provided a recording of the last 30 minutes of conversations in the cockpit on a continuous loop. That is discussion between the pilots and the flight engineers, and also from anyone else in the vicinity. Unfortunately, the clarity of the system in the DC-10 at that time was appalling. The recommended transcription procedure was only to use pilots and flight deck colleagues as transcribers who personally knew the flight crew. Only they were best placed to identify the individuals who were speaking, and then to transcribe their conversations.

The transcription team consisted Captains Arthur Cooper and Barney Wyatt, together with Don Olliff, who was the chief flight engineer of Air New Zealand, They were accompanied by accident Inspector Milton Wylie, who was nominally in charge. But Wylie did not know the flight crew of TE901 and so took no part in the actual transcription. It is believed that Barney Wyatt knew, prior to transcribing the CVR, that the flight path had been changed from McMurdo Sound by 27 miles to cross Mt Erebus. Wyatt's comments to Maria Collins prior to his participation in the transcribing team gave that game away. But Arthur Cooper had not been told of any change when he transcribed the tapes. They first heard the tapes at the Sundstrand Corporation in Seattle. They transcribed the tapes at the NTSB in Washington DC, where Colonel P Turner and the Audio Laboratory facilities there provided improved sound systems, and supposedly better clarity of the tape recordings.

It took five days of intense study to complete the transcription. The communications between Collins and Cassin took about half a day to transcribe. The rest of the week was spent due to the poor quality of sound of the talk between the flight engineers and Peter Mulgrew, who was the commentator for that flight. The US technicians told the transcription team that they should follow strict protocols so as to avoid miss-transcribing statements. Miss-transcribing is easily done with such poor-quality recordings from the CVR. The team agreed that Milton Wylie was to give their finished transcription to Chippindale. Arthur Cooper said it was agreed that it would be "typed, sighted, accepted and signed by all the members of the team that took part."

I have received a copy of the original Washington transcript. It was used in the USA case on 30th November 1987 as exhibit 3001.1. It is likely that it is the only one left in existence kept by Arthur Cooper and I am grateful for that. Two items in the transcript not mentioned elsewhere was the poor quality of the HF (High Frequency) radio quality and the attempt to use the 121.5 general calling frequency normally monitored by all aircraft and ground stations in the area around McMurdo Sound and Ross Island. First Officer Greg Cassin was clearly having trouble listening on HF as he had to repeatedly correct certain numbers he thought he heard. Collins at one stage suggested that the standard VHF monitoring frequency of 121.50 be tried. It is puzzling to me that no-one did answer Cassin on the VHF frequency of 121.50. There have been comments from a number of persons who claim they advised TE901 to stay away from Ross Island. What frequency were they using for these messages of "stay away" from Ross Island. Presumably, unless they were at Scott Base, behind Erebus, these folk must have monitored 121.50, and should have heard Cassin's attempts at communication on the VHF, particularly if they were on the west coast of McMurdo Sound. Why did they not respond?

That transcription, known as the Washington transcript, was rejected by Chippindale. Instead, he took the tape to his home and listened to it with Gemmell. This was strictly against all regulations and agreements for black box use. Later Chippindale travelled to the UK to review the tape at the Farnborough audio facility. There, Chippindale made his own transcription. He altered the Washington DC transcription in about 55 places. He inserted words into it that did not exist in the Washington transcription. An example of that were the words "Bit thick here eh Bert". The alterations that he made all supported his claim that the pilots caused the crash. He said that his CVR transcript was to support his report's conclusions. Anything that contradicted his conclusions was rejected or omitted. By this time, he must have been instructed as to what Prime Minister Muldoon wanted from him, and he obliged. He claimed comments had been made by the flight engineers that showed their dismay at Collins for his low flying. Chippindale's claim was untrue. They made no such comments.

On the advice of Arthur Cooper or Peter Rhodes, Mahon took the CVR tapes to the NTSB in Washington DC, and also to Farnborough in the UK. The same technicians who had previously helped Chippindale at Farnborough, now assisted Mahon and Baragwanath in listening to the tapes. It was on this visit that Mahon and Bill Tench met again. Tench had given evidence to the Royal Commission in Auckland. He now organised the facilities for Mahon at Farnborough. Tench had at that time written a book on air accident investigation, but it was not published until 1985. He would have been a very familiar figure to Peter Rhodes. Tench was the leading consultant for international air accident investigations.

Mahon used the opportunity to discuss with him the technical issues that arose from the Erebus tragedy. Tench was well aware of the controversies facing Mahon, because so many wrongful statements had been expressed by Chippindale. When Tench's book "Safety is no Accident" was eventually published in 1985, Tench knew of the Privy Council decision on Erebus. He knew that there were the claims in the pipeline in the US to be made by the families of the crew. He was therefore unwilling to write about Erebus. Those USA hearings were eventually held in 1987. Consequently, it was diplomatically necessary for Tench to omit any reference to the Erebus disaster and to the contradictory reports of Chippindale and Mahon. Chippindale surprised the claimants' US lawyers when, after he had given evidence by deposition for the claimants in New Zealand, he turned up unannounced to the hearings in the US and then gave evidence against the claimants on behalf of the US Navy ATC.

The judge, Justice Greene, in the US case, in his judgment he made many clerical errors of fact in the recounting of the evidence submitted. Very similar to the errors by Diplock of the Privy Council. Much of the evidence from Chippindale was questionable. The US lawyer Tim Cook claimed that he obtained out of court settlements for many of the families, albeit with NDAs (non-disclosure agreements). The broadcaster and film producer John Keir managed to uncover that story. He obtained an interview with Tim Cook in California, which he included in his 2019 podcasts. I was also able to contact Tim Cook verifying what he said earlier to John Keir.

Tench, in his book, went into the details about the corrections that were required to be made to the Dan Air flight 1008 report after the Spanish investigators had issued the first ICAO Annex 13 accident report on that crash in 1980 at Tenerife. I was fortunate to meet the Lloyds Insurance personnel who was involved in that case. Lloyds successful pressure on the Spanish investigators got the report heavily amended. The Air New Zealand ridiculously small area designated for flying below the MSA of 16,000 was similar to the impossible turning circles that the Spanish ATC had instructed flight 1008. That was the cause of the crash of Dan Air 1008. In both cases, under IFR rules, the turning circles were far too small for the rate 1 turns. Enough for any trained pilot to realise the falseness of the area ascribed for the MSA of 6,000 feet. Rhodes reported on this in Impact Erebus.

That point was not lost on Peter Martin, the UK lawyer for the Lloyds insurance syndicate that insured Air New Zealand. In fact, the Dan Air 1008 Lloyds appendix to the original erroneous Spanish report made it clear that Chippindale's report could be changed by Mahon's report. i.e. a similar appendix to the ICAO annex 13 report filed by Chippindale. But that would have spoilt the state sponsored fraudulent plan to restrict the payouts to the passengers to the Warsaw Convention low levels.

Chippindale broke every convention by amending the Washington transcription of the CVR. The 55 changes Chippindale made is a clear indication of the political pressure PM Muldoon put on those involved to blame the pilots. He did that so as to prevent massive accident claims being made by families of the passengers and crew. Chippindale achieved that required result by omitting from his transcript any pilot conversations that contradicted his theories. He heavily abridged the Washington transcription to achieve that aim.

At this point, I comment about the US Navy's tape recording of their ATC on the 28th November 1979. Peter Mahon made much of this in his book, Verdict on Erebus. When first arriving in Antarctica with Chippindale and Gemmell, Rhodes was advised by the US Navy personnel that they had accidentally erased the last 4mins 42secs of the tape that recorded their messages on both HF and VHF messages to TE901. Mahon interviewed Lt Commander Fessler on the subject and suggested the possible scenario some lawyers may make of this accidental deletion.

Mahon's suggested scenario was that the US Navy ATC did not follow procedure regarding HF and VHF conventions. The suggestion being that TE901 was briefly shown on the US radar for one minute according to calculations by New Zealand Land and Surveys [as requested by Mahon] of line-of-sight of the flight path. The US HF controller should have relayed the warning from the VHF radar operators messages, when they had not been able to make direct contact. TE901's transponder was being interrogated by the US radar. The CVR transcript evidences this IFF transponder contact. The US radar operators must have seen TE901. After this suggestion, the US Navy refuted their earlier statement about the accidental deletion of their tape by saying there were no messages to record during the 4.42 period. Nothing had been deleted. There were no messages during that time. Without written evidence of the earlier verbal statement to Rhodes that the tape had been erased, Rhodes was targeted by the US authorities and later he became targeted by Davis and Eden labelled as an unreliable witness by both sides.

3. Area Inertial Navigation System (AINS) (Clause 3.28)

In 3.28, Chippindale correctly states that the on-board navigation system operated normally. However, in 3.15, he criticised the pilots for not monitoring their actual position in relation to the topography adequately. This would have necessitated a chart table. The thought of using a knee or clipboard for such large charts was impractical. There are still a few YouTube wiseacres who claim the coordinates should have been plotted as the flight progressed. But Milton Wylie likewise was critical of Collins and Cassin. Wylie was employed by the Ministry of Transport and declined to acknowledge the whole of the research carried out by Vette which then became the standard for future accident studies. I should also observe that Wylie was not very successful in promoting the original CVR transcription by Cooper, Wyatt and Olliff. I cannot trust such an opinion, from Wylie.

But Collins was flying visually. The AINS monitor is on the ceiling of the flight deck. It would need to be continually checked for the coordinates to be continually plotted onto a map. That would have distracted the pilots from visual flight. In any event, that was not the purpose of the monitor. Its purpose was to enable the pilots to check the AINS accuracy at waypoints normally expected to be better than one mile out for every hour in the air.

In 1.17.7, Chippindale gave the impression that the final coordinate of 166.58, the TACAN waypoint, was correct, and that the coordinate of 164.48, which was the McMurdo Sound waypoint, which was given to pilots at the briefing was incorrect. Doubtless these words were suggested by Gemmell to Chippindale. He admitted that the shifted coordinate, that is the TACAN waypoint, that resulted in a flight path which crossed Erebus, should have been drawn to the attention of the crew of the accident flight. Air New Zealand did not do this.

Chippindale made a notorious statement in 2.5, where he wrote: "No evidence was found to suggest that they [the pilots] had been mislead [sic] by this error in the flight plan shown to them in the briefing". But it was later discovered that when he used the word evidence, all he meant was documentary evidence. He was so ignorant that evidence given verbally under oath is equally acceptable.

The minutes of the directors' meeting on 5th December 1979 showed that the flight path as briefed to the pilots was down the centre of McMurdo Sound. When a change is made to a briefed RCU flight plan, a company notice is supposed to be issued.

The absence of any such RCU Notice misled Collins and Cassin into believing that all the coordinates which they had been given at despatch were the same as those which they had been given at the briefing on 9th November 1979. That flight path would have taken them safely down the middle of McMurdo Sound.

Air New Zealand DC-10 pilots had been using the AINS for a number of years, and never had any pilots experienced issues with a break-down of the system. It was totally reliable. It was so accurate, that with flights to and from the same destinations, albeit that there was a different height of the ingoing and outgoing flight, the higher aircraft would experience a false audible warning of low flying caused by the body of lower aircraft flying in the opposite direction below.

The purpose of the AINS was to deliver the aircraft to the locality required with an error of less than a mile for every hour flown, so although it could not be used for landing purposes in IMC on a narrow runway, in practice every pilot had come to rely on the system to deliver the aircraft to the required waypoint, albeit that an error of just one mile for every hour flown was acceptable. For all practical purposes, it was much better than one mile.

In the case of the fatal flight, it was therefore reasonable for Collins and Cassin to believe that the AINS would deliver them to the centre of the entry to McMurdo Sound. That Sound was 40 miles wide, and the coastline had a distinctive shape. Unfortunately, the entry to Lewis Bay had the same distinctive coastline appearance as the entry to McMurdo Sound. Under 3.15, Chippindale expected the pilots to unfold large topographical maps, with their eyes looking down at a map, instead of looking outside as they were required to do under VFR flying rules. Chippindale also expected them to read the coordinates shown on the monitor in the ceiling, and then to re-plot that set of coordinates onto a topographical chart.

Collins had already planned the flight the night before. He must have marked (plotted) the flight path onto the topographical charts, based on the coordinates on the flight plan he had taken from the briefing. Collins was entitled to believe that, by using his plotted flight path, he could read the distance to run to the Dailey Islands waypoint, and therefore be able to see the exact position of the aircraft throughout the entire flight.

I find it interesting that the TAIC chief Inspector after Chippindale was Tim Burfoot. Tim's brother was Jeremy, an author/aviator of some repute and an experienced commercial pilot for Qantas. He regularly flew A380 airliners. His written advice to budding pilots was to plan ahead as much as possible before any flight to reduce workload on the day. This has to include any plotting of flight paths. Exactly what Jim Collins did on 27th November 1979. The absence of any RCU amendment notice should have confirmed the flight path was that as briefed. Collins relied on that mantra so that he could rely on the planning he had so meticulously carried out the night before.

AINS reflections

I have tried to place myself in the same position that faced Collins and Cassin. Of course, I did not have the advantage of a large passenger Jet with the AINS for navigation but even in small aircraft like the PA28 I flew on 17th March 1992 has the ability to use VORs and NDBs. It was on a trip to Plymouth and back in one day that I needed to use these radio beacons and their normally fixed coordinates.

The analogy is that the AINS (Area Inertial Navigation System) is like flying from one NDB/VOR radio beacon to the next except that with the AINS you go from one set of geographical coordinates to the next without the need to retune to the VOR/NDBs frequencies. On the return from Plymouth, I hit unexpected thick cloud very shortly after take-off over Dartmoor and was in IMC in the semi-dark. The first time on my own in IMC for real! Any pilot will appreciate what I went through mentally on that baptism of fire even though I had trained hard to obtain that coveted IMC rating, so I was legal. I had to rely on the VOR and NDB being where they were on the chart. I had to immediately start the scan of my instrument "T" and aviate. Thank you Brian Grant.

All pilots are taught that it was necessary firstly to Aviate i.e. fly the aircraft, secondly, Navigate and finally Communicate – in that order. Quickly my training came to my rescue and I kept G-AVNO under control. I then dialled in the frequencies. To be honest, I forget which ones I used that evening. I shudder to think what would have happened to me if the radio beacons had been "moved" the night before behind one of the high radio masts in the area, by the expert navigators of Air New Zealand (and not NOTAM'd). But I now think of Collins relying 100% on those AINS way points – exactly like a VOR or NDB. I relied on my chart with the chinagraph pencil line flight path showing those beacons that I had drawn for the outward journey to Plymouth.

In a way, Collins had flight planned similarly to my own planning for the 17th March. In his place, I would never have given it a thought that the position of those way-points or radio beacons might have been moved by the expert navigators, either by Air New Zealand or the UK topographical chart makers in the UK. Certainly not after the Route Clearance Unit (RCU) briefing of 9th November 1979 conducted by Captains Wilson and Johnson, who demonstrated the waypoint at Dailey Islands at the top of McMurdo Sound. Les Simpson could see the final waypoint was 27 miles west of Scott base.

On my flight, I did not have it completely easy. I was having to monitor my instrument panel, not looking out of the cockpit at that stage, when the DI started to play up and I had to use the magnetic compass in the monitoring loop. But that compass was not within the normal visual scanning position and focussing on that unlit was awkward. I very nearly lost my composure and ability to fly November Oscar. ATC were helpful, to a point. They instructed me to climb to 3,500 feet but then *report 1000 feet at Sandbanks*. If you ever can see a chart of the South of England, you will understand what was happening. Perhaps if you can get Google Earth, you might follow my flight path.

The mindset of all the DC-10 pilots with the AINS must have been that it was in fact a better nav system than flying from VOR to VOR in a Piper PA28 or Cessna 150. Effectively you have been given your own series of VORs. Then to have the terminal VOR put behind a volcano without being told! All those DC-10 pilots, in practice, had come to rely 100% on the AINS even if they were not, in theory, allowed to. Paul Holmes book relates the tale of inward/outward flights to LAX with the higher aircraft's low flying warning system being triggered by the lower aircraft flying the opposite direction, the system was so accurate.

Collins was 100% sure that the AINS had placed him at the centre of the approach to McMurdo Sound. As Vette discovered, in the conditions, the entry to Lewis Bay looked the same (albeit one-third in scale) as that for the shoreline cliffs of McMurdo Sound.

With hindsight, not a very good visual fix unless you add in the 100% accuracy of the AINS which you should be able to depend on.

With all IMC flying, the pilot has to rely 100% on his flying panel instruments even when physical senses are tricking one otherwise, first rule of IMC/IFR flying. Unless you have experienced this as a solo pilot, you cannot appreciate this. In the book "Turbulent Years" p91/2, Brian Waugh had a young 15 years old ATC cadet, Neville McLean, in the right-hand seat keeping a good lookout through the cockpit windows for the sea. He had encountered unexpected bad weather. I bet Brian would not have been able to maintain his monitoring of his instrument panel AND look out for the sea. But that is what I had to do near Poole Harbour and Sandbanks, albeit I was not in severe turbulence.

Fortunately I came out of the thick cloud over Poole harbour at 1000 feet after some quick calculations and dead reckoning, missing the Bovington mast just to the north. But my mindset was relying on that VOR. Thereafter it was easy for me to navigate visually along the Solent and the south coast. Easy for a yachtsman. But the incident did remind me of Jacks Sound and I had flashbacks of that near disaster when I was effectively responsible for three lives on that passage.

I am just amazed that the Air NZ executive pilots, as well as ex-Concorde pilots, continued to criticise Collins and Cassin for relying on their AINS. Richard McGrane must have known the truth but I expect he may still be alive so I am reluctant to suggest otherwise without trying to check the facts with him, as I did try with Bruce Crosbie

I was close to coming to grief on my return flight from Plymouth, only my training under the hood for the IMC rating and advice from Brian Grant saved me mentally. My family did not know of this incident -until now! - but it was one of my nine lives used! Blackout is as dangerous as whiteout if you are not expecting it.

I remembered my escapade in Jacks Sound during the struggle to fly and navigate November Oscar. On that 1978 sailing trip, I had the best night navigators beacon – the Moon. At least the Good Lord does not normally misplace that beacon and during this voyage in the summer of 1978, I came to rely on the position and height of the moon. I was the third person on board – as a cabin boy only - on a full Royal Navy exercise being carried out by Captain James Briggs and Commander Jake Backus. It involved repositioning a catamaran from Greenock Scotland to Padstow Cornwall including a night passage through a notoriously tricky narrow piece of water between Skomer Island and the Welsh mainland.

Being the least experienced, I still found myself useful on that night passage as I was an experienced helmsman and I was not involved in the navigation exercise being planned inside the cabin. The catamaran was "Bluefin", one of the most incredible multihull one-off designs ever built. I was also totally ignorant of what Jack's Sound passage was. For the record, it funnels the tide through a narrow gap at speeds of up to six knots. It was a south going tide against a south west wind about force seven, just below gale force. This combination provides several "stopper" waves in the Sound and it was essential that the catamaran went through these at full speed. My eyes had become accustomed to the dark and the effect of the moonlight on the surface of the sea. James and Jake did not have their full night vision so I was left at the helm.

The decision had been made to go through Jacks Sound at the very last minute, Captain Briggs' inspired astro navigation calculations confirmed that the moon's position for the transit of Jack's Sound lit up the passage perfectly, albeit midnight. James advised Jake who was fast asleep down below. Within seconds, he was in his full wet weather gear, life jacket, safety harness on and in the cockpit, holding on to the grabrail next to the helm. I could see the whites of his knuckles. That catamaran was exceptional and ploughed straight through the stopper waves just south of Horse Rock. Thereafter the exercise continued in safety, and we reached Padstow in the morning. I had just used the second of my nine lives, the first being with Brian Chadwick between Milford and Queenstown in 1962. (Chapter 3)

The catamaran Bluefin was sold later but I am pleased to note that it has returned to the Briggs family who will no doubt nurture and refurbish that incredible sailing craft which taught me so much about practical navigation. As for the Naval exercise by the Navy's expert navigators, it was useful for what happened less than four years later, briefly referred to in case study 6. Do navigate back to Broadlands Ben Russell. It was an accident.

These experiences confirm my view that moving TE901s waypoint from the Dailey Islands to McMurdo Station did affect Colins and Cassin. Chippindale's notorious opinion at section 2.5 of his report "no evidence was found to suggest that they [Collins and Cassin] had been misled by this error.." At least my VOR/NDB and the Moon were not moved by the remote navigator back at Air New Zealand House Auckland.

As we use Sat Navs on our iphones, we can appreciate more why Collins and Cassin relied on their AINS. As for the moon one kiwi aviation editor explained that having got lost using satellite navigation while navigating on the York ring road he used the moon to go due south!

4. Minimum Safe Altitudes   (Clauses 3.18-3.20)

The first flight as flown by Ian Gemmell on a direct line from Cape Hallett to the McMurdo

Williams Field waypoint did not go over the top of Mt Erebus. That was because Gemmell himself disconnected the controls from the onboard computer, and instead manually steered the DC-10 around Mt Erebus albeit under the control of the US Navy ATC radar surveillance. Flying over an active volcano is not safe . That was demonstrated when Gordon Vette was the captain. Erebus was throwing up lava bombs thousands of feet high. Even the Chippindale Report (Clause 5.16) included the recommendation not to flight plan over an active volcano.

On the day of Gemmell's flight, there was a considerable amount of cloud over the top of Ross Island. Gemmell claimed he never went below that nominal MSA of 16,000 feet. His claim was supported by his co-pilot Captain Tony Lawson. Lawson made an ass of himself over his definition of flying at 2,000 feet over Erebus during the Royal Commission. However, the commentator on that day was Bob Thomson, the chief of the Antarctic Division of the DSIR. His evidence to Mahon was that the flight descended to 9,000 feet. The passengers could hear the radio calls with the McMurdo ATC. These calls had been patched through to the intercoms in the passenger cabin.

One of Gemmell's passengers was Bruce Grierson, a high-profile lawyer. He was a keen 8mm cine cameraman, and he took eight reels of film on that trip. He wrote to Mahon on 30th April 1981 that was after the release of the Mahon Report. He stated the fact that when Gemmell was flying at 33,000 feet, he received a radar let down from the US Navy ATC, and that authorised him to descend to just 9,000 feet. That was exactly the height in Thomson's evidence. The radio calls from ATC had been relayed through the Public Address system so that all the passengers, but not Thomson because he was on the flight deck, could hear what was said. Grierson said Gemmell descended through thick cloud that came down to 9,000 feet. He said that on exiting the cloud, Erebus was close to the wingtip of the DC-10. Grierson said it was a very near miss. I provide more information on this in part 3

Anne Cassin had also borrowed a film like Grierson's, and that showed Gemmell had descended below 16,000 ft. It may be that she had Grierson's film. She wrote:

> Supt Brian Wilkinson came to my house to 'interview' me. I was delighted
> that the police were looking into it. Crosbie had stolen that stuff from my house
> without my permission so I thought that was a criminal offence. I also offered
> to get the movie that a passenger had loaned to me. He had been on Gemmell's
> flight. It showed the aircraft flying abeam the summit of Erebus - NOT 16,000' I
> had shown the movie to Paul Davison and Roger but they at that time said that it
> would be too difficult to prove and they felt there was enough evidence without it
> - if only we knew then. I had to return the movie.

It shows that Gemmell lied about his own altitude. It also adds to the evidence that the alleged MSA of 16,000 feet was not a rigid, never-break instruction of Air New Zealand.

That was only a myth put forward by Air New Zealand after the accident. The airline needed to claim that, so it could falsely claim the crash was caused by pilot error. That scheme must have been thought up after the crash, by Dalgety and Gemmell, or the board of directors.

5. Topographical Charts

Chippindale said that Collins had no topographical charts, and that he did not plan his route before the flight. In his press release dated 6 May 1981, he implied that Maria Collins and the two daughters Kathryn and Elizabeth lied in their evidence when they said what Collins had done. In effect Chippindale said that Collins did not possess such charts. He said that, despite the fact that he actually knew Collins had on the flight the US chart which matched the exact description Elizabeth had said her father had worked on. Chippindale said that, despite the fact that he knew how, why and from whom, Collins had borrowed one chart. He said that despite the fact that he knew, because he had read the Tait transcription of the radio conversation at Nelson between TE901 and Tait. He knew Collins was using it on the flight.

The reason Chippindale knew all that, was because he knew that when Collins was flying over the city of Nelson, his third pilot, First Officer Graham Lucas, put in a radio call to the airport. He asked to speak to Peter Tait of Helicopters NZ. He was given the frequency of 122.7 to speak directly to his friend there, Peter Tait. Tait had sent his friend, Lucas, the US map GNC21N. This was one of the two charts which Collins had been working on the evening before the flight as seen by his daughters. Tait asked Lucas whether he had received it, because he had sent it to Lucas by airmail only a few days earlier. Lucas answered - yes, it was onboard.

Chippindale had the transcripts of all TE901's radio communications. That included the one between Tait and Lucas. Chippindale recognised that the existence of this chart was important. Nelson police were asked to obtain a sworn statement from Tait, which they did so. GNC21N is a chart which covers the Air New Zealand flight path between New Zealand and McMurdo. It is an American Chart. I cannot emphasize enough that Chippindale knew Collins had it for his flight. The claim by Chippindale that Collins did not have that chart, and that Maria Collins and her two daughters committed perjury was a complete lie. Paul Holmes, in his book **"Daughters of Erebus"**, rightly made a big issue of this lie by Chippindale

It is impossible for Chippindale to have made his allegations in good faith that the Collins daughters were lying. He had known from the start that the GNC21N chart had been passed on from Tait to Lucas, and thence to Jim Collins. Holmes described Chippindale's duplicity against the Collins family, and the harm he deliberately caused them.

In case it is too hard to accept my word, these are Chippindale's words as taken from his press release:

> Again during my investigation I was unable to locate any map supply location with maps readily available which had provided maps for Captain Collins. Although available in Los Angeles by prior order, they were not readily available over the counter and the Air New Zealand briefing officer had to resort to a Photostat copy for his RCU briefings. Therefore from whence came his large map? [Comment: Chippindale knew exactly "from whence came his large map".]

These lies were written by Chippindale, despite the fact that he had the transcript that showed exactly how Collins had obtained this large US map, GNC21N, from Peter Tait. The ATC transcript between TE901 and Nelson Airport is the ultimate proof of Chippindale's knowledge that Collins had that map. I feel that anyone still supporting Chippindale was involved and guilty of lying themself.

Chippindale also said the "briefing officer had to resort to a photostat copy for his RCU briefings". The daughters were eventually able to identify the second map Collins was using that night. It was NZMS135. That was the map which Wilson, the briefing officer, had copied. Because NZMS135 is large scale, Collins would also have plotted his track from the Hallett waypoint to the McMurdo Sound (Dailey Islands) waypoint on it. He would have plotted his entire flight from Auckland to the McMurdo Sound waypoint and return onto his long GNC21N.

Chippindale's insinuation that Maria Collins and her two daughters Kathryn and Elizabeth were liars, whereas the real liars were key members of the executive of Air New Zealand, is for me the most abhorrent personal manifestation of this national scandal in New Zealand history.

Why did Chippindale lie? It could only have been part of his plan to blame the pilots. For me, it is the clearest indication that Chippindale became part of that conspiracy. Totally! Perhaps, like the investigating Police Superintendent Brian Wilkinson, he had been pressured likewise directly by the Prime Minister Muldoon and Des Dalgety. Wilkinson subsequently confessed to Peter Mahon that he had been instructed to find no one had lied. He did not tell Mahon who the instruction had come from. But Wilkinson told Anne Cassin that he had been charged by Muldoon to close the police inquiry into the perjury allegations by finding no perjury had occurred.

The incompetence of Chippindale

There are key issues that prove the incompetence of Chippindale. For example, his handling of the Harvie report into the crash of the Bay of Plenty Airways Aero Commander (per chapter 2) is evidence of Chippindale's low level of expertise. An easy comparison can be made of the difference in competence between the New Zealand accident inspectors, O'Brien, Harvie, and Chippindale on the one hand, and Bill Tench on the other hand as follows.

Bill Tench's book, "The Classic Accident" describes a Dan Air Boeing 707-300 crash as it was approaching Lusaka, in Zambia. Under ICAO Annex 13, the Zambians were responsible to carry out the investigation. But Zambia was not competent to do so. Nor was it financially able to fund the investigation. That was accepted by Zambia. On the other hand, the UK authorities were able to participate under Annex 13 regulations. Therefore they took over the investigation.

Is New Zealand's TAIC now in a similar position as Zambia was in 1977? Has TAIC been remodelled, funded and managed by real air accident specialists since Chippindale and John Britton?

The Dan Air Boeing 707 had a structural failure of the stabiliser (rear tailplane). A spar cap had failed through metal fatigue. Thus, a popular aircraft, the Boeing 707, had a structural weakness that was not previously known. Investigators rapidly realised that there were another 521 Boeing 707s still flying, and that they could all have the same structural weakness. Immediate international action was required. The knowledge across international boundaries by all the experts was combined. Every 707 was inspected. The inspections revealed how serious the problem was. Even though it was extremely difficult to carry out those inspections, over 38 aircraft were discovered to have these fatigue cracks.

Now compare that investigation with the New Zealand accident reports that were carried out by Inspectors Paddy O'Brien and Ted Harvie on ZK-BWA. That was the Bay of Plenty Airways Aero-Commander crash at Mount Ruapehu in 1961. O'Brien said the cause of the crash was pilot error. He said the pilot flew too close to Ruapehu. In fact, the real cause of the crash was the design weakness in the main plane spar cap. That should have been recognised by any competent air accident inspectors with the appropriate training in metal fatigue. ZK-BWA may have been the first Aero Commander to crash due to this design weakness. But there were many other Aero Commanders flying in 1961, and the manufacture of them was continuing.

I have provided full details in chapter 2. There were 23 further cases of Aero Commanders crashing due to this design weakness. Many lives were needlessly lost because of the inability of New Zealand accident inspectors to recognise the problem, albeit on that first occasion. That was so unlike the case of the Boeing 707 spar cap weakness which was dealt with by a combination of really competent international experts, such as Tench.

Paddy O'Brien in 1961 may be forgiven for his failure to recognise a design fault causing metal fatigue as it was the first complete wing failure. Likewise, the resources that could be devoted to the investigation of a small aircraft, such as the Rockwell Aero Commander, were not as great as could be devoted to the Boeing 707. But nevertheless in 1984, because of a public outcry against the ever-present mantra of blaming the pilots by the New Zealand aircraft accident investigators, a new review was carried out. In that review all the expert aviation reports on the Aero Commander's 24 crashes were given to the chief accident inspector, who was Ron Chippindale. Despite the overwhelming new evidence, and the history of the 24 Aero Commander's crashes since 1961, Chippindale still would not exonerate the pilot, Alf Bartlett. How many other accident reports produced by Chippindale over the 19 years after Erebus were as badly carried out as his review of ZK-BWA?

Chippindale may have simply been lazy in releasing Ted Harvie's 1972 report without revising it, ignoring events between 1972 and 1984. He was busy with Erebus. He continued in office as chief accident inspector for 19 years until his retirement. Then Tim Burfoot took over that position. Those subsequent years in which Chippindale remained in office must have been the result of the influence of various politicians, following his Erebus report with the blame the pilots mantra.

It was only in 1999 that Maurice Williamson was able to get Mahon's report accepted by the parliament as an official document. That is, it only happened after Chippindale's retirement.

The Chippindale Erebus Report 79-139 was supposed to have been prepared under ICAO Annex 13 terms and protocol. Doubtless much of the fine detail would have been prepared by a number of different members of the team of accident investigators. Not all the words and individual paragraphs would have been prepared by Chippindale himself. Reading between the lines, one can identify some of those paragraphs prepared by Chippindale, compared with those technical details prepared by other members of staff. It is easy to see who recommended that no flights be flown over active volcanos, especially when Ian Gemmell said it was safe. Chippindale by himself would not have embarrassed his technical assistant Gemmell by making such a recommendation. So some other more experienced accident inspector must have insisted that clause 5.16 be added to the recommendations.

Chippindale supporters who cannot see that the preceding factors are wrong will never be convinced that his constant attribution of blame to the pilots was also wrong. They will never be convinced that political pressures on him produced the amateurish report that Justice Mahon discredited in the key areas. I acknowledge that most of the technical factual data as required by ICAO guidelines in his report are correct. But most of the conclusions and emphasis have every appearance of having been provided to him by the chief pilot for Air New Zealand, Ian Gemmell.

The Chippindale Report was based on the premise that the "over the top of Erebus" evidence of John P. Wilson and Ross Johnson said was true. Chippindale may not have known of the directors' discussions on 5th December 1979, when they had minuted that "the crash site was well left of track". This is the clearest evidence from CEO Morrie Davis that the flight path as briefed to Collins, and all the preceding pilots, was not over Mt Erebus, but instead it was down the middle of McMurdo Sound. That completely contradicted the evidence given to Mahon by briefing officers John Wilson and Ross Johnson.

Chippindale completely ignored the evidence from the line pilots from 1978 onwards who denied what the briefing officers had said. The pilots said the track as given at the briefings was in the middle of McMurdo Sound. Therefore, any reference to alleged breaches of the nominal MSAs of 16,000 and 6,000 feet were irrelevant.

The contradictions in the Chippindale report's paragraphs 1.17.7, then 2.5 and finally 2.20 were not recognised by the Privy Council. In paragraph 2.20, Chippindale states:

> It was the result of a misconception shared by himself [Collins], the first officer [Cassin] and the flight's official commentator [Peter Mulgrew] that the approach path was over a sea level ice shelf to the West of Mt Erebus [i.e. middle of McMurdo Sound].

Compare that with Chippindale's paragraph 2.5:

> In the case of this crew [the Erebus crew] no evidence was found to suggest that they had been mislead [sic] by this error [changed final coordinates] in the new flight plan [that change not having been the subject of a notam] shown to them at the briefing.

In paragraph 1.17.7 Chippindale admits that flight ops intended "that it be drawn to the attention of the previous crew". It certainly was not drawn to the attention of the crew of the fatal flight.

These clauses in Chippindale's report, when taken together, are irreconcilable. Chippindale's statement that Collins and his crew were not misled by the waypoint change, whether that change was correcting an earlier mistake, or even worse, deliberately hiding that mistake, has to be one of the most perversely unfathomable opinions ever contained in an aviation accident report.

Unless of course you were to include his 1984 review of the Bay of Plenty crash of ZK-BWA! In that case Chippindale would not accept that there was already serious metal fatigue of the wing spar in that aircraft, and that it was ready to finally fail due to turbulence. The evidence from 23 years experience of metal fatigue of the wing spar was clear: 23 further crashes were caused by that same metal fatigue of the wing spar cap in each incident. (For more details see chapter 2 on the Bay of Plenty Airways 1961).

Case law on Mahon's use of words in para.377.

The key points in Justice Peter Mahon's report were referred to several times or more correctly by Ken Diplock in the Privy Council. Diplock repeated the relevant clauses 392, 393, and 394 of Mahon's report. That is, that the dominant cause of the disaster was the change of coordinates (from 164.48 to 166.58) and the fact that the change was not notified to the pilots. Mahon could not have made it clearer that the fundamental cause of the disaster was not the mistake by Brian Hewitt, but "that mistake is directly attributable, not so much to the persons who made it, but to the incompetent administrative airline procedures which made the mistake possible."

I take up the behaviour of the barristers at the Royal Commission of Inquiry into the Erebus disaster. Mahon's expression, which was much criticised by many legal commentators, was his phrase "orchestrated litany of lies". At an early stage, I thought that Mahon had gone too far. That was until I was advised of a crucial core piece of evidence which confirmed that Mahon was right. That information was contained in an email from one of the chief participants in the disaster inquiry.

Of the many pieces of the jigsaw of Erebus, that one piece changed my viewpoint, and I now agree whole heartedly with Mahon. I was advised that Des Dalgety sent a telex shortly after he received the news of the crash. That telex was physically handed in person to the Royal Commissioner. That telex contained the order that all records, relevant or otherwise, were to be destroyed. This followed the prior pattern of similar events of that era in the United States. Document shredding there had become a frequent defence tool used to conceal political and commercially embarrassing and costly incidents from the public eye and ear.

Des Dalgety was a long-standing friend and lawyer of the Prime Minister, Robert Muldoon. Air New Zealand was wholly owned by the state of New Zealand. Technically Muldoon was, as finance minister as well as PM, notionally the owner of all the shares in the company. Des Dalgety was the deputy chairman on the board of directors of Air New Zealand, and so represented Muldoon and the state.

Having been told of the leak of the Dalgety Telex, it became clear to me that Dalgety was the orchestrator of the cover-up of all the mistakes made by Air New Zealand. That was even before I had confirmation of the McGee meeting with Mahon.

Greg McGee in his book "Tall Tales" wrote:

> I was sitting across the table from [Mahon] at Brighton Road when he said, in his raspy, weakening voice, "The orchestrator was ... ", and I didn't hear the name he articulated.
>
> I can't miss this, I thought, the orchestrator of the notorious litany of lies, just

because I fear being rude or tiring the old man out, so I asked him if he would mind repeating it.

"The orchestrator", said Peter Mahon, quite clearly this time, "was Des Dalgety".

Mahon knew at this early stage who was lying because of this telex. Under the Warsaw Convention at that time, there was a limited payout for passengers of only NZ$42,000. But that limit only applied if there was no gross negligence. But gross negligence did not include errors such as pilot errors, and possibly individual personal mistakes by employees, such as navigation errors made by someone like Hewitt. That would be the safest defence that Air New Zealand could make against the risk of the massive payouts similar to those that were being obtained in US courts against airlines and aircraft manufacturers.

Dalgety was one of the cleverest lawyers in New Zealand. He decided that both the pilots and the navigation section should be blamed. As is usual in any crash, the two pilots, Collins and Cassin, would always be in the firing line. That is simply because they were the proximate cause of the crash. The proximate cause used to be the normal quote in ICAO accident reports under the original conventions of that organization. However, dispensing with a navigator from the flight decks and replacing with the new AINS computerised navigation had not been tested under the Warsaw limitation of liability provisions. Dalgety saw the chance to not only blame the pilots to restrict the compensation payable, but also to blame the office-based navigators, in this case Brian Hewitt.

Air New Zealand therefore offered up Hewitt as the sacrificial lamb alongside Collins and Cassin. Peter Mahon worked out that Dalgety had this plan to blame Hewitt in order to cover up the Air New Zealand blunders, and he clearly spelled that out in paragraph 393.

At the Royal Commission hearings there were a large number of barristers. They all supported differing conflicting interests. Mahon had to remind those barristers that the commission was not an adversarial court hearing, but instead it was an inquiry into the facts. Technically under the barristers' code of conduct, they should not have deliberately tried to mislead or withhold relevant information from the Royal Commissioner. But in fact with hindsight, it is clear that most did. It seems that the New Zealand establishment is slow to criticise its members in this regard.

Under "discovery" regulations, Air New Zealand was obliged to provide relevant documents such as the directors minutes of 5th December 1979. Such breeches of "discovery" legislation are being investigated in the UK in relation to the Post Office Horizon computer scandal. Inquiries into prosecution of those who failed in this regard are well under way as I write.

Such behaviour should provide lessons about the cause of the crash so that there would not be a repeat of such a disaster. This is precisely what an investigation under ICAO Annex 13 is intended to achieve. I have been reminded many times of this, from the third man who accompanied Chippindale on the ice, Peter Rhodes.

Dalgety ensured that Air New Zealand had the most experienced counsel to defend it. He was Lloyd Brown, who was a close friend of Mahon. Lloyd Brown was instrumental in the selection of Mahon to be the Royal Commissioner. But was such a close relationship between a Judge and the Senior Counsel for the main interested party such a wise choice. At this point, I raise the issue of the Bill Wilson case when an appeal court judge was a great friend and business partner of one of the barristers representing a litigant in a case being adjudicated by Wilson. Ted Thomas ensured that Wilson resigned.

To this day, there are still excerpts from the original video of the Royal Commission hearings of some of those cross-examinations on YouTube. One example is TVNZ's Lookout: The Mt Erebus Disaster. In one section, the video demonstrates exactly how Gemmell dealt with questions from Mahon. It has to be remembered that Gemmell and Chippindale were at the crash site together, prior to recovery of the CVR and the flight data recorder DFDR. Chippindale was not told, until two weeks later, that the route had been shifted prior to the fatal flight without the air-crew being told of the change. It was important to know if Gemmell, the chief pilot, had known of the change in the coordinates from before he left New Zealand for the crash site.

It has since been confirmed that Greenwood had briefed Gemmell on the coordinates change before he left for Antarctica. When Gemmell gave evidence at the Royal Commission, there was an exchange between Mahon and Gemmell as to when he knew of the last minute change in the coordinates. It is now certain that Mahon had already known at that stage in the hearings that Gemmell had been privately briefed by Greenwood that the coordinates had been changed after Collins RCU meeting On one occasion the mountaineer with Gemmell found Collins's flight bag with the chart and atlas. But when you view the actual video on YouTube of the cross-examination at point 38.08 on the video, the body language of Gemmell is plain. Mahon was astute at reading body language. This is the point that appellant courts must always take care when declining to accept the judge's opinion of the veracity of the evidence being given at first instance. - probative evidence!

The question that had been put to Gemmell was whether he had been told of the change in co-ordinates before he left for Antarctica. Because if he did, then that would have given him the necessary early motive/opportunity to collect and hide all the documentary evidence of that change that he could obtain from the Scott Base store or from the crash site, including taking the pilots' flight bags. This action had been ordered by Dalgety.

Back at Scott Base Rhodes saw Chippindale pass the documents found on the crash site to Gemmell who was returning earlier taking with him the CVR box and DFDR box to Auckland. This did not take place on the crash site but back at the fire station depository under Mitchells guardianship. This led to Mahon's report paras 345-348. These were key issues such as the blue envelopes that were discussed right through to the Privy Council's judgment. The transcript of that video of the actual hearing follows.

> Gemmell: I had no knowledge of any error.
>
> Mahon: It was known in Auckland on the night of the accident.
>
> Gemmell: I don't recall where your honour having been told of that evidence or that knowledge.

Whilst Gemmell denied that prior knowledge, his response to Mahon's intervention when Mahon said that it was "known in Auckland", was not a straight denial. Instead Gemmell in effect, questioned Mahon, by asking "where did you get this evidence from?" Because this evidence had not yet been provided at that stage in open evidence at the hearings, Mahon had learnt this from some leak. It was quick of Gemmell to spot this. But in giving such a quick response, he gave himself away to someone as astute as Mahon. It confirmed that Gemmell was lying, and that he did know the waypoint had been changed before he left for Antarctica. Gemmell knew what he needed to do to hide any evidence that Collins had been briefed with the flight path down the middle of McMurdo Sound. With the hindsight of history, Mahon was dead right.

Brian Hewitt was duly humiliated for his mistake in transposing the 166.48 to 164.48. Nobody admitted to noticing his error, despite the fact that 164.48 was in the middle of McMurdo Sound, not at Williams Field 27 miles away. That is nobody until Les Simpson, and he was surprised that the distance was so far. Simpson was captain of the flight on 14th November. It is at this point that the shambolic internal communications within Air New Zealand were demonstrated.

It is just not credible that experts like Amies and Lawton had not noticed that the flight path had been moved 27 miles to the west, completely unbelievable. Unless they were not so expert that they thought themselves to be. This was Mahon's dilemma. Who to believe?

Mahon's paragraph 393 must have caused Dalgety considerable shock and consternation. It almost wrecked Dalgety's plan. Hence Air New Zealand applied for judicial review of the Mahon Report.

Paragraph 393 reads:

> **393**. In my opinion therefore, the single dominant and effective cause of the disaster was the mistake made by those airline officials who programmed the aircraft to fly directly at Mt. Erebus and omitted to tell the aircrew. That mistake is directly attributable, not so much to the persons who made it, but to the incompetent administrative airline procedures which made the mistake possible.

The High Court was bypassed in the application for judicial review, and the case went direct to the Court of Appeal. That court included Sir Owen Woodhouse. The fact was ignored that he and another Court of Appeal colleague, Duncan McMullin, both had offspring who were employees of Air New Zealand, and so they should have recused themselves.

McMullin's sitting on the case was an appalling judicial misbehaviour because Richard McGrane, Air New Zealand's lawyer, was a close friend of McMullin's family. He visited the McMullins' Remuera home a number of times before and during the inquiry.

Pilots objected to McMullin sitting, so Mahon told Cooke, the acting president of the Appeal Court, the following:

> He has some tie-ups with the company.
>
> Now, they are great friends with this boy McGrane who is the third counsel for Air New Zealand.
>
> McGrane briefed all the evidence for weeks and weeks and weeks.
> And he is a constant visitor to their [McMullin's] place as I know myself.
>
> I saw him there. But I know apart from that. He was there before the inquiry started and while it was on.
>
> And he [McGrane] was the person who briefed the evidence that I disbelieved ... Now, the pilots don't like it.
>
> I conveyed this message to Cooke and he came back with the reply that, no, he [McMullin] insisted on sitting. He was entitled to sit.

Cooke should never have allowed McMullin to sit. Here you have McMullin, who is an enemy of Mahon, and he insists on sitting so as to spite Mahon. He refuses to stand down, despite being asked to because of his friendship with a lawyer who acts for one of the parties. Not just actual bias requires a judge to stand down, but the mere appearance of bias requires a judge to stand down, or recuse themselves. That is a scandal on McMullin's part.

It's even worse than that when he gives a judgment which is so biased against Mahon. He later visits the Privy Council. Diplock in The Privy Council judgment tells a series of lies about the facts, all of which are to the detriment of Mahon. That is extraordinary. It can be explained only by the fact that Woodhouse and McMullin lobbied Diplock and the members of the judicial committee – in person. Another clue to the illicit lobbying can be found in the use of the words "let bygones be bygones" repeated at the conclusion of Diplock's judgment. These were the very words used by Morrie Davis during his meeting with Maria Collins one year after the accident when he was trying to make a new start for Air New Zealand's public relations. Doubtless Woodhouse and McMullin were made aware of that meeting and Davis' attempts at mollifying Maria Collins.

In addition, I have been told that there was also another direct connection between Maynard Hawkins of Air New Zealand management and McMullin. That is the fact that

Roger Hawkins, son of Maynard, flatted with Richard McGrane. And McGrane was a regular visitor to McMullin's household. McGrane was a barrister for Air New Zealand. McGrane had the considerable technical knowledge on aviation matters, because he was a qualified pilot.

That knowledge was lacked by Lloyd Brown and David Williams, the two other senior counsel for Air New Zealand. There was a fourth junior barrister for Air New Zealand – Denise Henare. She should have directly informed the Royal Commission that Davis and Dave Eden were handed the Brizendine low flying article and were well aware of low flying. The fact that these judges had children employed by Air New Zealand was not known by the public until after the Court of Appeal judgment was announced.

There had been many legal confrontations between Woodhouse and Mahon. There was no love lost between them. On one occasion Mahon was quoted as saying something along the lines that "Woody may take the broad view but this was a convenient substitute for thought." This applied particularly to the difficulties that the High Court judges had in divorce cases where Woodhouse's broad view was that as a starting point, an equal division of property should apply. Mahon's view was that Woody did not give guidance as to how to implement this broad view in practice when, for example, a business or farm had to be dealt with where there was insufficient finance to achieve that broad view without having to end the business or to sell the family farm.

The Court of Appeal split into three and two. It was no surprise that Woodhouse and McMullin provided the most damning denial of Mahon's ability to recognise lying. They were no better than the Uk's Lord Bridge who also could not recognise witnesses who lied. The other three members of the court, Somers, Cooke, and Richardson, were not happy to criticise Mahon's ability in that direction, but they still decided the Air New Zealand case was valid and they rescinded the NZ$150,000 contribution to costs which Mahon had awarded against the company.

Technically Mahon's award of NZ$150,000 was wrong, because the law set down that it could not be more than NZ$600. In both judgments, this is a common factor. What a waste of time over that NZ$150,000. At the end of the day, that $150,000 was coming out of one or other government bank account. Either the account of Air New Zealand or account of the Ministry of Justice.

It is a UK bar tradition that junior barristers assisting a silk (i.e. Kings Counsel) would do any research into the relevant law and other technical issues. Likewise with a Commission of Inquiry, counsel "assisting" the Commissioners are suppose to provide a similar research facility. I find it hard to believe that Mahon did not discuss with Baragwanath and Gary Harrison the possibility of awarding unnecessary costs to compensate for time wasting against Air New Zealand and CAD. Mahon did at one stage near the end of the Royal

Commission hearings request views on costs. Why did nobody answer that question and draw Mahon's attention to the maximum NZ$600?

The New Zealand public and media were appalled by the clear bias of Woodhouse and McMullin against Mahon that had arisen from the fact that their children could have been affected by an adverse judgment. I shudder to think what could have happened, had the publicity machine of Air New Zealand been subject of examination at the Royal Commission with respect to the Brizendine affair. Woodhouse' daughter was part of the publicity department. As the Appeal Court was the court of first instance and subject to hearing prime evidence, Baragwanath being unaware of the relationship, he could have called the daughter to give evidence. In front of her father – that would have been controversial and the whole trial would have had to be abandoned. As it is, it was a subject of controversy still referred to in the present day. This bias may have been why Woodhouse and McMullin were not chosen to sit in a case when the Arthur Allan Thomas inquiry became the subject of yet another appeal on a judicial review of another Commission of Inquiry. That case involved the notorious Crewe murders when police had planted evidence to gain a conviction.

That judicial review was about the behaviour of the chairman of that Royal Commission, Justice Taylor, towards the police and their barristers. It was no coincidence that Woodhouse and McMullin's services had been dispensed with, and instead they had been replaced by Sir Ronald Davison, and by Maurice Casey, who was famous for his intervention into the rugby All Blacks and Springboks tour cancellation. Alternatively Woodhouse and McMullin may not have been available due to their secret assignations with Diplock and the Privy Council. I provide more detail below.

Air New Zealand and its executives claimed in the Court of Appeal that Mahon had denied them natural justice. They falsely claimed he had not warned them that he did not believe them and had failed to offer them the right to call further evidence to prove they had told the truth. Both the Court of Appeal and Privy Council made a big factual error in this regard. Justice Thomas Thorp, was well aware of the application of the notorious case of Robert Maxwell and the Pergamon Press, as did Stuart Macfarlane later when investigating the errors of the New Zealand Appeal Court and Privy Council in the UK.

It would be useful to digress to review this case and to explain its relevance to the Mahon Report. Robert Maxwell was an infamous entrepreneur in the 1970s. His bullying behaviour would have made Muldoon seem like St Francis of Assisi. Maxwell and his lawyers used the delaying tactic of pleading the requirement to give time to call more evidence during Board of Trade inquiries into his running of Pergamon Press, one of his companies. The tactic eventually was called Maxwellisation.

Lords Denning, Orr and Lawton put a stop to Maxwell constantly delaying the publishing of the reports of the lawyers and accountants who were criticising him and his involvement in Pergamon Press. Lord Denning gave the lead judgment rejecting the Natural Justice claim of Maxwell.

Denning's judgment:-:

> "Just think what it means. After hearing all the evidence, the inspectors have to sit down and come to tentative conclusions. If these are such as to be critical of any of the witnesses, they have to re-open the inquiry, recall those witnesses, and put to them the criticisms which they are disposed to make. What will be the response of those witnesses? They will at once want to refute the tentative conclusions by calling other witnesses, or by asking for further investigations. In short, the inquiry will develop into a series of minor trials in which a witness will be accused of misconduct and seek to answer it. That would hold up the inquiry indefinitely. I do not think it is necessary. It is sufficient for the inspectors to put the points to the witnesses as and when they come in the first place. After hearing the evidence, the inspectors have to come to their conclusions. These need not be tentative in the least. They can be final and definite, ready for their report."

Those inquiries were carried out under the UK Companies Acts, and so they were not New Zealand Royal Commissions. But the principles regarding Natural Justice were the same.

Mahon was under pressure of time to deliver his report as quickly as possible to the NZ government. Mahon could have given Air New Zealand and its witnesses the opportunity to provide more evidence to support their evidence already given, but Mahon did not find them believable.

It was also curious that the attorney general was willing to finance Mahon's appeal to the Privy Council in London, but remained parsimonious as regards Mahon's pension. It was the attorney general's counsel who stabbed Mahon in the back during the Privy Council submissions by urging their Lordships not to overturn the Court of Appeal's judgment unless the decision of the NZ Appeal Court was "manifestly wrong". The Denning Judgment re Maxwell proved that the Appeal Court was manifestly wrong!

In 1982, the other judicial review case in the Court of Appeal was held shortly after delivery of the Erebus Appeal. It was the Court of Appeal case on the Arthur Thomas inquiry about the behaviour of the chairman of the commission, the Australian Judge Robert Taylor. The court decided in favour of that chairman that it was OK to be offensive to the witnesses for the police as well as to their counsel.

On one remarkable occasion, Justice Taylor was rude enough to call the counsel for the police "thick in the head". The court still held he was not guilty of any bias against that barrister and his police clients. By comparison, Mahon always maintained a very polite attitude to all the witnesses and to their barristers at the Commission hearings, even when he suspected them of lying. Perhaps that was the problem. Maybe Robert Taylor was right to openly display such dislike of liars during the hearings.

It was a surprise to those who lied and who thought they had been able to hoodwink Mahon. During the hearings, he did not say anything except for the private warning he gave to David Williams, counsel for Air New Zealand, about the bad impression the company and its witnesses were giving as to the veracity of their evidence. He also told Peter Martin, who was the lawyer for Air New Zealand's insurers, of his concern as to the veracity. It was therefore dishonest of David Williams to allow Lloyd Brown's submissions that no warnings had been given. Is this not a breech of the barristers code not to mislead? Diplock was led to believe these submissions were true, when they were completely untrue.

Those paragraphs 348, 376 and 377 of the Mahon Report were also referred to by Stuart Macfarlane. Paragraph 348 involved Dave Eden, Air New Zealand's director of flight operations. Dave Eden had been talking to Peter Rhodes about his evidence that Ian Gemmell had transported documents from the crash site for Chippindale. As Rhodes did not have any documentary proof, he was forced to withdraw the claim, or he would be sacked.

In his book, "Verdict on Erebus", Mahon confirmed that he did not think Davis was involved in the preconcerted plan of deception. Mahon said: "was he the person responsible for the planning of the altitude and navigation evidence which I believed to have been false in both branches? I did not think so."

Davis, Gemmell, and Eden all gave evidence on behalf of Air New Zealand. The one person who did not give evidence was Dalgety. Mahon had already received the leaked Dalgety telex which contained the instruction to shred documents. It would have been cruel to have filed that document in evidence to the Royal Commission, as that could have enabled Air New Zealand to trace the whistleblower. The person who leaked the Peter Martin letter was traced. Mahon knew that the person who leaked the telex would have been sacked. There was a steady source of intelligence that Mahon had come to rely on, until the whistleblower was assigned to an overseas flight base, well away from Mahon.

Simple answer for Erebus

There are still some who believe that the pilots of the fatal flight should share some responsibility for the crash. Most of them base their opinion on what they claimed was the pilots' breach of the nominal minimum safe altitude (MSA) of 16,000 ft although in practice, even 16,000 feet was not sufficient to cope with an eruption from the very active volcano. There was near disaster of a British Airways flight to Perth. It had to divert to Jakarta when the Boeing 747 lost all four engines due to volcanic ash.

That proved how stupid it would have been to have a flight plan that ran over the top of an active volcano. Originally the flight plan had been agreed between Gemmell and the

Civil Aviation Department behind Keesing's back who was still supposed to have been in charge. Their reason for specifying such a flight plan was that the straight line from Cape Hallett to McMurdo Station went over the top of Mount Erebus.

In 1978 that nominal direct flight path from Cape Hallett to McMurdo Station and the New Zealand Scott Base was replaced by Brian Hewitt. He accidentally typed the waypoint coordinate as 164.48. That resulted in a flight plan that ran safely down the middle of McMurdo Sound. That flight path down the middle of McMurdo Sound to the Dailey Islands was ideal. It suited the US Navy ATC for the avoidance of conflicting traffic. Hewitt said that he should have typed 166.48, the Williams Field waypoint, so that the flight plan crossed Erebus, as it did before he made that mistake. It remained down the middle of McMurdo Sound until Air New Zealand changed it on the morning of the fatal flight once again to the TACAN waypoint, so it crossed Erebus.

Roger Dalziell gave evidence of what the briefing officers, Wilson and Ross Johnson, had said at his briefing. Dalziell said that at no time did the briefing officers ever say the flight path ran over Erebus. They never prohibited breaches of MSAs of 16,000 and 6,000 feet. The word prohibition had to be used under aviation lore. The reason they didn't was due to the route always being down the middle of McMurdo Sound in 1978 onwards. If there was bad weather at Scott Base, then the alternate flight path was nominally to the South Magnetic Pole (SMP). Wilson's only trip to Antarctica was to the SMP with Dalziell. So Wilson never experienced the middle of McMurdo Sound flight path, only the diversion to SMP. The board of directors was told by Davis, at their meeting on 5th December 1979, that the crash site on Erebus was considerably left of track. This was the ultimate confirmation that the track was known by Air New Zealand to be down the centre of McMurdo Sound. And that was 27 miles west of Erebus.

Mahon disbelieved this evidence given by Wilson and Ross Johnson. It was the main factor in Mahon's decision to reject their evidence. No doubt those two had been coerced by Air New Zealand to say that they had briefed pilots that the flight path crossed Erebus throughout 1978 and 1979 and that the route was over Erebus. During those years the flight path was really down the centre of McMurdo Sound, 27 miles away from Erebus.

Many people, including expert aviators, were taken in by this blatant lie. Had Air New Zealand obeyed the order for document discovery of any directors' minutes such as those which recorded the 5th December meeting, that is, those minutes which should have been disclosed to Mahon, then that lie would not have been successful. As it is, the allegation of breach of MSAs was the only basis with which Air New Zealand could blame the pilots.

This muddied the waters of the compensation claims limit, and saved Muldoon and the politicians from bankruptcy of the New Zealand economy. It was not helped by Muldoon declaring what was technically a domestic flight, to be an international flight. The New

Zealand Compensation scheme known as ACC was far more generous than the Warsaw convention of NZ$42,000. Another totally dishonest tactic to defraud the passengers relatives of the appropriate compensation.

This Accident Compensation scheme had been instigated as a result of an Inquiry led by Sir Owen Woodhouse. Legal commentators claimed that his report included statements beyond the remit of his commission. Exactly the perceived wrong that Woodhouse claimed Mahon had committed. Pure hypocracy on Woodhouse' part but that was nothing more than one of the battles between these warring giants of the legal profession in New Zealand.

This was not the only time New Zealand court orders for "discovery" were thwarted by the corruption of process. Another example was when the New Zealand Government colluded dishonestly with its armed forces, when the NZ Army built a bridge at Te Rata for the Berrymans. That complete story has been told in "The Justice Mirage" by Rob Moodie. The army staff, the attorney general, the coroner, many crown law barristers, and a few judges such as John Wild, acted injudiciously in keeping secret an army report, the Butcher Report under privilege regulations. That privileged secret report said the army was negligent in the construction of a bridge for the Berrymans.

Had the army properly acceded to discovery and declared that report to the Berryman's lawyer, Rob Moodie, then the inquest into the death of the victim of the bridge collapse, and all the subsequent claims would been in favour of the Berrymans, without the delay of many years. The legal establishment members would then have lost their fee-earning opportunities from the taxpayer. Apart from Baragwanath, another Erebus lawyer was able to benefit from the bottomless pit of the taxpayer, Kim Murray. He had been a very junior part of the Civil Aviation Division's legal team.

Kim Murray had become entangled in the army cover up in the Berrymans case and the Attorney General's disingenuousness. The army had deliberately not briefed Murray on the existence of the army's secret Butcher Report which had admitted negligence by the army. So he was able, in all innocence, to deny discovery demands by Moodie. As it was, Rob Moodie had to disobey an injunction not to disclose the truth about the NZ Army's shoddy construction contained in the Butcher Report. I feel sad that it was Baragwanath, despite having worked with the ultra honest Mahon, who was the judge who fined and suspended Rob Moodie for this technical breach of the injunction incorrectly applied by Judge John Wild which was nothing more than an attempted cover-up by the authorities to save yet again money. Most of the legal establishment was implicated in that cover-up, right up to the level of the Governor General of the time. I have also seen documentary evidence of an ex parte injunction which delayed the sale of a book due to the solicitor general of the time being economical with the truth. John Wild needed little persuasion on the false evidence of that Solicitor General.

At the time of writing, the latest person who has been released because of a conviction which was falsely obtained by corruption and incompetence is Alan Hall. His case was so bad that there is now supposed to be an investigation in progress to see whether certain police and prosecutors were guilty of perverting the course of justice. At the least, in Hall's case, the competence of all those involved from police to prosecutors was in question as they could not tell the difference between a small slight person (Hall) who was just five feet seven inches and the main suspect who was over six foot tall.

In the UK, another inquiry is currently being held into the scandal of the sub-postmasters. They were falsely prosecuted for fraud in the Horizon software case. Horizon was the name given to the Post Office computer accounting system for 12,000 sub-post offices around the country. Eventually it was demonstrated that the system was full of software glitches and bugs which caused cash shortfalls leading to prosecution and jail for some postmasters. The Post Office and its officials constantly denied the existence of these software glitches and bugs. It is becoming clear that even when these officials were aware of the problems, the lax adherence to the rules for prosecutors and barristers, they continued prosecuting despite knowing that the sub postmasters were innocent. It has taken years for the cases to be exposed for what they are. Most such cases were caused by breaches of etiquette and codes of conduct that barristers and prosecuting lawyers are supposed to adhere to. It seems that government officials were also complicit in the cover-up. Much like the Erebus scandal in New Zealand.

All these cases should have been the subject of inquiry by the professional bodies, but in New Zealand's case it appears that the establishment is too strong to allow its members to be accountable for malpractice. The perjury by witnesses at the Mt. Erebus Inquiry was investigated by a police team led by Brian Wilkinson, but not a single charge was ever made.

It has been revealed that behind the scenes, Brian Wilkinson was ordered by the Prime Minister Muldoon to wind up the inquiry into Mahon's allegation of perjury by the Air New Zealand management pilots, and to find no evidence that they had committed perjury. I repeat that had the 5th December 1979 directors' meeting minutes been correctly revealed under the order for discovery made by Mahon, it would have been a different matter. As it is, the myth that Air New Zealand briefed the pilots that the flight path crossed Erebus and the claim of the airline that the pilots breached the MSAs, may still remain in the minds of a few ill-informed so-called expert aviators as the only mistakes made by Collins and Cassin. Basically, the judiciary and the police were not independent of the politicians in New Zealand at that time.

All the Air New Zealand executive pilots were under pressure in various ways for different reasons. Macfarlane has reported on Mahon's reliance on the Pergamon Press and Robert Maxwell's machinations in 1970-1974. In that case, the Companies Act investigation was carried out by the Board of Trade Inspectors, including Chartered Accountants. Maxwell used every trick in the book to prevent and delay that accountants report using this old natural justice defence. Denning LJ et al eventually put a stop to these claims for natural justice tactics in 1974.

Diplock cited his agreement with those judges, Denning, Orr, and Lawton in 1975 during one of the many House of Lords cases into the Hoffmann La Roche pricing disputes.

Diplock said:

> Even in judicial proceedings in a court of law, once a fair hearing has been given to the rival cases presented by the parties the rules of natural justice do not require the decision maker to disclose what he is minded to decide so that the parties may have a further opportunity of criticising his mental processes before he reaches a final decision.

Why did Diplock have such a lapse of memory, when instead of quoting Maxwell, he quoted the Ex Parte Moore 1965 case? I reveal the answer to that question at the end of part 3.

Appendix to Part 2 —Exhibit 164

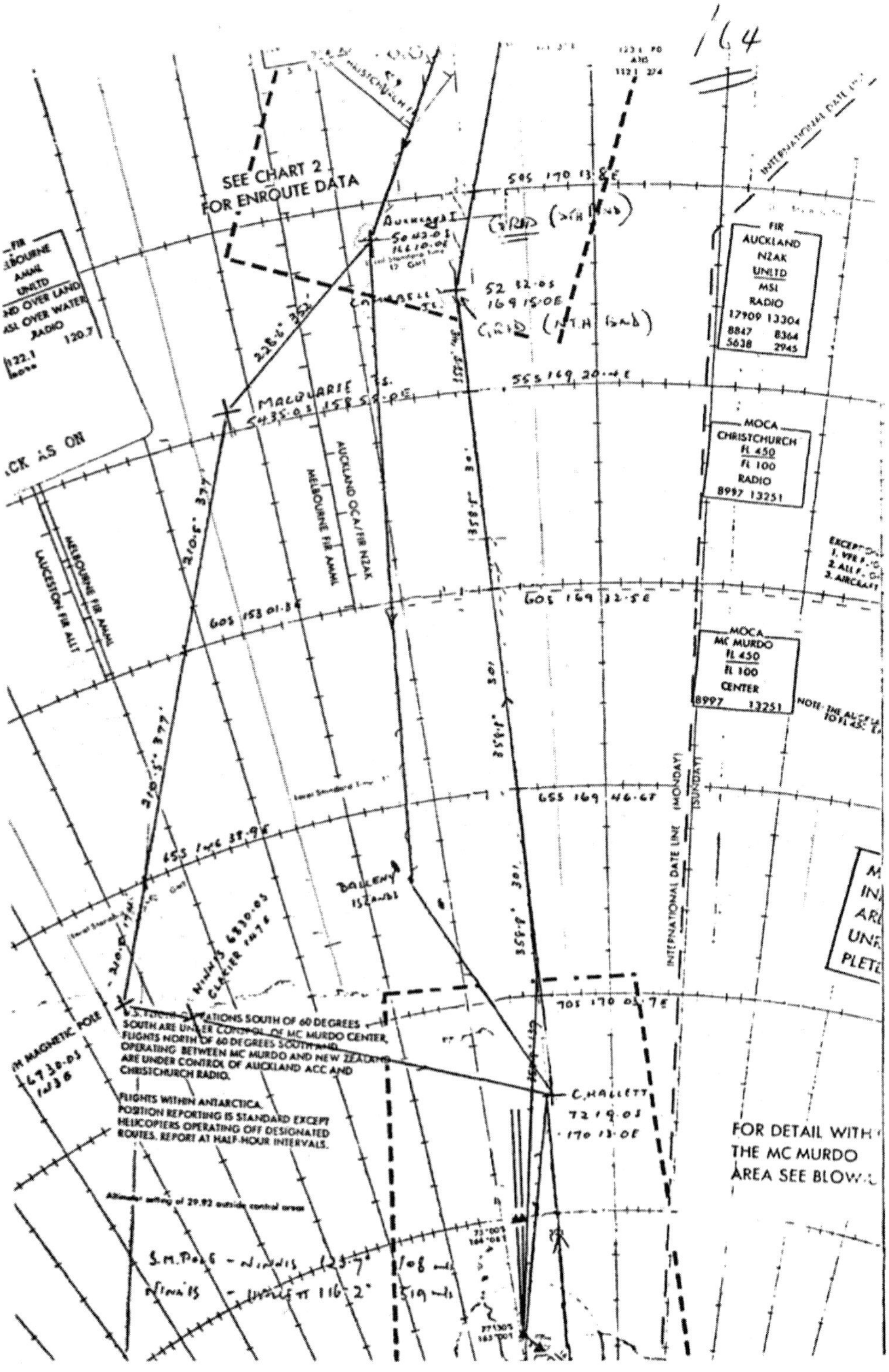

The Mahon Report at pp. 91-92 explains the significance of Exhibit 164. It shows the flight path down McMurdo Sound past the Byrd Reporting Point. At approximately the same time as Air New Zealand shifted the flight path from one that crossed Erebus to one down the middle of McMurdo Sound, the airline started to brief pilots on it and to give exhibit 164 to pilots on despatch.

Why would Air New Zealand do that, if its intention was not to tell pilots that the flight path did run down McMurdo Sound? That shows Air New Zealand did know that the flight path did run down McMurdo Sound.

Exhibit 164 was a diagram produced at the Royal Commission of Inquiry into the Erebus disaster, to show that the flight path of Air New Zealand DC-10s from Cape Hallett to McMurdo was down the middle of McMurdo Sound. According to Macfarlane, it was first introduced to the Inquiry during the cross examination of Brian Hewitt on 28th August 1980. The lines on the diagram show that the flight path was not over the top of Erebus as was claimed by Air New Zealand. The airline admitted it was a diagram prepared by the expert navigators Amies and Lawton. They claimed that it was only a draft working document as a route feasibility study drawn up some time before 1978. They claimed it was not intended to be used for navigation. The document itself appeared to be a photocopy of a copy of a xerox diagram with the bottom part of the original diagram being missed in the copying.

Mahon was criticised by the Privy Council with respect to this exhibit 164. The Privy Council said first:

> there was not any material of probative value before the Judge that could justify a finding that Exhibit 164 incorporated a track and distance plan for a route southwards from Cape Hallett down McMurdo Sound.

The Privy Council is wrong in their first point. Mahon actually said:

> **238. …** This is a track and distance diagram prepared by the Navigation Section, which contains headings and distances for the area north of the Auckland Islands down to the two alternate routes available to Antarctic flights. The principal feature of this document, which it turned out Mr Amies had in part prepared, was a plotted track from Cape Hallett down McMurdo Sound on a path which appeared to lead it not only to the east of the Byrd Reporting Point but also to a position situated somewhat further to the true south.
>
> Now this flight path (making due allowance for the imperfections of what is a fairly poor photocopy of an original) appears to be almost indistinguishable from a flight path running from Cape Hallett down to the altered McMurdo waypoint. In addition the draftsman had run a dotted semi-circular line around the south of

Ross Island, and then a straight line had been drawn back to Cape Hallett along 170° meridian of east longitude. On that line had been drawn an arrow pointing towards Cape Hallett.

239. Mr Amies, who appeared disconcerted when Exhibit 164 was placed in front of him by Mr Davison, was cross-examined closely about its content. He asserted that it was only a draft track and distance diagram and pointed out that there was no track and distance notation for the southern or northern legs of the Cape Hallett/McMurdo sector. He also alluded to certain other slight inaccuracies in the chart. As to the arrow pointing in the direction of Cape Hallett after a presumed circuit of Ross Island, Mr Amies agreed that he had drawn this arrow but maintained that it was not intended to be an aircraft track.

The Privy Council in their second point said:

> or was intended or would be understood by any experienced pilot to be intended to be used for purposes of navigation

Mahon never said Exhibit 164 was intended or would be understood by any experienced pilot to be intended to be used for purposes of navigation. Instead, the point Mahon made was that in 1977, when the flight plan crossed Erebus, Air New Zealand handed out to pilots a diagram, Annex J, which showed a track that did cross Erebus. In 1978, when Air New Zealand shifted the flight plan to run down McMurdo Sound, the airline handed out to pilots Exhibit 164. This was a diagram which showed a track that ran down McMurdo Sound. Mahon's point was that this showed that Air New Zealand knew they had shifted the McMurdo waypoint from Erebus to McMurdo Sound.

Mahon also said:

> As to the arrow pointing in the direction of Cape Hallett after a presumed circuit of Ross Island, Mr Amies agreed that he had drawn this arrow but maintained that it was not intended to be an aircraft track. He maintained that he had drawn it there only to indicate the position of true north, and this was because he had been working with grid navigation when entering details on this chart.

But what Amies, an expert navigator working in grid navigation meant by that arrow is not relevant. The real point is that Air New Zealand, when they shifted the route to McMurdo Sound, handed to pilots a diagram with an arrow which appeared to show a track back to Hallett. That confirms the appearance of a McMurdo Sound flight path.

The intention of Amies has no bearing on that. All that matters is that the airline gave pilots a diagram which appeared to them to show a McMurdo Sound flight path. Pilots thought it was important evidence of that, so they gave it to Davison.

No doubt Amies never intended it to be used for navigation. No doubt Amies intended the arrow to show north and not a flight path. But what was in Amies's mind is of no relevance whatever.

Gemmell falsely told Chippindale Annex J had been recovered from the crash site. His intention was to persuade Chippindale that having Annex J onboard showed the pilots had been told the flight path crossed Erebus. Annex J looks much like Exhibit 164.

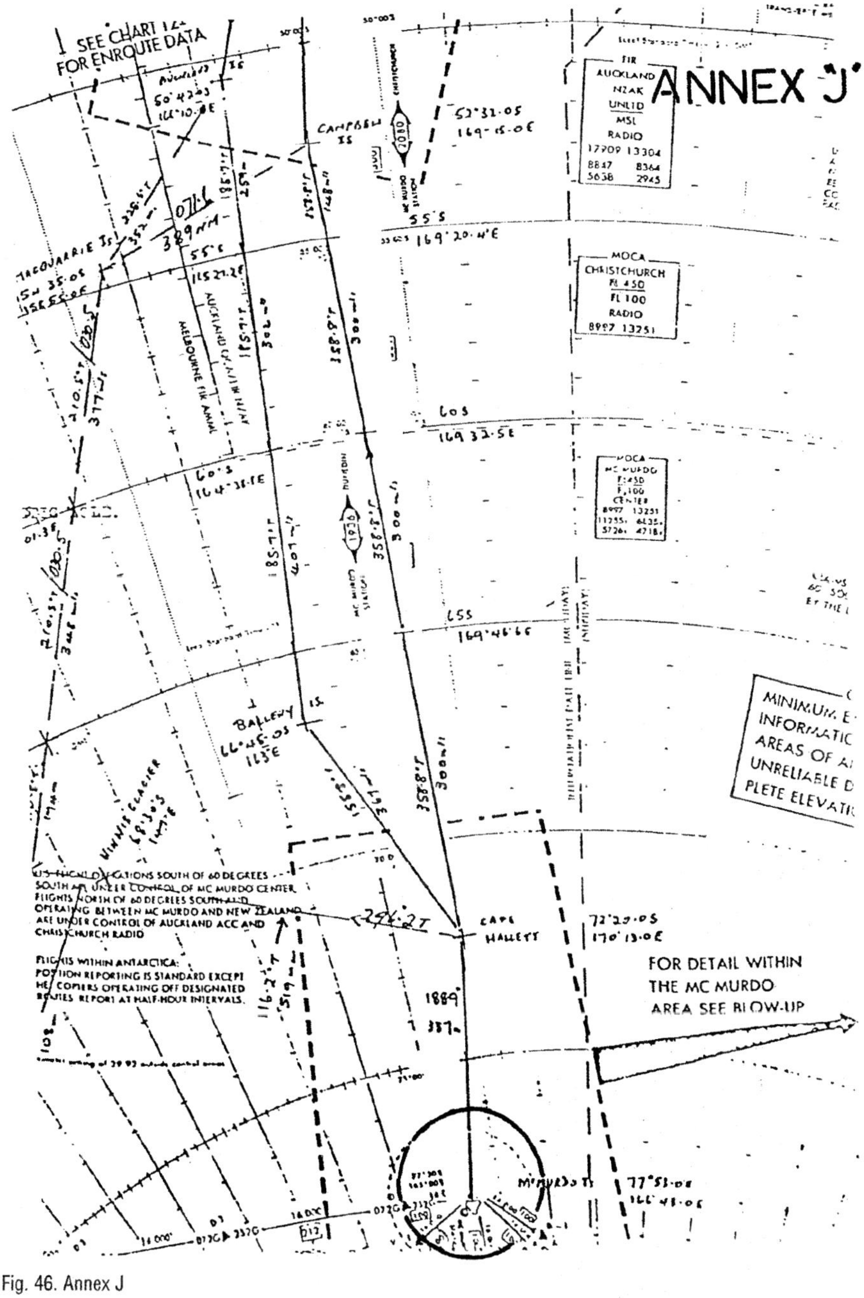

Fig. 46. Annex J

I regret that in reproducing both exhibit 164 and annex J, it is not very clear where the flight path was indicated at the very bottom of both these diagrams. However, in the docudrama written by Greg McGee, there was one sequence where both diagrams were filmed side by side with annex J on top of but to the left of exhibit 164. The actor playing Baragwanath was seen using a pen to highlight the flight path on exhibit 164 from Cape Hallett down the middle of McMurdo Sound to the US reporting point Byrd, then turning further south to encircle Ross Island, returning back to Cape Hallett on the track with Amies' notorious arrow hand drawn on the meridian, as he claimed. I hope I can reproduce this as a blow up:-

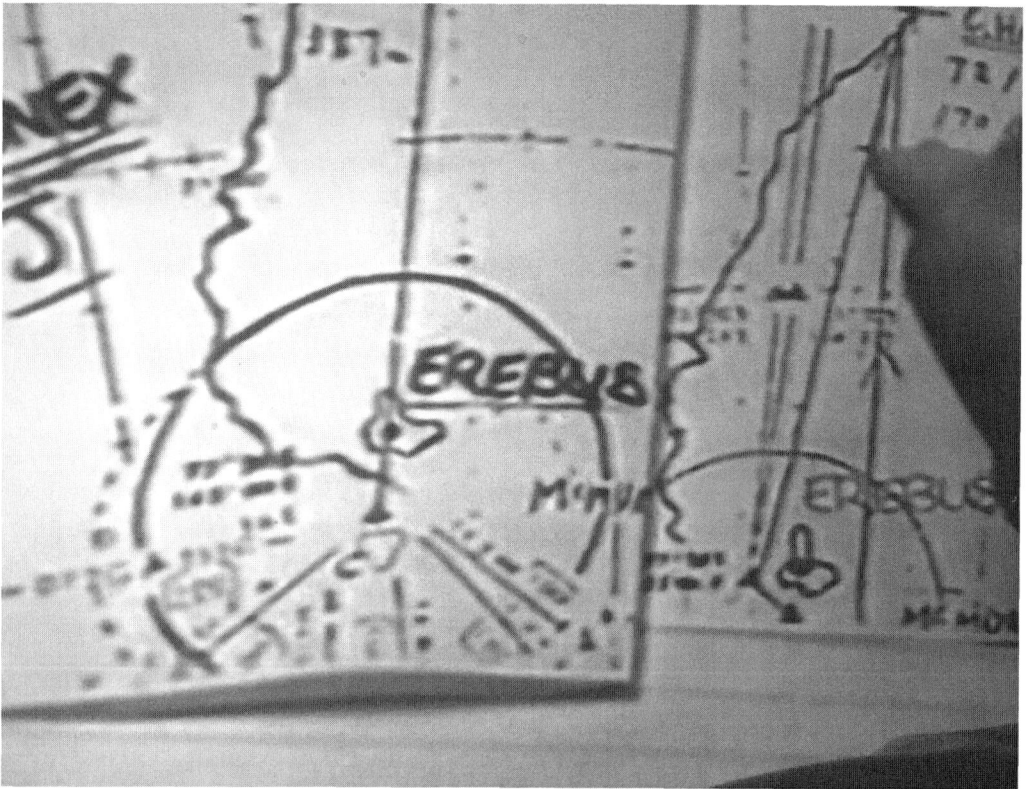

Lord Diplock of the Privy Council wrongly ignored the evidence that the flight path was in the middle of McMurdo Sound. I am referring to the physical documentary evidence that the directors' minutes of 5th December 1979 said that the crash site was well left of track. Whilst the directors minutes were not strictly part of the evidence available to Mahon for his Royal Commission report, they were available for the NZ Appeal Court. It is not clear why Mahon's barristers were unable to present those directors minutes either to the Appeal Court or the Privy Council as they were so important as evidence. It was a perversion of the course of justice not to allow these to be presented to the Privy Council.

It is just more evidence of the unjustified criticism by the Privy Council claim of the lack of probative evidence if they refused to allow that probative evidence to be admitted. There was also all the line pilots' verbal evidence that the flight path was in the middle of McMurdo Sound. It shows the success of Des Dalgety's telexed order to destroy all the documentation when exhibit 164 was the only document left that had not been shredded.

What was significant was the timing of first presentation of exhibit 164 to the Royal Commission. That date was after Amies' first appearance to give evidence on 28th August 1980. Amies had to be recalled on 16th September 1980 to give further evidence to rebut the meaning of 164, significantly after 11th September and the Cooper/Rhodes meeting with Davis and Eden. Hewitt had been examined on 28th August 1980 when Davison presented him with exhibit 164, and then cross-examined him on its details. The next witness was Lawton, the other author of exhibit 164, and he was examined on 9th September.

The way in which the evidence was being extracted piecemeal from the Air New Zealand witnesses was causing considerable concern to Arthur Cooper (a CVR transcriber at the Washington NTSB laboratory) and to Peter Rhodes. Arthur Cooper accompanied by Peter Rhodes has described this meeting with Morrie Davis shortly after the debacle of Lawton's cross-examination on exhibit 164. Rhodes and Cooper found it impossible to discuss with Davis the bad impression the airline's management's evidence was giving at the Royal Commission.

Twenty-one years later, that date (now known as nine-eleven 2001) became fixed in American history as that of the tragic destruction of the World Trade Centre in New York with over 2,000 lives lost.

The evidence given by Air New Zealand and CAD executives was far-fetched. I quote a passage from Sam Mahon's "My Father's Shadow".

> I remember my brother who had been visiting the hearings regularly, reported that from time to time the whole court would be trembling with mirth at some of the evidence being given, it was palpably unbelievable.

There had been an earlier row between Richard McGrane and Paul Davison after the latter had introduced Exhibit 164 during Hewitt's cross examination. The ever-alert Peter Mahon was aware of that row. It was Richard McGrane's involvement in preparation of submissions at the Privy Council's hearing in late October 1983 that may have resulted in their lordships' rejection of Exhibit 164 as being "not any material of probative value". McGrane's connection with Maynard Hawkins, who was a witness for Air New Zealand, may not have been well known. Much has been made of McGrane's friendship with Duncan McMullin, the judge in the Court of Appeal. I repeat that McMullin should have recused himself from sitting as a Court of Appeal judge in the case for the same reason as Woodhouse. Both had children working at Air New Zealand.

A further reason why McMullin should have recused himself is that McGrane shared a flat with Maynard Hawkins's son Roger. Roger claims he did not discuss the Royal Commission evidence with McGrane whilst it was in progress. Roger said that only after the hearings ended, did he and McGrane discuss the Erebus matters. Roger and Maynard Hawkins doubtless continued these discussions up to the preparation of the Privy Council submissions. McMullin and Woodhouse were in London and attended Privy Council meetings in 1983. Doubtless they were trying to influence Diplock and the other Law Lords.

I can never reconcile how a democratic country could allow such judicial misbehaviour. The 2019 apologies were made on behalf of the NZ government by its Prime Minister, likewise Air New Zealand's chair person apologized for the company's behaviour 40 years earlier. The current 2024 Air New Zealand is not the same as that in 1979. It has to be time that the New Zealand judiciary and professional disciplinary authorities also add their apologies to those of 2019 – with the promise that behaviour like that of Woodhouse and McMullin will never be permitted in future. But not in the way that Bill Wilson's case was dealt with.

The reason why Davison produced exhibit 164 was to show that Air New Zealand had adopted the middle of McMurdo Sound flight path by including that diagram in all the flight envelopes. The directors' meeting minutes of 5th December 1979 likewise demonstrated that fact. Mahon had issued an order for discovery of these directors' meeting minutes. However, Air New Zealand disobeyed that order. Had those minutes been produced, then Air New Zealand's whole case based on their claim the pilots had been briefed that the flight path was overhead Erebus would have blown up. How this breach of an order for discovery was covered up and kept from the Privy Council is to me one of the mysteries of the Erebus affair. That evidence should have been pushed hard.

Lord Diplock, in the Erebus case, had a memory loss about Maxwellisation and natural justice. His judgment in the Erebus case contradicted his former concurring judgment with Denning, Orr and Lawton in his 1975 Hoffmann La Roche speech, "that one could go too far in giving natural justice yet more time".

Diplock's concluding words of his judgment: *"The time has come for all parties to let bygones be bygones so far as the aftermath of the Mount Erebus disaster is concerned"* was inappropriate and childish. No doubt those words were supplied by Morrie Davis via Woodhouse and McMullin! Diplock was totally unaware of, and insensitive to the feelings of the families of the 257 victims of Erebus. Diplock was oblivious to the harm his failing memory of Maxwell's case had on the majority of the New Zealand nation. I cannot imagine that the fate of the UKs sub postmasters following the Horizon debacle would be ended by a "bygones be bygones" recommendation.

Part 3 — Erebus in perspective

Whilst this part may repeat some information provided within the main body of the book, I have included those items for ease of reference.

There are strong parallels with case of the Dragonfly ZK-AFB that went missing on 12th February 1962, and with its sister aircraft Dominie ZK-BCP that completed sightseeing excursions in the previous weeks. Those flights were pure sightseeing day trips. The intention was to show the passengers the snow and ice of the mountains of the Southern Alps, or, in the case of the Antarctica flights to show the snow and ice, with the additional thrill of seeing Scott's hut, McMurdo Station, and Scott Base on Ross Island where Operation Deep Freeze was situated.

Despite the differences in distances flown, the differences in speeds of the de Havilland biplanes compared those of the DC-10 large jet airliners, they both made their return trips in the same time. The biplanes were operated by only one man, Brian Chadwick. The DC-10s were operated by Air New Zealand with about 8,000 personnel. The important limiting factor for both was the range available from the fuel load able to be carried. It had to be sufficient for the distances covered.

The Air New Zealand trips were first planned well before 1977 and were to be with DC-8 aircraft. One trial trip was carried out, but it required landing in Antarctica to refuel. On that test trip, the aircraft was grounded at McMurdo due to adverse weather. That adverse event demonstrated that there were no facilities for the many DC-8 passengers at Scott Base, had the aircraft been held up by adverse weather. So there was no further consideration of repeating the sightseeing trips with DC-8s.

The purchase of a DC-10 fleet enabled a reassessment of Antarctic trips, as the extended range of the DC-10 allowed it to fly from Auckland to Antarctica and back to Christchurch without the need to refuel. The hazard of a refuelling stop at McMurdo was thereby avoided. However, careful monitoring of fuel consumption was still required, and all the usual cruising speeds and heights had to be maintained.

On reaching Antarctica, it was hazardous to reduce the cruising speed. The use of flaps that was needed for flying at lower speeds was not wise. If flaps were in deployed, then the extremely cold weather might have caused the flaps to ice up, and to remain deployed. An aircraft afflicted by this would not have the range and fuel capacity to fly back to New Zealand with those flaps extended. At 250 tonnes, the DC-10 was too heavy to land to refuel at McMurdo's Williams Field, even in an emergency, if the flaps were frozen solidly extended due to icing.

As for navigation, there had been a revolution in technology with the DC-10. It was equipped with the Aerial Inertial Navigation System (AINS). This was based on inertial gyroscopes that were able, by computing the twists and turns, ups and downs, to calculate where the aircraft was at any time. The DC-10 system had three inertial sensors. They were all linked, so that if one failed, it was obvious which one had failed. The remainder of the flight could continue safely on the remaining two sensors. The American C141 Starlifter's AINS system, that followed flight TE901, only had two sensors. So, if one went wrong, it needed a decision as to which sensor had malfunctioned. To do this, it had a navigator on board with charts, and it had a chart table.

The flight deck configuration of the DC-10 with its three sensor AINS had no navigator and more importantly, no chart table. Total reliance was made on the accuracy of the AINS. The system, at the worst, had an error of only one mile for every hour flown. In some respects, it was a more reliable system than the Sat-Navs of today. That was because it was not affected by satellite glitches or by external reliance on international cooperation. The AINS was so accurate, that it had been useful in identifying incorrect coordinates attributed to NDBs, VORs and TACANs. These were types of radio lighthouses. On paper, pilots were not supposed to rely 100% on the accuracy of AINS, but in practice, due to the three sensor AINS equipment on board, they all did. This applied to all airlines with the DC-10s, not just Air New Zealand.

The fact that the DC-10 had no chart table and no on-board navigator were major factors in the Erebus accident. The system did not have a visual display unit which displayed visually the aircraft's position on the screen's chart for the area. That is unlike present day Sat-Nav systems.

However, the AINS did display map coordinates in a monitor in the ceiling of the flight deck. This was outside of the standard instrument scan required for full instrument flying. In theory, these co-ordinates could be written down and then transcribed onto a topographical map. But in practice, without a chart table, this was cumbersome and time consuming, and distracted pilots from visual flying. That was the reason why Collins prepared his charts on the evening before the flight. His daughters, Kathryn and Elizabeth, saw him doing so.

Most pilots, certainly of my vintage, would plan a VFR flight by using a china-graph pencil on a topographical air chart that showed the intended flight path. There would be useful details printed on these charts, such as the radio frequencies of NDBs, VORs etc as well as airports. In my days as a novice pilot, by law one had to carry a topographical map of the area being flown. That was needed even on my first solo, when it was only a simple, take off, cross wind, downwind, base and final approach, all within four miles at the most of the airfield. The reason was that these bumps and circuits, as they were affectionately known, could always be disrupted by an incident that closed the runway, and so it could become necessary to divert to another airfield or airport. The topographical chart would provide back-up information.

The use of topographical charts on regular commercial flights had virtually ended, but it was still a requirement that one was carried. In practice, British Airways printed out an IFR chart for all its flights. Each individual flight would have its own printed chart to be discarded after this one use. They rarely showed any topographical features. All that would be shown would be the VORs, NDBs, airports with their coordinates, radio frequencies, ILS etc relevant to the planned flight, and any divert information. All of that would be uncluttered by visual flight rules details. Those charts would contain up to date information on everything the commercial pilot would need without having to recheck NOTAMS etc. Had Air New Zealand in 1979 provided the same type of charts, there would have been no crash on Erebus.

I have kept a number of these charts of flights to and from Birmingham courtesy of a British Airways captain and former student at Seawing Flying Club. These look similar to the IFR charts shown in the books and exhibits about the Mt. Erebus saga. Much detail is not clear in the reproduction of those exhibit 164 or annex J charts as printed in those books.

The following are some of the relevant factors that happened on the fateful flight of 28th November 1979 with Jim Collins and Greg Cassin as pilots. At the Route Clearance Unit (RCU) briefing were Collins and Cassin, as well as three other pilots. The other pilots were scheduled for trips on 14th and 21st November. Flight plans with the co-ordinates for the Dailey Islands waypoint in McMurdo Sound were handed out. These coordinates had first been copied from a paper-based file (alpha sheet) into the Air New Zealand computer when the physical files were computerised.

The flight plan digital storage and computerisation was carried out in 1978 by the Chief Navigator, Brian Hewitt. Co-ordinates were fed into the computer for a number of waypoints that showed the route that had been devised in 1977. The terminal waypoint supposed to be for Williams Field at McMurdo Station after the penultimate waypoint of Cape Hallett.

The geographical longitudinal coordinate was 166.48 E. The flight paths for all six of the 1977 trips were straight lines from Cape Hallett to McMurdo station. These flight paths were directly over the active volcano of Mt Erebus. At 12,450 feet it was a real barrier. However, the 1977 flights were flown in good weather except for one flight. Or so it is alleged.

In 1977, after Cape Hallett, the clarity of the polar atmosphere usually enabled the AINS guided autopilot to be disconnected from its Nav Mode and instead it was flown manually, that is on Heading Select. Flights followed the west coast of McMurdo Sound. That flight path was over the sea and so it was completely safe to fly at a low altitude. The flight path over a mountain of 12,500 feet requires nominally for IFR flights a minimum safe altitude (MSA) of 16,000 feet. However, that should not apply as Erebus was a very active volcano. One that had little notice of quick bursts of eruption. There was no real MSA for Erebus. The 1977 flights all had the McMurdo waypoint with a coordinate keyed into the AINS that would take the flight over Mt Erebus. But in practice none of those 1977 flights ever flew over Mt Erebus.

What did happen in practice was that the Air New Zealand DC-10s were flown in VMC on VFR down the middle of McMurdo Sound past the Byrd reporting point. They used the pilots' eyesight and were guided by the US Navy Air Traffic Control (ATC) radar in McMurdo Sound for flight separation. It was vital for the US Navy controllers to identify and monitor the Air New Zealand DC-10 for this traffic separation. It was impossible to provide radar coverage had the flights been over Erebus as the radar aerials could not be raised to cover an overhead join. There was considerable traffic from Operation Deep Freeze which included much helicopter traffic. It was essential for the ATC to provide separation services to avoid conflict with that other traffic. Radar let down services were provided to maintain separation. Altitudes down to 1,500 feet were quite normal. Hence Collins and Cassin had no problem with the 2,000 feet cloud base.

This is where there is some conflict of evidence. One management pilot, Maynard Hawkins, denied in his evidence ever flying below 6,000 feet over McMurdo and Scott Base in his attempt to lend credibility to the "never below 6,000 feet MSA - even though the US Navy had offered him a let down to just 1,500 feet. Justice Peter Mahon disbelieved his evidence, because his evidence conflicted with other passenger reports, and an article by a newspaper reporter on board that flight.

Maynard Hawkins was a controversial character. Hawkins gained his management position on 21st November 1979, so he was a training officer at the time of the accident. Should he have borne some responsibility for ensuring that pilots were appropriately trained?

His criticism of the pilots Collins and Cassin was that to fly VFR "you must not think you know where you are, you must know where you are." I find it hard to resist thinking that when you are a training executive, your job means that you are responsible for the training of your pilots. That surely must include training the pilots how polar VFR is so different to temperate VFR. Was Hawkins responsible for one of the chief failures of Air New Zealand because he did not brief (that is train) pilots to be able to cope with the normal phenomena of the polar weather? Or was he just as ignorant as all the pilots as Gordon Vette admitted – "it could have been me"?

A pilot who gave evidence that he never flew below the nominal MSA of 16,000 feet was Ian Gemmell, the chief pilot of Air New Zealand. He was the originator of the Antarctic sightseeing trips. His flight was the first non-stop day trip on 15th February 1977. He was accompanied by co-pilot Captain Tony Lawson, who also was co-pilot to Hawkins later on 18th October 1977. Gemmell had on board as commentator for the passengers the director of the Antarctic Division, Bob Thomson.

Bob Thomson gave evidence that confirmed passengers' stories that Gemmell flew down to the cloud base of 9,000 feet that covered Ross Island. Bruce Grierson was one such passenger. He happened to be one of the best-known legal brains in New Zealand. He was a partner in one of the best-known firm of lawyers in Auckland. Grierson wrote a letter to Peter Mahon shortly after publication of the Mahon Report. It was a pity that Grierson did not offer his evidence previously to the Royal Commission.

Old 8mm film

Grierson was a keen amateur film buff, and he said he took eight reels of film. The radio communication between the DC-10 and the US Navy ATC was relayed to the passengers to hear via the public address system in the aircraft. ATC had identified Gemmell's DC-10 after it turned at Cape Hallett. It was still at the cruising height of Flight Level 330, that is 33,000 feet. Gemmell immediately accepted the ATC Radar guidance. He was flying in cloud on the direct route that went overhead Mt Erebus and Ross Island. The US Radar gave flight directions enabling Gemmell to descend from the 33,000 feet down to 9,000. That was just below the cloud base.

According to Grierson, Gemmell, on coming out of cloud at 9,000 feet, had only just missed the mountain. From a passenger's point of view, it may well have seemed like that. But, in reality, there would probably have been a much greater clearance of the mountain than it appeared to the passengers. Grierson praised some extremely skilful manoeuvres by Gemmell after he descended below the cloud base. It is quite likely that he descended much lower than the 9,000 feet as claimed by Thomson. Grierson's 40-minutes' worth of film, that showed the descent to 9,000 feet, had it ever became public, would have been the ultimate evidence of the true altitude that Gemmell descended to. By comparison, my heavily edited 8 mm film of one of Brian Chadwick's last flights to Milford Sound, amounting to only seven minutes, shows the details of that flight and the low altitudes flown. (Chapter 3)

The film footage from Grierson, which showed that Gemmell had descended beneath the level of Mt Erebus, was similar to the film borrowed by Anne Cassin, the wife of co-pilot Greg Cassin, some years later. That also showed that Gemmell had descended beneath the level of Mt Erebus. The two films, the public address commentary, and Bob Thomson's evidence all show that Ian Gemmell gave false evidence, and that in truth he flew below what Air New Zealand claimed was the MSA.

When Brian Hewitt was programming the AINS coordinates for the computerised flight plans, instead of keying in the NDB waypoint of 166.41E, he mistyped two digits. He keyed in 164.48 E for the McMurdo waypoint for the flight path. The coordinate of 164.48 E provided the ideal flight path, because it resulted in a flight path down the middle of McMurdo Sound. 166.48 was the Williams Field runway coordinates.

That flight path was safe from any mountain, as it was all at sea level, and the entrance to McMurdo Sound was about 40 miles wide. That more than accommodated the theoretical maximum error of AINS of one mile, that could have arisen on that hour long sector from Cape Hallett.

The first flight which incorporated the coordinate of this 164.48 E into the AINS was when Ross McWilliams was pilot in command. At this stage, it is useful to record that the then International Director of Flight Ops – prior to Dave Eden – was Doug Keesing. He was a passenger on that day and Japanese TV was making a documentary on the flight. The publicity for the flight was considerable because of the presence of this big boss as well as the TV cameras and reporters. One report was as follows:

"We seemed almost to hang over frozen land at 2,000 feet, we were low enough to see huts and vehicles clearly – yet high enough for passengers to be comfortable flying a mountainous land."

The Air New Zealand claim that descent below the MSAs of 16,000 and 6,000 feet was prohibited, without Doug Keesing taking action after his flight was clearly stupid. It just reinforced Mahon's belief that Wilson and Johnson were lying like troopers. For the judiciary of both the NZ Appeal Court and the Privy Council to believe such ridiculous claims and counter claims by Air New Zealand was appalling judicial incompetence.

Coming back to the co-ordinates, the original compass heading from Hallett to the Scott Base with the 166.48E coordinate had not been changed. That would have suggested that the amendment of the McMurdo waypoint to 164.48 E was an accident. But note what Mahon said.

> I agree that there is considerable validity in this point.
>
> The track and distance details of the Cape Hallett/McMurdo sector would have required amendment in the manner indicated by the Navigation Section witnesses.
>
> As opposed to this, I observe that when the Williams Field waypoint was changed to the NDB waypoint, there was no amendment of the track and distance details, minor though such amendments would have been.
>
> In addition, the Navigation Section may have thought it not necessary to alter the track and distance criteria from Cape Hallett to McMurdo for the reason that the pilots were accustomed to flying on Heading Select down this sector and not by reference to the fixed heading programmed into the AINS.

The difference in compass heading of a change from 166.48 to 164.48 is so small that it probably would not be noticeable by human eye on a standard compass in a bumpy boat or aircraft, let alone one so close to the South Magnetic Pole. More than likely, as most experienced polar navigators would know, the compass would not be used at all. In any case, grid navigation was applied after 60 degrees South.

So far, I have been charitable to Hewitt, inasmuch as I have not referred to Mahon's para 229. But, to put everything in perspective, I now quote it.

> 229. At this juncture I must pause to consider whether the Williams Field co-ordinates were in fact accidentally used. Certainly the latitudinal meridian was also the same as the Williams Field latitude. But this version of events allowed Mr Hewitt to say that he had only made a mistake in one digit, namely typing in 164° instead of 166°. If, in fact, he had intended to use the current NDB co-ordinates for McMurdo, then there would have been a mistake in two digits, namely 166 degrees 41 minutes east would have been typed in as 164 degrees 48 minutes east. Since it was the case for the airline that this alteration in the destination waypoint was purely accidental and not by design, it was therefore essential to show, if possible, that only one digit had been involved in the typing error. It was scarcely conceivable that two digits could have been mistakenly typed in out of a total of five. I have gone to some lengths to explain all this, because the explanation of the Navigation Section, based upon a mistaken alteration of the McMurdo waypoint, was not accepted by some counsel and, in particular, was doubted by both counsel assisting the Commission. In their submission, Mr Hewitt must have been fully aware of the McMurdo waypoint currently operating, that is to say, the NDB waypoint. What he could have done, so it is said, would have been to leave the Williams Field latitude as it was, but to alter the NDB longitude so as to move it 2 degrees to the west, which would programme the aircraft to fly to a destination point just to the west of the Dailey Islands. This would conform with what was known to be the standard practice of antarctic pilots which was to fly down the centre of McMurdo Sound and then turn left into the McMurdo area at a point somewhat to the south of McMurdo Station, the purpose being to give passengers the best possible view of the McMurdo Station-Scott Base area. In other words, it was suggested that the four 1977 flights, commencing on 18 October 1977, had all flown down the Sound in approximate conformity with the military track, and the shifting of the McMurdo waypoint was done deliberately so as to conform with this general track.

> 230. All this was strenuously denied by the Navigation Section. I can summarise the objections in this way:

Mahon then listed those objections and gave his answers to all six of them.

Within Air New Zealand, advertising and brochures for passengers were printed that extolled the low-level views. If flights were above 3,000 feet, then none of those promised views could have been fulfilled. Likewise, the flight path Air New Zealand promised was down the middle of McMurdo Sound, despite denials by evidence from the navigation section and from the briefing officers, Wilson and Johnson. The Artistic licence claimed by Hewitt at one stage was hardly believable when the passenger brochures showed the middle of McMurdo Sound flight path. Likewise the photographs were virtually all well below 6,000 feet if not nearer to 1,500-3,000 feet.

The flight path with the 164.48 coordinate was ideal as regards the US Navy ATC. The US Navy ATCs were able to monitor the DC-10s by radar if they flew down McMurdo Sound. On the other hand, I repeat that US Navy ATC could not see by radar if the DC-10s descended to the alleged MSA of 16,000 feet, flying over Mt Erebus. It just never happened. It was all part of the orchestration of the lie by Dalgety with Gemmell's help. The problem would have persisted well after the DC-10s had cleared Erebus. The simple reason was that the upward angle of the radar scanner would have needed to be over 30 degrees. Rhodes was not popular with Air New Zealand when providing the technical details of the radar at MacBase. But the radar scanner was programmed to go up to a maximum of 15 degrees, because it had to monitor and control all the Operation Deep Freeze aircraft and helicopters flying much lower ie ground level upwards. In any case, Mac Base's radar was just a portable model. It did not have the modern abilities of radar sets that are now taken as standard. Rhodes thereafter became a target when he was first told verbally of the erased MacBase tape and the loss of four minutes and forty two seconds of the US Navy radio messages. Later the US Navy denied erasure of tape. Instead they changed their story and said it was a period when there were no messages exchanged. That was hardly credible and I personally believe Rhodes first version, as did Mahon, in conversation with Lt Cmdr Fessler. Rhodes gave a description of the ability of the US Radar which could not monitor any aircraft coming over Ross Island.

The planners of the Air New Zealand Antarctica flights gave no consideration to the problem of overflying an active volcano. With one exception, Ian Gemmell gave evidence there were many flights over active volcanos. He said that if Erebus was erupting, then this information would be provided to pilots, so they could take appropriate action to avoid the eruption. We now know thanks to the research since and as recorded by Colin Monteath, Erebus is not that type of "safe" predictable active volcano, if there is ever one! (White Island NZ -9th December 2019).

The incident with the British Airways 747 scheduled Singapore to Perth, Flight 009 had not occurred at that time. That aircraft flew through an invisible at night ash cloud from a volcano. It caused all four engines to stop. The aircraft was only just able to glide to make an emergency landing at Jakarta. Some engine power had been restored, and that enabled the pilots to make a safe landing at Jakarta. Without some engine power, it would have been an absolute disaster, as the aircraft would have had to ditch in the sea. There would have been little chance of a Sully Sullenberger successful Hudson River type ditching. Few of the Air New Zealand pilots had the training that Rod Lovell had, the DC-3 pilot who ditched in Botany Bay in 1994.

The flight of Gordon Vette would have been dangerous to have followed the original 1977 flight path overhead Mt Erebus on that day. Erebus was erupting, it was throwing lava bombs 6,560 feet higher above 12,450 feet, and ash would have been much higher, whereas the MSA was 16,000 feet. The president of McDonnell Douglas, John Brizendine, was on board on that occasion. He wrote the now famous article advertising the low-level Antarctic Air New Zealand sightseeing trips. A million copies of that article were printed and distributed to every household. Morrie Davis, the Chief Executive Officer of Air New Zealand, said he had not read the article extolling the trip and the low flying. According to letters from Denise Henare who later was the fourth counsel for Air New Zealand at the Mahon Inquiry, she had distributed draft copies to Davis, Dave Eden and 23 other executives - in person! I have copies of her letters to that effect including Russell McVeagh's David Williams.

This sets the background to the tragic events of Air New Zealand and flight TE 901. The parallel is the sightseeing flights by Brian Chadwick with his Air Charter biplanes 17 years earlier. It is remarkable that 60 years after Chadwick disappeared, new evidence of his flying emerged from old amateur family films. I was that guilty party who had inadvertently hidden the truth about Brian's flying. What further evidence is likely to emerge about the murky past of Air New Zealand in 1977 and the inauguration of the Antarctic flights? The official apology for the Erebus disaster was given by the Prime Minister Jacinda Ardern at the 40th reunion of the families of the 257 victims in November 2019. That apology was followed by an apology in the same terms by the chairperson of Air New Zealand.

I have suggested that the legal profession also needs to apologize for its actions or more correctly its lack of action against its members and judges who broke their codes of conduct, even if it was not considered that they were involved in perverting the course of justice. Better monitoring of these codes was required then, "The Justice Mirage" indicates nothing had changed for 30 years and it would not be unreasonable to ensure that currently there is no breech of codes of practice. Again the Alan Hall case indicates that nothing has changed.

It was not clear whether those two apologies extended to the behaviour of CAD, Ministry of Transport/TAIC inspectors investigation mistakes and their misguided ICAO Annex 13 report delivered by Ron Chippindale. Was Chippindale a central part of the conspiracy that Mahon labelled an orchestrated litany of lies? Or was he no more than a victim of the same lies and misinformation from the management of Air New Zealand? What about his civil servant colleagues who were part of the Civil Aviation Division? Were they equally culpable of inexcusable gross negligence by their failure to monitor Air New Zealand's flights?

I keep in mind Chippindale's behaviour when he accused the two children of the pilot Jim Collins, of perjury. I refer to those Daughters of Erebus as Paul Holmes names them. Their evidence when they recounted the story of their ever-diligent father preparing for his flight to Antarctica in their last conversations with that loving father is more than I can comprehend. Then for an accident inspector to call them liars in his press releases is beyond that comprehension. Collins was doing what all good pilots should do – thorough preparation for an unusual flight and drawing the coordinates on those charts. Chippindale knew one chart had been provided from the co-pilot's friend in Nelson.. I also repeat my criticisms of Chippindale's intransigence when he covered up mistakes made by O'Brien and Harvie, his predecessors, concerning the 1961 tragedy of the Bay of Plenty Airways incident. In that case, due to metal fatigue, a wing had separated in flight near another volcano, that of Ruapehu. He and his predecessors were fixated with the blame the pilots mantra of the air accident investigation inspectors. He was aided and abetted by CEO John Briton of TAIC in 2000/1.

The Erebus disaster was caused by a number of factors. One was the numerical transposition of the number four replacing the number six. The coordinate 164.48 was wrongly typed instead of the correct 166.48.

Simpson was one of the pilots at the same briefing on 9th November that was attended by Collins and Cassin. At that briefing, the flight path was briefed as being down the middle of McMurdo Sound to the Dailey Islands with the 164.48 waypoint. The flight path briefed was not over Mt Erebus. All the line pilots agreed with Simpson that was the case for the whole of 1978 and 1979 flights. Only the executive pilots, Gemmell, Grundy and Hawkins on the 1977 trips had tried to convince Mahon that the flight path planned was over Erebus. As for the claim never to be lower than 6,000 feet, Ross Johnson admitted he broke that MSA regulation. Hawkins clearly flew below 6,000 feet but had forgotten that his co-pilot Ken Mulgrew was photographed perfectly with Mount Erebus towering 10,000 feet above him. That photo was reproduced in Air New Zealand's publicity material. Absolute proof of Hawkins failing memory!

The subsequent communication between Ross Johnson and Brian Hewitt as reported by them in evidence may have been influenced by the cover-up of the true facts that was imposed by Air New Zealand.

Irrespective of that, using the Alpha sheet, Hewitt proceeded to type in the longitude for McMurdo's Williams Field coordinates 166.48 but typed 164 degrees 48 minutes east. He went on to say that although it was standard practice to check such figures by looking at the visual display unit on the computer, comparing these figures with the work sheets, he did not detect his error. The result of typing in this wrong meridian of longitude was to place the McMurdo waypoint about 25 miles safely to the west of the McMurdo NDB.

Hewitt continued to use his original alpha sheet in November 1979, when amending the terminal point of the flight from the Williams Field longitude (166.48) to the TACAN waypoint (166.58). He had not realised he was changing 164.48 to 166.58 – 27 miles difference. Whereas in actual fact all the pilots since Ross McWilliams flight on 7th November 1978 had a Dailey Islands waypoint based on 164.48. That resulted in a flight plan down the middle of McMurdo Sound.

The new coordinate of 166.58 that Hewitt entered on the Antarctic flight path changed the flight path back to the nominal 1977 flight path, so that it once again crossed Mt Erebus, all of 12,450 feet. Hewitt claimed he had not been told that the flight paths for 1978 and 1979 (which used his incorrect coordinate) had been adopted by the expert navigators within Air New Zealand. This was one of the most serious management errors of the internal communications systems. Hewitt was prone to error. Nobody checked his work. Even a change of a briefed flight plan of two miles should have been advised to the pilots. It was unforgivable that it was in fact a change of 27 miles without the pilots being told.

Had the weather been as good as it had been on most of the previous flights, then the change would not have mattered. It would have been obvious to Collins, using his mark one eyeball, that the AINS guided flight path was leading the DC-10 straight at Erebus.

None of the Air New Zealand pilots were given the training that the Operation Deep Freeze airmen of the US Navy, the RNZAF, and the AAF were given. Regulations were that those military pilots had to have had the experience of three previous trips under supervision before they were permitted to be pilots in charge of any flight to or around Antarctica.

The original Civil Aviation Division (CAD) licence to Air New Zealand included the stipulation that pilots had to have previous experience of Antarctica before they could be pilot in command. It was vital that they were trained to recognise that VFR flying in the whiteness of Antarctica, with the insidious optical illusion of whiteout is hazardous. It was this lack of relevant Antarctic training that became another serious factor in the eventual tragedy. None of the pilots were trained that flying under an overcast sky with the unbroken whiteness of the ice and snow could produce the visual mirage of an unbroken clear vision for forty plus miles, in other words whiteout.

That stipulation by CAD that pilots must have previous experience of Antarctica before they flew in command was quickly removed for Air New Zealand's convenience, as there were no pilots with that level of experience to train the subsequent executive pilots. The Antarctica sightseeing trip was also regarded as a perk for those executive pilots. The only pilot who flew on more than one occasion was Captain Tony Lawson. And his definition of flying at 2,000 feet over Erebus brought the biggest laugh of those attending the Royal Commission.

Collins and Cassin rightly had every faith in the AINS to deliver them to the centre of the entrance to McMurdo Sound. This is what they had been briefed. This is what all their colleagues had experienced except for Roger Dalziell. He had to divert due to poor weather to the alternate sightseeing flight path that included a visit to the South Magnetic Pole. He had the briefing officer Captain John P. Wilson on board.

Whatever Air New Zealand claimed to the contrary, the briefed flight path after Cape Hallett was down the centre of McMurdo Sound based on the minutes of the directors' meeting held on 5th December 1979. The CEO, Morrie Davis, had inadvertently let the cat out of the bag, when he informed his fellow directors that the crash site was considerably left of track. That could only mean that the track was to the west, down McMurdo Sound. Exactly as it was briefed by Wilson and Ross Johnson, and confirmed in all the evidence given by the line pilots. It was only after the crash that Wilson and Johnson gave sworn evidence that the briefed route was over Mt Erebus.

It was this conflict of evidence that the Commissioner, Justice Peter Mahon, had to decide who was telling the truth. The discovery notices that were issued to Air New Zealand to reveal all documentation concerning flight TE901 were not complied with. It was not until the Court of Appeal hearing that these minutes of the directors' meeting were disclosed. Had they been properly revealed to Mahon as required by law, the outcome would have been entirely different. But such was the cover-up presented to Justice Mahon.

The last words between Collins and his wife Maria were that he must remember to buy the blue cod at Christchurch on his return from Antarctica. That personal story is comparable with that of the rainbow trout that Brian Chadwick was given by Don Nairn and Dick Hutchison in my film at Queenstown on our way back from Milford Sound in January 1962.

There were the radio communications between First Officer Graham Lucas and Peter Tait in Nelson about Collins having the map GNC21N on board. The cockpit voice recorder and the flight data recorder were found fairly quickly by Ian Gemmell and his mountaineer escorts, only for them to be misused by the ever-intransigent Ronald Chippindale.

Analysis of Privy Council Judgment

An extract from the Privy Council judgment follows. Ken Diplock, on behalf of their lordships dealt with lying as follows:

> It is an understandable human weakness on the part of individual members (of the airline management) having responsibility for flight operations that they should shrink from acknowledging, even from themselves, that something they had done or failed to do might have been a cause of so horrendous a disaster.

My first encounter with the Erebus saga was Diplock's detailed Privy Council's full judgment. Shortly afterwards I read John King's book on New Zealand Air Tragedies. As a result, I had a clear unbiased mind, unaffected by the shenanigans of the Court of Appeal fiasco. I have also had the experience to observe the development of some the top legal minds in the UK, from the time when they were pupil barristers to their elevation as silks and then judges in the High Court up to the ultimate elevation in UK judicial circles. I was used to reading their judgments over the years. That has helped me to understand and to read between the lines of judgments in the Supreme Court or Privy council. His Honour Peter Mahon most certainly could read between the lines far better than myself.

We now know with hindsight that Mahon was aware of many matters not derived from the verbal and written submissions. There were leaks to him from Air New Zealand employees who were fearful of losing their jobs if the source of the leaks became known. The most surprising leak being the telex from Des Dalgety to Air New Zealand staff to shred all documents. It was closely followed in importance by the Peter Martin letter.

CEO Morrie Davis was highly critical of Mahon. For example, Macfarlane in Erebus Papers p.7 quoted Davis:

> He became prone to advice he was receiving outside the court, which he was entitled to do provided he brought it back to court, so if there were accusations consequently arising, they could be sorted out in court. He did not bring it back to court – and went on and on totally disregarding fact and relying more on mystery and presumptions.

This demonstrates the problem with Morrie Davis. The Royal Commission was not a court. Davis and his fellow directors were quick to intimidate employees who gave evidence that was contrary to Air New Zealand's interests albeit strongly denied. I am aware of one occasion when an employee was sacked, albeit he was later re-instated by the board of directors. It overrode Davis's sacking. Mahon was an exceptional person in being able to recognise when he was being lied to. Even Diplock's Privy Council judgment included comments about the lying Mahon faced. It is well known in legal circles that after someone has been caught lying under oath, from then on, those liars' evidence is said to be unreliable. Often when these liars do in fact tell the truth, judges will be reluctant to accept their evidence. The judges in both the Court of Appeal and Privy Council acknowledged the power of being able to observe witnesses giving evidence, because body language can often indicate the veracity of that evidence. I will never forget viewing that one critical question asked by Gemmell of Mahon of evidence yet to be given. Gemmells body language gave him away.

The witness reports of the mountaineers who accompanied Gemmell on the crash site ice confirm that the flight bag of Collins, when it was found, did contain Collins's atlas and a chart. Greenwood had told Gemmell, before the latter flew to Antarctica, that the McMurdo waypoint had been shifted from McMurdo Sound to that over Erebus. Gemmell was fully alert of Air New Zealand's need to conceal any documentary evidence which could prove the flight path had been briefed as being down the middle of McMurdo Sound. As well as that, shortly before he died, Gemmell admitted that the papers from the ring binder of Collins had been impounded by Air New Zealand.

What of the briefing notes of Cassin that were taken from Cassin's home? They could also have contained the same details as Collins noted from the briefing. Anne Cassin's sister Celia and brother-in-law Don Richens were probably unaware of the importance of Greg's notes. They were inadvertently very helpful to Air New Zealand, because they enabled the airline to make Greg's papers disappear into the company shredder. How deep Captain Crosbie was involved in persuading them to release Greg Cassins papers is not clear, except according to Mahon's surprise, Crosbie received a letter from the Richens acknowledging that it was their responsibility for providing these papers.

John Keir attempted to obtain Crosbie's version of these events prior to his 2019 podcasts on "Erebus Flight 901 – Litany of Lies". Crosbie made it very clear he was not willing to cooperate, although Maynard Hawkins was only too happy to add his own views for the podcasts. When I contacted Bruce Crosbie, he stated that he had not been pressurised by Air New Zealand, his employers at the time but was kind enough to wish me luck with this book. One can only have sympathy for any employee caught up in his employer's fraud. Not everyone was as principled as Mahon's father, or Mahon himself.

Mahon said he had been told an orchestrated litany of lies. In cold, hard fact he was told exactly that. I hold detailed proof of dozens of lies that Mahon was told.

Mahon could only record his opinion as to what had caused the crash after he had decided who had been lying to him in their evidence. Take one example. Wilson and Johnson said they told the pilots at briefing that the flight path crossed Erebus. It follows that if what they said is true, then the pilots caused the crash, because they flew on the flight path at 1,500 ft. That ignores Keesing's flight as a passenger with McWilliams on the first 1978 flight after Hewitt had set the flight path down to the Dailey Islands.

On the other hand, the other pilots at that briefing, told Mahon the briefing officers had told them the flight path was in McMurdo Sound.

The Court of Appeal (Cooke judgment p. 666) said of Mahon's finding he had been told an orchestrated litany of lies. They said:

> If, contrary to the view just expressed, the Commissioner did have jurisdiction to consider allegations of organised perjury, natural justice would certainly have required that the allegations be stated plainly and put plainly to those accused. That was not done. If it had been done, what we have said earlier is enough to show that they could well have made effective answers.
>
> So we conclude that in making the findings or allegations stated in para 377 of the report the Commission acted in excess of Jurisdiction and contrary to natural justice.

They were wrong, very wrong and the 1974 Appeal Court judgments of Denning, Orr and Lawton clarified that Buckley's high court judgment in the Pergamon Press case [1970 1 WLR 388] did not overturn Mahon's right to add his reports paragraph 377. Warnings had been given by Mahon.

Did Mahon warn the witnesses he believed they were lying? Firstly, he did warn Peter Martin, who was the lawyer for Air New Zealand's insurers. Peter Martin wrote a letter about Mahon's warning. Mahon said of that letter:

> But the significant point about the Martin letter was that no one speaking on behalf of Air New Zealand ever denied the validity of Mr Martin's letter, and it has never been denied to this day. I had deliberately warned the airline, through its insurers, that the altitude and navigation evidence, in my opinion at that time, was false evidence given in concert, and the airline had immediately acted in response to that warning.

Secondly, Mahon warned Air New Zealand's lawyers he believed their witnesses were lying. Paul Holmes (p. 344) explained:

> One afternoon in October 1980, with the navigation evidence all in, Mahon called Air New Zealand counsel into his room. Only David Williams, one of the Air New Zealand counsel was still there. He also asked one of the counsel assisting the Commission to come in as well.
>
> When he arrived, I said that I felt I was under an obligation to tell him that I was concerned at the possibility that he and the airline witnesses might think I had made up my mind against them on the issue of credibility. I referred to the executive pilots who had given evidence on the altitude question. I said that at this juncture, and especially having regard to the unexpected evidence of Captain Wilson, I had no option but to have doubts as to the credibility of those witnesses,

or at least as to some of them. As to the navigation section witnesses, I again had no alternative but to maintain at the present time a considerable degree of doubt as to whether they were telling the truth.

Mahon made it clear that despite the 'air of profound disbelief' in the courtroom about the navigation, or flight path, evidence, he assured counsel that he had not made up his mind and would not, until all of the evidence had been heard.

Was it honest of the Air New Zealand's lawyers, after he had given them this warning, to claim in court in their submissions that Mahon had not given any warning that he did not believe them? In particular David Williams of Russell McVeagh should have insisted that Lloyd Brown withdrew his statement that no warnings had been given. I question his shocking memory.

Macfarlane's Erebus Papers and the Judicial Committee of the Privy Council

The Privy Council's judgment in the case of the Erebus saga has puzzled commentators because it contained so many contradictions. It contained a message that was completely clear to Mahon. Stuart Macfarlane in his Erebus Papers listed most of the misstatements made by their Lordships. I will not repeat this long list of factual misstatements by the Privy Council that Macfarlane listed on pages 537-626 and 703-706 of Erebus Papers. Those misstatements were so regrettable. They constituted a rewriting of the factual basis of the case.

As Macfarlane said the misstatement by the Privy Council of Justice Mahon's case in regard to altitude, which is now permanently recorded in the Law Reports, was by far the worst of their misstatements in the entire judgment and it must have done incalculable harm both to his reputation and to the reputations of his counsel in the eyes of the judiciary and of the legal profession. Their Lordships revealed either an inexcusable failure to comprehend the factual and logical basis of the case before them or a deliberate intention to discredit the Judge.

Unfortunately for Stuart Macfarlane, when he came to advertise and market Erebus Papers, the New Zealand legal establishment in 1991, in the shape of the solicitor general and the attorney general, prevented advertising of the book in the New Zealand Law Society's periodical LawTalk. It was an attempt at censorship. Allan Richie executive director of the NZ Law Society said "any ads suggesting that the Judges of the Privy Council have acted in bad faith or for improper motives will not be accepted." It seems that the Attorney General of the time, Paul East, took more notice of complaints from an anonymous High Court Judge as well as from the Solicitor General. In fact, Macfarlane accused the judges of incompetence, bad faith and improper motives. He explained about 28 cases where the judges wrongly stated what the facts were to the detriment of Mahon.

It is so surprising that Attorney-General Paul East PC was so hypocritical in attempting censorship. In his paper "Life as the Attorney-General: Being in the Right Place at the Right Time" he wrote about parliamentary privilege and freedom of speech. His job included that the Attorney-General "owes a duty, not only to the Government but also to uphold the New Zealand constitution and to ensure that the Government both acts lawfully and is not prevented from acting lawfully". Paul East.

Stuart Macfarlane was right to be concerned about the Government's response. Friends in Wellington legal circles had told him that as soon as his book appeared in the bookshops the Attorney General instructed the Wellington Crown Law Office to buy the book, read it and prosecute Stuart for scandalising the judiciary. The Crown Law Office response was to say that Stuart had been very, very thorough and that any publicity from such a prosecution would not go in the Government's favour and would only serve to increase sales of the book. The Attorney General quietly withdrew his demand.

Peter Mahon believed that he did not need to allow any more time or warning to be given to those persons who were providing palpably false testimony to the Royal Commission. He was right. His reliance was on the notorious Pergamon/Maxwell case that has been widely studied and quoted. His thinking was backed up by the judgments of one of the most eminent of the British judiciary, Lord Denning. The central character under scrutiny in that case was Robert Maxwell. Nobody over 50 in the UK needs reminding of the horrors that man inflicted on thousands of pensioners as well as many others who suffered at his hands. Even today, the name Maxwell and his offspring still sends shivers throughout the highest families in the UK. That includes the Royal Family. The case was that of a Board of Trade inquiry into Pergamon Press, one of Robert Maxwell's companies.

The inspectors mostly accountants were stymied time and again by Maxwell who delayed the report on the grounds of Natural Justice that he should be given the time to respond to the inspectors' criticism of his actions. This is exactly the same natural justice claimed by the Air New Zealand executives in their fight against Mahon's attribution of orchestrated litany of lies to the false evidence they had given to him.

Eventually in the English Court of Appeal judgments by Lords Lawton, Orr and Denning in 1974, it was made clear that these types of inquiry (admittedly under the auspices of the UKs Companies Acts) that Maxwellisation could not be allowed to delay the reports into the suspicious transactions within Pergamon Press. The delays which had been caused by Maxwell's claims for natural justice were rejected.

Maxwell v DTI [1974] QB 523. I have already quoted Denning's judgment when he rejected the argument that fairness required that tentative conclusions be put to the witnesses after the hearing of evidence had concluded. He stressed the unacceptable implications of such an approach.

Mahon's legal argument was based on Denning's judgment. He knew that he did not need to give any more time to Davis, Gemmell, and other witnesses for Air New Zealand to defend themselves against his finding they had lied to him or that Orchestration was an appropriate term. But he was surrounded by incompetence when Denning's 1974 judgement was not quoted.

Even more surprising that Woodhouse had the cheek to accuse Mahon of exceeding his terms of reference when in the Inquiry into Accident Compensation schemes (ACC), Woodhouse had also exceeded his own terms of reference. I realise that the New Zealand ACC no fault accident compensation system resulted from the Woodhouse Inquiry, but Woody did exceed his terms of reference if strictly interpreted. But he was not prepared to concede that Mahon should have been equally treated. Woodhouse was a hypocrite.

The Court of Appeal failed badly when it ignored the Pergamon Press precedent that showed it was unnecessary for Mahon to constantly tell the Air New Zealand witnesses that he did not believe their evidence, and to give them the opportunity to call further evidence to prove that they did tell the truth.

This is where the Privy Council made it clear to Mahon that they agreed with him about the liars and why they lied. They praised his diligent investigation in a manner never granted before to a judge

There was so much happening behind the scenes with Mahon. For example, his meetings with Bill Tench, who briefed him in air accident matters and ICAO Annex 13, then his meeting with Peter Martin detailing the insurance aspects. As well as that, through his relationship with ALPA pilots, doubtless he came to understand modern aviation better than a number of out-of-date pilots and other pterodactyls who continued to criticise the fact that Mahon had not been a pilot like Chippindale. These dinosaurs prevented the benefit of learning by mistakes in their repeated wrongful claims of pilot error when there was instead a valid reason. Such as The ZK-BWA Aero Commander, which was the first of a genre to lose a wing due to a design and construction fault that caused metal fatigue in spar caps.

The one case quoted by Diplock was *Regina v Deputy Industrial Injuries Commissioner, ex parte Moore.* I believe that case was a red herring, because the facts in that old case had little in common with those in the Erebus Inquiry. Admittedly the words natural justice were used. What is not so well known is that in *ex parte Moore* Diplock was the judge at first instance. One of the lawyers who represented one of the litigants in *ex parte Moore* was the young Nigel Bridge. He was later to become Lord Bridge. Doubtless Lords Bridge and Diplock were able to reminisce on that case 18 years earlier. But the application of natural justice on a claim by a crane driver's injury in *ex parte Moore* had little to do with the natural justice due to be shown to 257 subjects in the Erebus case.

The case that really is closest to the Erebus case was that of the Pergamon Press case with Robert Maxwell in the English Court of Appeal. In that case Lord Justices Orr, Lawton, and Denning could not be clearer in their 1974 judgments. What is surprising is that less than a year later, Lord Diplock, in the House of Lords, approved their judgments that held it was not necessary for a tribunal to give a party more time to produce more evidence that they had told the truth. Diplock's approval was given in his judgment on the *Hoffmann La Roche* case of 1975. That is only eight years before Diplock accused Mahon of not giving Air New Zealand witnesses more time to produce more evidence that they had told the truth. That was a complete contradiction by Diplock, of his own earlier judgment.

Perhaps the situation with the Birmingham Six fiasco that was initiated by Nigel Bridge's comments confirming his view of the guilt of the Birmingham Six in that case was becoming a problem. Lord Scarman, whilst it is acknowledged that he was nominally part of the Privy Council that failed Mahon, was instrumental in obtaining the release of the Birmingham Six and in proving their innocence.

The full case reference containing Diplock's approval of his forgotten decision that Maxwell had used in his claim to natural justice is *F. Hoffmann La Roche & Co. A.G. v Secretary of State for Trade and Industry* (1975) AC 295, 368 D-E and 369 D-F.

This is part of the statement made by Lord Diplock when he approved the judgments of Lords Orr, Lawton, and Denning in the above case. Diplock said:

> I would accept that it is the duty of the commissioners to observe the rules of natural justice in the course of their investigation — which means no more than that — they must act fairly by giving to the person whose activities are being investigated a reasonable opportunity to put forward facts and arguments in justification of his conduct of these activities before they reach a conclusion which may adversely affect him.

But why then did Diplock issue such a perverse judgment against Mahon in 1983? The judgment of the Privy Council agreed that Peter Mahon did a brilliant job under such circumstances. As a result of the Mahon Report, though many years later, ICAO and accident investigatory agencies changed the system of investigation of many types of accidents, not just those relating to air accidents.

The judges in the Privy Council were normally of the highest repute for their intelligence and ability to produce quality resulting judgments that should stand the test of time. I fear that on this one occasion, they may not have been as wise as they should have been. I smelt a rat! When one examines the individuals and their personal track records, those reputations are at risk. To give one example, Lord Bridge in the Birmingham Six saga prevented justice for 16 years. He caused a combined total of 100 years of incarceration for those innocent defendants. He was not alone, there were 18 other judges who were similarly wrong in their assessment of the innocence of the Birmingham Six.

The reasons for the perverse and contradictory judgment of Diplock and the other four Privy Councillors in the Erebus case were probably even simpler. When Woodhouse and McMullin attended Privy Council business in London in early 1983, as Caterina de Nave reported, they undoubtedly lobbied the Privy Council to find against Mahon. Caterina was the brains behind "*Erebus: The Aftermath*" the docudrama which must have had a massive effect on the New Zealand populace. The equivalent docudrama "*Mr Bates v The Post Office*" just screened on UK TV about the Post Office Horizon scandal is breaking all records and the whole country is up in arms over the mishandling by the UK establishment. Changes will be made in the UK that were not made in New Zealand to the establishment. It is a pity that "*Erebus The Aftermath*" did not cause the long term changes in New Zealand that the UK Horizon cases is having on UK politics and society.

That, together with the personal pressures on Lord Bridge with the rumblings of innocence of the Birmingham Six, may have been two levers on Diplock and the other judges to make the decision that they did. The Birmingham Six were convicted in 1975. Their guilty verdicts were quashed on 14th March 1991. Each of the six received compensation ranging between £800 thousand and £1.2 million.

I believe that the current members of the judicial committee of the Privy Council and Supreme Court would not be impressed by Woodhouse and McMullin. The comparison between the judgments of the majority in the Court of Appeal and that of Woodhouse and McMullin has to be clear proof of their bias. Bias in judges is supposed to be taken seriously. For example, Justice Bill Wilson was sacked because of his perceived bias, and the problematic incestuousness of the New Zealand judiciary in that case should have rung alarm bells.

The case of Saxmere v Wool Board litigation blew up in Wilson's face when one of Peter Mahon's old friends, Sir Ted Thomas uncovered the connections of Justice Wilson with the lawyer for one of the litigants in question. This ultimately forced Wilson to resign, albeit with a large payoff. Those connections were Wilson's financial indebtedness to Alan Galbraith QC, one of the lawyers. Even the highly respected Judge Sian Elias became involved, because of her partnership in a race-horse stud and property business with Wilson. Rich Hill Ltd was the business tied up many different interests.

But then I think of Mahon and Lloyd Brown. They were very close friends and Brown was instrumental in getting Mahon appointed as sole Commissioner. Brown was then appointed as senior counsel for one main key party – Air New Zealand. Mahon and Brown were so close and had Mahon found in favour of Air New Zealand, would the pilots' families felt that it was a case of bias, as did the lawyer for Saxmere, which eventually led to Wilson having to resign after Ted Thomas did the dirty on Wilson. I find it hard to understand this part of New Zealand law. Or should I spell this LORE. Double standards and hypocrisy go together as related in The Justice Mirage by Rob Moodie.

My personal view is that New Zealand is too small for the judicial system it has adopted from the UK system. I have seen reports about this small size problem that was particularly the case when the decision to remove the Privy Council as New Zealand's final appeal court was being debated. There are bound to be too many occasions of legal incestuousness. The book "The Justice Mirage" provides detailed length case studies of the inter-connections between lawyers and judges who were all willing to cover up each other's mistakes, failings, and, on some occasions, even blatant dishonesty.

When researching the comparisons of Mahon and Brown with that of Wilson and Galbraith, in the latter case, most of the hierarchy of the New Zealand legal establishment were involved incestuously. All had various connections, similar to that of Galbraith and Wilson. My own experience is that in such situations, any imbalance in funding between partners is not considered until the annual accounts are prepared by the accountants. It was this perceived imbalance that Wilson's critics used to pressurise him. Sian Elias used Rich Hill, the stud in question near Matamata, for her own horses. She had given approval of the relationship with Galbraith on Wilson's first elevation to the bench. But it was the perceived bias that ultimately led to Wilson's downfall. That the whole of the legal establishment let Woodhouse and McMullin off the hook in 1981/2, is evidence of the failings of those self same individuals.

The Attorney General Chris Finlayson had to stand down from deciding the case and Judith Collins was appointed acting Attorney General to deal with Wilson's situation. It was a complete mess to sort out. But Wilson's transgressions were minor by comparison with the actions of Woodhouse and McMullin. When Saxmere v Wool was re-litigated in the Appeal Court for the second time, the result was the same and Saxmere's appeal rejected. But with such a mess left behind.

Diplock criticised Mahon's lack of natural justice shown to the liars of Air New Zealand and CAD. In fact Mahon did not have to tell the Air New Zealand witnesses he believed they were lying and to offer them the chance to delay and call more evidence to prove they had been telling the truth. That proposition was examined in detail, together with many other similar cases, in a review commissioned by the UK Treasury Committee in 2016. For full details see "A Review of Maxwellisation" November 2016 by members of UK's Blackstone Chambers.

I will not repeat all of the 47 pages but the cases referred to in it concerning the Pergamon Press issue with Robert Maxwell make it clear that Peter Mahon was completely correct in 1980-1981 in that he did not need to provide further time for the liars of Air New Zealand or Civil Aviation Department to call more evidence to prove they had told the truth.

What did happen at the Privy Council in 1983?

The Privy Council is a name for a collection of senior judges – Law Lords. It is worthwhile considering the individuals. After much research into Erebus Papers and the stories behind the many mistakes Macfarlane uncovered, I was sure that much more was happening behind the scenes. It all came to a head when I realised that Diplock's mental faculties were declining after 1975 and that due to his reputation and power, he was able to persuade his fellow judges to agree his own opinions. This is the result of my inquiries.

Judges of the Judicial Committee of the Privy Council

The Presiding Chairman who delivered the speech was Lord (Kenneth) Diplock (1907-1985) He was accompanied by Lord Keith (1920-2002), Lord Scarman (1911-2004), Lord Bridge (1917-2007) and Lord Templeman (1920-2014). The dates of births and deaths have a strong significance. Clearly Kenneth Diplock was by far and away the most senior judge and he died just two years later from emphysema. He was also the very last judge to be appointed before the introduction of compulsory retirement being imposed on judges on attaining the age of 75. Diplock was with good reason a highly respected judge of the old school and had even been a squadron leader in the RAF during World War II. His colleagues on this committee likewise had some involvement in the armed services during that war, but Diplock outranked them all. He had been involved in Special Operations Executive and was a spymaster on secret missions such that Churchill would never reveal exactly in what operations Diplock partook.

In 1975, Diplock was at the top of his mental faculties sitting as a Law Lord in the House of Lords as it was then (now the Supreme Court). In particular, he supported Lord (Tom) Denning's judgment in Maxwellisation with Pergamon Press Inquiries. He was also the most powerful judge in the country including the setting up of the special juryless courts, appropriately named Diplock Courts specifically to deal with the difficulties with juries in Northern Ireland

Extracts from Commercial Court Website

I was able to glean the following observations from the above website:

"Diplock's personality deteriorated during his time in the Lords, to the detriment of his reputation. His cleverness sometimes led him to over-think things.

At best, this conflation of rights and remedies shed little light on the nature of contractual liability. At worst, it was confusing. More serious than such gratuitous intellectual showing-off, Diplock's self-assurance gradually turned to conceit. Still intensely hard-working, he prepared thoroughly in advance of each appeal and, almost inevitably, had usually formed a view before the hearing."

[Comment: The secret lobbying by Woodhouse and McMullin no doubt had influenced Diplock.]

Pre Conceived Judgments

"There was no harm in this so long as he was prepared to treat that view as a preliminary conclusion, up for debate in the hearing. But Diplock became increasingly convinced that his opinions were always right and that all other opinions were essentially irrelevant. Preliminary views hardened into fixed decisions, from which he could not be swayed. He became increasingly intolerant of oral advocacy, and was known to write his judgments before the hearing. This closed-mindedness was compounded when Diplock began to share with Lord Wilberforce the responsibility for presiding over appeals. He used his position (as president) to cut counsel short and slap-down any judicial interventions which ran counter to his own thinking. He also tried to bully, rather than persuade, his colleagues into supporting his own view, and imposed a system of single judgments (very often written by him) to ensure that decisions reflected his own reasoning."

[Comment: The Mahon v Air New Zealand case fits this scenario perfectly)]

Diplock's deterioration between 1975-1983

"Diplock's judgment also became less reliable. In truth, Diplock went on past his prime. If he had left office at the end of the 1970's, he might well have retained the deservedly high reputation of his heyday. But he was the last serving Judge who had been appointed before the introduction of the compulsory retirement age, and could not be got rid of."

Clearly in 1983 Diplock had forgotten his support of Denning's judgments in Maxwell eight years earlier when it was decided that it was not necessary to delay reports on the grounds of "Natural Justice". Lord Diplock had become such a bully that his subordinate judges usually acceded to his written judgment, prepared no doubt on the whole in advance affected by the private lobbying from Woodhouse and McMullin. There was no CRM "Crew loop" failsafe system in the Privy Council in 1983. It was a pity that Mahon's counsel had not done the necessary homework in listing Denning's and Diplock's previous decisions precedent re Maxwell. It is traditional that junior barristers carry out this research for their senior colleagues. Peter Mahon had done so many years earlier in the Parker/Hulme case. Mahon had been prosecuting barrister and the defending junior barrister Brian McClelland stayed up all night searching through law libraries for precedents to help the defence. That was before the Internet. Mahon was an honest prosecutor, unwilling to win at any cost. Justice was more important to him and his conscience. Beware of "win at any cost" Prosecuting Barristers.

Strategic Pressure from the UK Government, Woodhouse and McMullin

We will never know what pressure, if any, Diplock was under from the UK government. Likewise what was said by Woodhouse and McMullin. The Falklands conflict in 1982 involved some assistance from the New Zealand government. There was a chance of a strategic defence hole in the Pacific due to the weakening of the New Zealand economy. That is if Air New Zealand and CAD were to be successfully sued by the passengers for gross negligence as this would have had severe repercussions for the UK as well. Muldoon was prepared to attempt to invoke the Warsaw convention and keep compensation down to NZ$42,000 by declaring what had been described before as a Domestic Flight as an International flight. That became necessary under the Warsaw convention, otherwise the New Zealand compensation scheme known as ACC was likely to be many times the NZ$42,000. Even worse had Peter Mahon's Royal Commission been accepted and filed in place of the Chippindale ICAO Annex 13 report, then compensation could have completely bankrupted the New Zealand economy as the New Zealand Treasury would have been caught up due to the negligence of the Civil Aviation Department (CAD).

LAST WORDS

From Ian Hambly

Ian Hambly told me who was the orchestrator of the "orchestrated litany of lies. I have edited his following statement to Stuart Macfarlane.

"As to who was the orchestrator, there are two parts to this. Several years later I was told by Mike Neville, Air New Zealand's in-house solicitor, that the whole event was "orchestrated" by Des Dalgety from the Board Room at Air New Zealand House. He used the word deliberately. Des Dalgety was Robert Muldoon's personal solicitor and on the Board of Air New Zealand. With its travel privileges, this was the plum board appointment in the country.

Des Dalgety was the Deputy Chair of the Air New Zealand Board at the time of the crash. He had been appointed to the Board by Muldoon.

When I met Peter Mahon to give him Dianne Keenan's diary, I told him what Mike Neville had told me. I don't know when, in relation to that conversation, did Mahon speak to Greg McGee who reported his conversation with Mahon when he named Dalgety as the Orchestrator."

Mahon was right when he told Greg McGee that Dalgety was the orchestrator. McGee wrote in his book *Tall Tales (Some True)*, page 244:

> I was sitting across the table from him at Brighton Road when he said; in his raspy, weakening voice, 'The orchestrator was', and I didn't hear the name he articulated. I can't miss this, I thought, the orchestrator of the notorious litany of lies, just because I fear being rude or tiring the old man out, so I asked him if he would mind repeating it. "The orchestrator", said Peter Mahon, quite clearly this time, 'was Des Dalgety'.

> Des Dalgety was a director on the board of Air New Zealand, and was also personal attorney to Robert Muldoon, on whose behalf he had fought various defamation battles, Muldoon was Minister of Finance, as well as Prime Minister, and was therefore Air New Zealand's shareholder, on behalf of the nation.

However, the above is only a small part of the picture. There is no doubt that Dalgety 'orchestrated' Air New Zealand's part in the 'pre-determined plan of deception'. The plan had to be developed without the input from Air New Zealand's senior counsel Lloyd Brown QC who led the airline's case at the Royal Commission. Incidentally, there is evidence that it was Lloyd Brown who suggested Peter Mahon's name to Muldoon for Royal Commissioner. I understand he never spoke to Mahon again after his report was published. There is no suggestion that Brown was aware of what Air New Zealand were up to. Dalgety had to make sure that all the ducks were in a row before presentation to Brown and then the Royal Commission.

It is obvious that Dalgety would have had no influence over the Chief Inspector of Air Accidents, the Director of Civil Aviation nor the Commissioner of Police. The only person in a position to 'monster' these people was Muldoon. Both Eddie Kippenberger (Director of Civil Aviation) and Morrie Davis (Chief Executive of Air New Zealand) made complete fools of themselves in the witness box at the Royal Commission. Only Muldoon had the ability to put them in such a position. And only Muldoon had the ability to prevent them being charged with perjury. Only Muldoon had the ability to ensure Ron Chippindale (Chief Inspector of Air Accidents) was rewarded with free first class travel on Air New Zealand after his Report.

It is possible (probable?) that Dalgety provided Civil Aviation with advice on how Air New Zealand intended to mount their case, so that both organisations were in sync. I have no evidence to support that, but I believe it likely.

Why did Muldoon take such action? It comes down to money. Muldoon was trying to save the government from substantial costs. It was Muldoon who went on national television to declare TE901 an international flight (in breach of the ICAO Convention). The intention was to limit damages to NZ$42,000, and shift it away from the State. Air New Zealand had insurance cover for that. When it was realised that Air New Zealand had problems in their navigation section, so removing the NZ$42,000 limit, it was decided to blame the pilots. Pilot error was covered by the Convention, mistakes in the administration of the flight by the airline were not.

It's worth noting that at the time of the crash, the Office of the Chief Inspector of Air Accidents was part of the Ministry of Transport. This function was removed from the Ministry on 1 September 1990 and became part of an independent crown entity, the Transport Accident Investigation Commission. In 1992 rail accidents and in 1995 marine accidents, were added to its jurisdiction. This was a necessary move after the debacle exposed by the Royal Commission. Although that was not admitted at the time, nor was it during Muldoon's tenure as Prime Minister which finished in July 1984.

Main sources of Information

"The Erebus Papers" – Stuart Macfarlane

"Verdict on Erebus" – Peter Mahon

"Impact Erebus" – Gordon Vette

"Flight 901 to Erebus" – Ken Hickson

"The Justice Mirage" – Rob Moodie

"My Father's Shadow" – Sam Mahon

"Daughters of Erebus" – Paul Holmes

"Towards the Mountain" – Sarah Myles

Numerous Law Reports

Many email and skype exchanges with key participants including Arthur Cooper and Ian Hambly

Podcasts including White Silence – Michael Wright

Erebus Flight 901 : litany of lies? – John Keir

erebusengravedonourhearts.com – Lizzie Oakes

Internet and YouTube Commentaries
Caterina de Nave and Greg McGee and their docudrama Erebus the Aftermath

"Concorde" – Mike Bannister

Accident report on AF 4590 – F-BTSC 25 July 2000 – Bureau Enquetes – Accidents (B.E.A.)

"Flying Concorde. The full story" – Brian Calvert

CHAPTER 7

SEA FOG IN THE ISLES OF SCILLY

Details for chapter 7 - G-BEON S-61 Sikorsky 03/07/1983 – Isles of Scilly Helicopter White Out – Lawlor Captain. 20 Dead six survived.

Background

This was the accident with a British Helicopters scheduled flight from Penzance to St. Marys, Isles of Scilly on 3rd July 1983. Brian Waugh's favourite in the UK, The Isles of Scilly referred to at p37 "Turbulent Years". The helicopter accident happened before the causes of the Erebus crash had been fully agreed and understood, with particular emphasis to white-out and vision perception. The detailed knowledge of the generally accepted lessons from the Erebus Royal Commission and Vette's work was delayed by the lies of Air New Zealand and the Privy Council hearing later in 1983. That inquiry was supposed to have been a fact-finding mission as conducted by Justice Peter Mahon and the important lessons concerning pilots vision and illusions were delayed for the international community.

Synopsis

The helicopter was a 26 seat Sikorsky S-61 with every seat occupied on the flight from Penzance to St. Mary's Isles of Scilly. It crashed into the sea at full cruising speed just a minute from landing at Scilly, at St Mary's Airport.

The weather was reported to be poor and some patchy sea fog when approaching the islands. Visibility was down to ¾ of a mile with a cloud base reported of 250 feet. The pilots were briefly disorientated. Both failed to notice an unintentional descent when approaching the Islands after receiving ATC clearances. That is the official view and the pilots accepted some responsibility for the accident. However, the lessons were learnt. Audible ground warning equipment was to be fitted in future flights.

An unofficial private report. There were the conversations between the six survivors who were swimming in the water together helping each other to keep afloat. Those conversations between the survivors whilst in the sea were a bit different to the official accident reports!

The seats in the helicopter were mostly dual seats. However, in the crash into the sea, it appears that the dual seats may not have been sufficiently anchored to take the exceptional G-loading of two passengers in such a sudden stop. All 26 seats were occupied. It was the middle of the holiday season. There were only six survivors. Two of these were both the pilots, obviously in their individual seats, and two children who were said to have been in dual seats although being much smaller, the anchorages of their seats may not have been so stressed due to the lighter weight of those children. The other survivors were the two ladies well known throughout the Islands. They had single seats. Was that the factor in their survival of the initial crash? The dual seats appear to have collapsed but there is little comment about this common factor in the official reports.

Whilst treading water in the sea, waiting for the RNLI Lifeboat in the charge of the famous Scillonian coxswain Matt Lethbridge, the term white-out was overheard by the ladies without understanding the significance. The Erebus saga was less than four years earlier. This could not have been the same type of white-out suffered by the Erebus Pilots in Antarctica which was sector white out due to the reflecting light on snow and ice white surfaces. But the sea fog had a similar effect on a VFR flight. The surviving adult ladies had no idea what whiteout was and were never told but it was a word repeated to me by the sibling of one lady.

Whiteout?

The visual perception problem had not happened before to those pilots. They had not realised that they were descending from visual reference points that would normally be picked up by the mark one eyeball. Gordon Vette's work over a period following Erebus in chapter 6 led to a better understanding for all pilots of the problems with vision and perception. Not just sector white-out.

Unfortunately, Captains Dominic Lawlor and Neil Charleton were not likely to have been aware of Vette's detailed work about pilot perception at that time. As pilots, they may have had access to the accident report of Ron Chippindale. Had Air NZ been open and cooperative during that enquiry/investigation by both Mahon and Chippindale, the lessons of visual perception may have added to the training of pilots like Lawlor and Charleton to cope better with any visual problems they encountered and to recognise possible meteorological illusions. Twenty lives were lost out of the 26 on board the helicopter. Twenty lives out of Scilly's tiny permanent population of 2,000. Every Scillonian knew most of the lost souls. What may not have been widely known outside of Scilly is that due to the timing of the trip, most of those passengers on board would have been Scillonians as it was the middle of the day and the special offers for regular flyers would have been in operation. Most holiday making passengers would travel on the early mornings and late afternoons flights.

The tragedy of Erebus had a profound effect on New Zealand. 257 lives were lost out of a population of just over three million. But the disaster of helicopter G-BEON with the loss of 20 lives on a Scillonian population of 2,000 had a massive effect on tiny Scilly thereafter, even to this day. The 26 seat Sikorsky is no longer used for the trip and currently has been replaced by the Sikorsky S76 which only carries nine passengers at most.

How do I know what Lawlor and Charleton said to their surviving passengers? Just by chance, it so happened that my wife and I accompanied the sister of one of these survivors on her first visit after the accident, to meet her sibling. Understandably she was extremely nervous. She latched on to Helen and me in the Penzance terminal building prior to boarding the helicopter. She sat next to Helen on the helicopter as we made our way to St Mary's. She needed comforting. Helen was the friendly soul needed and held her hand for the whole of the flight. That flight was only 20 minutes, one I would not want to repeat.

The lady was met by the sister who had survived the accident with G-BEON and everyone was then able to calm down. We were told of the unofficial discussions between the pilots, once again the visual perception errors of experienced pilots flying VFR.

This was just another coincidence that has found me personally affected before or after a tragedy. The grim reaper will get me eventually. I have had a lot of close shaves, not least the flight with Chadwick as well as my own flying experiences with the small Cessnas and Pipers flying in the UK's miserable weather. That is why I feel the need to relate these incidences as many of the lessons that should have been learned from those experiences, clearly have not been learnt, whether in general aviation of the UK or New Zealand.

Main sources of information

The internet has provided most of the official facts which include the accident report as well as newspaper articles.

But the truth was learnt in the unforgettable incredible journey to Scilly with thanks to the sibling of the survivor.
"This is your life – Matt Lethbridge" UK TV documentary.

CHAPTER 8

MISSING HELICOPTER NEAR THE ROUTEBURN TRAIL

Details for chapter 8 -ZK-HNW – Lost 03/01/2004 –Found 21/11/2012. Helicopter Hughes 369 HS. Pilot - Cam Montgomerie and passenger from UK Hannah Timings. Difficulty with authorities for Layla Timings family.

Synopsis

The pilot was a low-hours (200) pilot who was flying in Fiordland, New Zealand. He had come from Wanaka and landed for the night at Howden Hut, and had intended to proceed to Milford Sound on the next day. The weather was awful and with hindsight, he should never have attempted to fly in those conditions, as it is all too easy to overestimate one's ability to fly in IMC.

At first glance, this appears to be a straight forward case of an inexperienced pilot albeit with a commercial licence, the pilot having been caught out by the weather and get home itis. And it may so have been. But this aircraft was lost and not found for the best part of nine years. The members of the family of the passenger did their best to arrange searches well after the official searches had ceased.

Nine years later, they were found just two miles from their last reporting point. How could they have been missed? There is tiger country in New Zealand which cannot easily be ground-searched. Photographs and video published in the NZ media following the discovery in 2012 showed the wreckage halfway up a grassy slope. It was not the impenetrable jungle country New Zealand is famous for, but rather it was in the open. But it was so close to the Routeburn trail, one of the most popular trekking areas.

It was only by chance that another helicopter pilot happened to see the sun reflecting light on a piece of metal that caught his eye. Brendan Hiatt after a quick recce then completed his flight with the fare paying passengers. He returned with extra observers on board. Even then, it took him some considerable time to re-spot the wreckage seen earlier. It was not helped by the helicopter's green paint with the green grass background. In earlier times, the air accident expert W.H. (Bill) Tench was involved with safety for the North Sea helicopters. One safety feature following the difficulties with ditched helicopters was to find a suitable colour scheme that would show up in the North Sea. Green was very much out. But for ZK-HNW it provided the camouflage that may have helped to hide the wreckage for nearly nine years.

Part of the cause of the crash may have related to the pilot's satellite navigation display that was linked to true north, instead of magnetic north. It is easy to confuse the use of magnetic or true north on modern sat nav equipment. It should not happen but it does. On board ZK-HNW was a Garmin Sat Nav that may have shown 272 degrees True, from Wanaka, and not Magnetic. Radio calls with this number from Cam Montgomerie confused searchers, including Gavin Grimmer, who takes great effort to keep alive the searches for many other missing aircraft.

Compare sat navs with the AINS in chapter 6 – Erebus. They work on entirely different principles. It is said that with sat navs, pilots are less likely to be unaware of their exact position navigation wise. This does tempt greater risk taking by ill prepared pilots who rely only on their sat navs.

In the period 2004 and 2012, on many occasions, Hannah Timings' family had tried to obtain information from the NZ authorities but were hampered by a considerable amount of Kiwi red tape. Trying to investigate during the missing period was almost impossible for that family. They came from the UK (Cheltenham, Gloucestershire). It was thanks to people like New Zealander Gavin Grimmer keeping these incidents in the news that pilots like Brendan Hiatt are always alert to the possibility of finding any of the many missing aircraft. Grimmer has been collating information on missing aircraft over a number of years. He has self-funded many searches, including that for the Dragonfly and Brian Chadwick and his passengers. (See chapter 3.)

I think it reasonable to compare the search for ZK-HNW with the search for helicopter ZK-HTF that went missing on 4th November and found just a few days later on 19th November 2005 after privately funded 975 helicopter search hours.

ZK-HTF went missing for just a short time, not the nine years of ZK-HNW. It took away the record for the largest search for a missing aircraft that of the Dragonfly ZK-AFB (Chapter 3). It was during that time when ZK-HNW with Cam and Hannah had not been found in Fiordland for an additional seven years. In some respects, it is not important as to which was the largest search in New Zealand, the search for ZK-HTF was controversial due to the disorganised searching with hundreds of fruitless duplicated costly helicopter hours. Helicopters are a very expensive aircraft for such a blanket search.

There was an inquiry as to the way the ZK-HTF search was carried out. The hapless pilot's family (Erceg), one of the richest in New Zealand up to that time, paid privately for this additional 975 helicopter hours that cost over NZ$1.5 million. The publicly funded costs were much less. Dazza Sherwin is one of Gavin Grimmer's contacts involved in findlostaircraft. co.nz website. Dazza and Gavin are currently searching for ZK-FMQ, Ryan Moynihan's Cessna 180 that went missing on 8 November 1997 and G-AUN2 10 January 1928! There are a number of other missing aircraft noted on that website.

Despite the millions of wasted dollars in the search for Erceg and his passenger, Dazza simply applied his experience and knowledge of radar with a little common sense. He located ZK-HTF precisely where the corrected radar tracks indicated where the final flight path was. It was exactly where the missing helicopter had come to rest in an open paddock within a small dense glade of trees. Most importantly in that short time span, there were the tell-tale signs of yellowing of leaves from the broken branches in the glade's trees which were losing their greenery in those short 15 days. Like ZK-HNW (green), ZK-HTF's colour was the perfect camouflage once again. But not before the family had been charged so much for their privately funded wasted helicopter time.

I had been involved with multihull yachts in the 1970s and reviews of Search and Rescue (SAR) following the 1979 Fastnet tragedy. We tried to persuade all our offshore racing craft owners to paint the undersides of the bridge decks dayglo orange before they were permitted to enter the offshore racing fraternity. The purpose was that if they capsized, then the high-definition colour would be easier to spot, whether from air searches or by other watercraft. Just as Tench specified years earlier for North Sea helicopters. As for ELTs (emergency locator transmitters), if an aircraft crashes, that is the time when the ELT should be able to issue radio signals. But if, when an aircraft crashes, the ELT is useless due to separation of transmitter from its antennae by the crash, that is just plain stupid. Are lessons still to be learnt?

The most obvious lesson is that searches are best carried out in an organised way, and that where dense jungle is involved, signs of yellowing after the critical period, usually 14 days after a disappearance, should not be the time for official searches to be discontinued. In the case of the Dragonfly in 1962, the official searches were called off just when signs from the yellowing of jungle flora are beginning to appear. Professional thinking?

ASIDE

Gavin Grimmer is also looking for the first two Boeing Aircraft ever built. They may possibly be in part of the old military fort at North Head, Auckland Harbour. But the NZ authorities (so honest and expert) deny that there is any chance that they could be in the long blocked up labyrinthine passageways. The idea of old disintegrating ordnance has also been dismissed officially so these passageways will not be re-opened. I think of Beirut and the promises of the Lebanese politicians. Those officials must be responsible if there was disintegrating ordnance. If anything like that was to happen in Auckland, there will be many officials likely to be guilty of involuntary manslaughter. The danger is well recognised in the UK of the old liberty ship, the Richard Montgomery. Much care is taken by the UK authorities with this wreck which is in the middle of the Thames Estuary. It sank in the Second World War with thousands of tons of bombs and other ordnance intended for the D-Day beaches. Most of these bombs are still on board.

In correspondence between Hannah's sister Layla and Gavin Grimmer, Layla and her family had mentioned synthetic aperture radar (SAR) equipment early in 2009. Such equipment may hold the key for many other future searches. Greater progress is supposed to have been made in technology over the past five years than the previous 55 years, which would take us back to 1962 as I write. Go back another 60 years from 1962. The Wright Bros did not get off the ground until December 1903.

As a final twist, my step-son was the vicar at St. Pauls in Auckland from 2003 to 2013. He conducted the memorial service for Hannah Timings. Hannah was a close friend of his wife and family from Cheltenham, so I knew that there was a personal connection, similar to Chadwick as well as the Scillonian Helicopter incident. What I did not realise until very recently was that Hannah and her family, Layla, Pippi and Sam were guests at my step son's wedding in the UK. I felt quite emotional to see them and their names on the table plans when looking at the old wedding videos and photos. I am aware from this personal experience that even with an accident involving just two persons, there is still that heartache for their families and until found, there is no closure for grieving hearts.

Recently, there was a reunion of the families and friends of the pilot and passengers of the missing Dragonfly ZK-AFB as described in case study no.3. It was the delayed 60th anniversary due to Covid but I repeat, nevertheless, there continued to be considerable interest with over 100 people who attended the Christchurch Airport meeting. This was where the biplane departed on that day in 1962, but was never to be found. Close relatives, brothers and sisters still alive from New Zealand and Australia were among the attendees. I made a brief presentation introducing the film of the Dominie (ZK-BCP) flight of Chadwick. It showed the scenery as it was in 1962 when Chadwick disappeared. At the conclusion, one person stood up clearly very emotional saying that he too had been on exactly the same flight just a few days before 12th February 1962 and seeing the film for the first time, he realised how lucky he had been. I shared that emotion from 13,000 miles away.

Main sources of Information:

Findlostaircraft.co.nz and special thanks to Gavin Grimmer.

"Traced but still Missing" by Gavin Grimmer
New Zealand Coronial Office

FULL CIRCLE: LESSONS LEARNT

We have in fact come full back circle to the Dragonfly search. The success in finding the missing helicopter of Cam Montgomerie and Hannah Timings was entirely by chance, even though it was so close to where it was last positively placed. Erroneous reports diverted the attention being paid by the findlostaircraft.co.nz team. Random searches based on reported sightings in the NZ bush, hills, and mountain screes are highly unlikely to be successful. Only when equipment like synthetic aperture radar is developed which can be used to survey the ground from the air over the impenetrable jungle, is there any chance. There is so much tiger country in New Zealand.

Unless you have been to New Zealand, and walked in the tiger country, as I believe to be an appropriate description, it is hard to understand how thick and dense the vegetation is in that country, or how large and unpopulated parts of the South Island of New Zealand are. There are raised walkways over a number of these spectacular trails. Go off these walkways, you would not be able to get very far physically. If any of these missing aircraft crashed in those areas, there is little chance of finding those aircraft. If you still cannot imagine how dense some of the vegetation is, try a quick visit to Google Earth and press the Street View button. Some show these walkways and you will then appreciate how dense is the vegetation so impossible to penetrate. Then imagine it with a 45% slope, it becomes dangerous to attempt to leave the pathways. Some of Lew Bone's excellent photographs around the Mt Aspiring area and in particular Rainbow Valley show the physical difficulty of searching in those areas. Had those searches been carried out during the "window of opportunity" with the tell-tale signs of yellowing of broken flora and greenery, there would have been a better chance of success following the example of ZK-HTF and Erceg's helicopter.

It still does not excuse not finding the Hughes helicopter in open country. Those early searches must have been deficient to an extent. A defence to this statement is that the aircraft was green, not the easiest colour to detect. Doubtless there may be some secrets somewhere being hidden from the public and the families of the victims. There was a directive/recommendation by WH Tench for the helicopter fleet servicing the North Sea oil drilling platforms that the aircraft had to be painted a distinctive colour easily detected against the background of the sea. Should there be a similar directive in New Zealand for all aircraft?

However, such equipment as synthetic aperture radar (SAR) could also be very important for other purposes to the NZ economy. Hunting for minerals from the air as well as the side benefit of finding old aircraft engines and landing gear, there is the additional benefit of finding rare elements like Lithium. This is the new gold for prospectors. Perhaps old gold too, which is so important in the space industry. There are prospecting companies internationally who already have such equipment now. It may come on-line in the next few years economically, and light enough to be installed in gliders and other small manoeuvrable aircraft.

The importance of finding these old missing aircraft cannot be overstated. There are a number listed in Gavin Grimmer's website findlostaircraft.co.nz. as well as Chris Rudge's "Missing". Grimmer also includes the first two Boeing Aircraft on his website. The importance of the search in New Zealand history for the Dragonfly in February 1962 was demonstrated by the many hours taken in the official search. There were only five persons on board, compared with ZK-EBU with seven. It merely illustrates the New Zealand authorities' recognition that a pioneer of the mountain flights of the time, Brian Chadwick, must be found. Lessons will be obtainable from a full investigation of the crash on its site when and where the Dragonfly is found.

Finally, ICAO (International Civil Aviation Authority) has to be confident that its member countries are capable of regulating flying safely and that when accidents happen, proper competent inquiries under Annex 13 are carried out. The reasons for the accidents have to be ascertained by competent trained investigators, so that any mistakes made or structural deficiencies are ascertained and the lessons learnt for the benefit of all countries. Prosecutions under alleged health and safety at work failures is a retrograde political step. The first essential has to be to find out what happened to prevent a recurrence. Likewise, this cannot take place without finding the accident sites. New Zealand's missing planes list is one of the worst in the civilised world. I was challenged by a proof reader about this statement. I had consulted a database of all missing aircraft throughout the world, and I took the period from 1945 to 2012, and New Zealand had more missing aircraft than any country on that database. Chris Rudge's book "Missing" is a revelation of the period 1928 to 2000 for aircraft disappearances in New Zealand. New Zealand's South Island being in the way of the roaring forties explains much and then there is the impenetrable jungle. As Brian Waugh said in his book "Turbulent Years" *The Queen Mary could be hidden in this type of country"*. I can add that a small Dragonfly DH90, the size of ZK-AFB would be completely swallowed up and lost for ever in most parts of that jungle.

To me, the most surprising missing aircraft in New Zealand is that of ZK-WAC. It was a Piper Tomahawk which on 7th January 1982 took off from Ardmore Airport. This is very close to the largest city in New Zealand, Auckland. That in UK distance terms, it would be like a plane from Stapleford, Biggin Hill or Elstree going missing well within the circle of the M25, closer to the centre of London than Southend. Both Chris Rudge and Gavin Grimmer have made recommendations for search and rescue organisational changes and improvements. Such a pity that these knowledgeable folk are regarded as amateur by officials who continue to make the same type of errors in their search and rescue operations.

Other search techniques

There are many old aerial photos of New Zealand on the internet, all with the dates of those photos. A computer programme to allow a co-ordinated search could be prepared. Interested volunteers could then be organised and allocated to various areas with dates of aircraft going missing. It is a numbers game to see tell-tale signs of a crashed aircraft never spotted before. This would be much cheaper than improving SAR equipment and may be more effective in the short term.

In the Second World War, aerial photographs were useful for reconnaissance purposes. Those techniques could easily be applied to searches through the New Zealand jungle using these historic photographs.

Who has aviation knowledge of the likely areas in New Zealand? Obvious candidates are gliding pilots. They are familiar with the mountains around Mounts Tasman, Aspiring, and Cook. They fly without the use of engines over most of the territory that needs to be covered in the photographic search. A number are computer programmers. They have the knowledge to create appropriate search APPS. One glider pilot gave evidence to the inquiry into the Kaimai tragedy (Chapter 4).

Funding must be found, if the words uttered on 28th November 2019, by the New Zealand Premier and Chair-person of Air New Zealand are to have any real meaning for there to be a revival of New Zealand at the forefront of world aviation and regain its reputation with ICAO. Accident reports directly involving Chippendale have to be reviewed, and not just Bay of Plenty and Erebus sagas. But all cases involving metal fatigue should be re-examined by the New Zealand inspectorate.

When asked by a monarch of New Zealand aviation writing, the appropriately named John King, as assisted by the Reverend Dr Richard Waugh QSM, "Where is the Dragonfly?" I can now only reply:

> Of course, I know exactly where Brian Chadwick, Louis Rowan, Darrell Stanley Shiels, Elwyn and Valerie Saville can be found. They are resting in a spectacular country in its most beautiful part, The Southern Alps. RIP

There is still one other missing person in our family and that is the sad case of cousin Ben Russell who disappeared after the tragic accident to Kim, his father (uncle to my step children). Ben is particularly associated with the instigation, development and marketing of the computer search engines we all now take for granted. If anyone knows of the whereabouts of Ben Russell born 6.6.1970, one of the best computer boffins ever, please ask him to contact his one and only aunt, my wife, Helen.

MEMORIALS

There have been a number of memorials to those who lost their lives at various tragedies from accidents in New Zealand. The Kaimai memorial near to Gordons Quarry was dedicated at the 40th anniversary of the accident and again hundreds were present in mid-winter at that memorial for the 60th anniversary. The number of folk attending these services demonstrate that these are very important in the lives of the 23 victims' friends and relations. However, there still has not been a dedicated memorial to the lives of the 257 souls lost at Mount Erebus. It nearly happened at Dove Myer Robinson Park in Auckland. It was delayed so often by NIMBYs. Earlier in 2023, the planned site was affected by catastrophic weather and it was felt unsafe to lay a permanent memorial at such a vulnerable site. The search for a new site is underway.

As the memorial is likely to be sited in the Auckland area and ease of access is a factor, there is a conflict of interest in that those living very close to a suitable site may behave similarly like those residents around Dove Myer Robinson park had done for a number of years. My own childhood memory of Auckland is the ever-present view of Rangitoto island on the skyline of the main harbour. It was a volcano like Erebus but without the snow. Perhaps a memorial there which can be seen from much of Auckland would stand to have an outside chance of selection. Perhaps on the side of Rangitoto, large enough to be visible, at 1467 feet above sea level to match the exact height of the site of TE901's accident, a suitable monument with the names of the passengers and crew of flight TE901 could be erected quickly, without the NIMBY problem. It would then mean a very easy "pilgrimage" to cover the short distance to that island. Alternatively Albert Park, Auckland? So central! Or Auckland National War Memorial.

Special thanks go to the Reeve family who first realised the significance of the unique 8mm film, Gavin Grimmer of findlostaircraft.co.nz, Lew Bone, and John King. These New Zealanders forbearance of this POME over such a time has been appreciated. Then without the help given by Alec and Richard Waugh, I would never have considered this book. Finally the immense help with the manuscript from Stuart Macfarlane, Ian Hambly, Arthur Cooper and again Richard Waugh cannot be overstated. There are other persons who wish to remain anonymous but have exchanged and provided information that has never seen the light of day before due to the need for confidentiality but trust me to relate their story accurately and in confidence. They know who they are, and I thank them profusely.

Post Script

Blame the pilots mantra has ceased as being the first line of defense - that was until the Boeing 737 MAX and the MCAS (Manoeuvring Characteristics Augmentation System). Boeing stated that all it needed after the 29 October 2018 Lion Air 610 crash was an updated checklist. Enough for any competent pilot to manage.

But then the Ethiopean airlines Flight 302 10th March 2019 crash - were lessons learnt?

APPENDIX 1

Chief Executive   Plant Representative

Attention: Manager Public &   our ref. MDR 3
            Corporate Relations   your ref.

                                     date   May 9, 1978

Dear Morrie:

I believe John Brizendine indicated a willingness to write his
impressions of our Antarctic flight for our publications purposes.
Today I have received John's reflection on his trip and I enclose
same for your use.

                    Best wishes,

                    Phil Le Couteur

                    P. F. Le Couteur

PFL:ds

Enclosure: Antarctica -- With Air New Zealand
            By J. C. Brizendine

✈ air new zealand | memorandum |

to   Chief Executive   from   Plant Representative

Attention: Public & Corporate   our ref.   MDR 3
            Relations Director   your ref.

copies to   date   May 11, 1978

            ANTARCTICA -- WITH AIR NEW ZEALAND
                          BY
                  J. C. BRIZENDINE

Dear Morrie:

The attached enclosure on the above subject supersedes and replaces
the enclosure sent with my memo MDR 3 dated May 9, 1978.

                    Best wishes,

                    Phil Le Couteur

                    P. F. Le Couteur

:ds

Enclosure

This shows the original letter and article from John Brizendine, president of the DC-10 aircraft manufacturers extolling his flight's low level sightseeing trip with Gordon Vette in 1977 that Morrie Davis claimed not to have read.

ANTARCTICA -- WITH AIR NEW ZEALAND

BY

J. C. BRIZENDINE

We had just flown non-stop from Long Beach, California to Auckland in something over twelve hours on the delivery flight of Air New Zealand's eighth new DC-10. When Morrie Davis casually suggested we should take Air New Zealand's last "flight-seeing" trip of the season to Antarctica, I must admit that the thought of another twelve-plus hour flight so soon found quite a bit of competition with visions of a pleasant spring day on a beautiful New Zealand golf course.

However, after a brief contemplation, the lure of the land seen by so few, and described so dramatically by great explorers from Captain Cook to Sir Edmund Hillary, made the decision easy. The opportunity was too great to miss for anyone with the least urge to see the "other side of the mountain."

So by 8:00 a.m. the morning of 15 November 1977, my wife, Shirley, and I were aboard the Air New Zealand DC-10 at Auckland's International Airport -- along with about 200 other kindred souls.

There were New Zealanders, Australians, Japanese, Americans (and probably other nationalities), most of whom had journeyed to Auckland to join this odyssey. We were a group of all ages -- children to great grandparents -- and varied interests from all walks of life. There was a man with his leg in a cast and others needing aid to move around, but everyone had a sparkle in the eye in anticipation of a great adventure. There were many new friendships to be made that day. I was interested to meet a number of residents of Christchurch where many Antarctic expeditions have been launched, and, indeed, is the main supply base for today's scientific operations in Antarctica.

Actually, we were airborne from Auckland at 8:45 a.m., Air New Zealand having taken its usual care to assure that our vessel was well provisioned for the comfort of all on board. Once aloft and aligned to our southward track, Captain Vette greeted us warmly and outlined our flight plan which would traverse 5500 nautical miles and keep us airborne the next twelve hours or so.

Captain Vette reported the latest weather outlook for our primary destination, McMurdo Station and Scott Base on the Ross Ice Shelf. He explained that weather conditions are always "subject to change without notice" at those latitudes, but the chances were good for fine weather some six hours hence. Should we not find the McMurdo area clear, we had an alternate flight plan to the vicinity of the magnetic south pole. Our optimism was heightened and one could feel the excitement build already.

Once our DC-10 had reached the stable air near our initial cruising altitude, Captain Vette switched off the fasten seat belt sign and so advised the passengers, as is normal. This may have been the last "normal" aspect of the flight in the passenger cabin for some hours!

Immediately, almost everyone was out of their seats. As if by some magic the mood in the cabin was instantly festive. Everyone was instantly friends to everyone else. The most experienced air traveler had never seen a flight like this!

We were, of course, amply provided with refreshments, appropriate to the hour, depending on one's individual inclination. Somehow our gracious, efficient and patient cabin staff persuaded enough of us to be seated to permit them to serve a champagne breakfast.

Our knowledge of the Antarctic continent was both refreshed and expanded by pertinent fact sheets and glossary "Antarctic Fragments" provided each passenger. Two documentary movies were shown on historical expeditions, including Sir Edmund Hillary's five-man trek to the South Pole in 1957/58.

One of the highlights of the flight was meeting and talking to Peter Mulgrew who Air New Zealand had invited to be our "resident Antarctic expert" for the trip. New Zealanders will know that Peter Mulgrew was one of Hillary's team to the South Pole and again in his historic conquest of Mt. Everest. A most unique and remarkable fellow! A quiet, unassuming gentleman, Peter had spent about three years in Antarctica. His patient and ready answers to all of our uninitiated questions added greatly to our already heightened interest.

Flying due south at longitude 165°E, we sighted the first drift ice about four hours out of Auckland and reached the Antarctic Circle a few minutes later as we passed the Balleny Islands. By this time the passengers were all on the move again, particularly to the windows for a clear view and an opportunity for photographs.

Captain Vette assured everyone that all would have plenty of opportunity for viewing and photography, and in the mood of camaraderie in the cabin, the windows were cheerfully shared. Everyone seemed to have one or more cameras along and the film usage was phenominal! From past experience, Air New Zealand had stocked fresh film aboard, and doubtless it was needed.

The mainland was sighted at Cape Adare. With the clear weather we had enjoyed enroute continuing, the vistas which unfolded were awesome as we flew southward, passing Cape Hallett and with the Admiralty Range of Victoria Land on our right and the Ross Sea on our left. With our DC-10 still at cruising altitude we could see for a distance of perhaps 200 miles. There didn't appear to be a level spot on Antarctica, from where we sat. Jagged mountain peaks rise above 5,000 feet. Valleys appear filled with enormous rivers of ice -- the glaciers. It seems the glaciers were countless. The landscape, of course, was white and "shades of white" with an occasional black cliff bare of snow and ice. Even though we were sitting comfortably in our shirt sleeves, in a living room environment flying through bright sunlight, looking down on the endless mountains, ice and snow, gave one the feeling that Antarctica is indeed a forbidding land.

The distance from Cape Hallett to McMurdo is nearly 400 miles, which gave everyone on board ample time to view the massive world of white. The sunglasses which Air New Zealand had advised us to bring were welcome apparel.

As we neared the Ross Ice Shelf, Captain Vette began a gradual descent which would bring us to approximately 3000 feet above the ice. Ahead could be seen 13,200 foot Mt. Erebus, a live volcano emitting clouds of white smoke. Another remarkable feature of wonderous Antarctica!

At 2:20 p.m. New Zealand time, (5 1/2 hours after leaving Auckland) we were abeam of Ross Island, dominated by Mt. Erebus, flying over the Ross Ice Shelf at relatively low altitude. Surface features could be seen distinctly. We flew past Mt. Terror with considerable black basalt rock on its slopes uncovered by snow.

Captain James Ross had named many geographical features of the area in 1841 when he sailed his wooden ships, Erebus and Terror, south in the Ross Sea to a point 78 degrees 10 minutes south latitude... An almost unbelievable fete considering the obstacles we could see from our vantage point.

Circling over the Ice Shelf, we turned northward to fly overhead Scott Base and McMurdo Station. From our height of perhaps a half-mile, we could view the layout of both bases and the airstrips located on the Ice Shelf. Aircraft and other equipment stood out sharply against the mottled, gray-white background created by sunlight and shadows of some scattered clouds. We could also see personnel on the surface, waving, and perhaps wondering "what is that strange bird with a koru painted on its tail doing in these parts?".

We had time to cruise about the area for about forty-five minutes at our close-up sightseeing altitude. All the while, Peter Mulgrew provided us with an excellent "guided tour" monologue through the DC-10's public address system. Being very familiar with the geographical and topographical features of the region as well as the sites of current and past expeditionary events, Peter helped bring us as near to being "Antarctic explorers" as we could be without actually setting foot on the surface. One had the impression that it was all an exciting experience to Peter too, viewing so clearly this area of great historical significance and he, himself, having participated in a phase of that history. Pointing out such sites as the route taken to the Pole, Shackleton's Shack, and the spot where Captain Scott died, only 11 miles from supplies, must have been a moving experience for Peter. It certainly added an ingredient of drama for the rest of us on board.

The natural beauty of the area led to a steady buzz of camera shutters operating. Particularly vivid were the great sheer cliffs of ice at land and sea juncture, from which fell enormous masses of ice to become icebergs. The 20 per cent above surface and 80 per cent below feature of icebergs was clearly identifiable from our DC-10. The "blue ice" of the Ice Shelf is vividly blue, as we could see. And Peter Mulgrew noted the blue ice is hard as quartz and very sharp-edged; so sharp, in fact, that he had found it necessary to make leather boots for his dog team in order to cross it on foot.

The time to depart McMurdo Sound on our return leg to New Zealand was determined by our flight planners on the basis of fuel remaining on board to comfortably reach Christchurch plus reserves for any contingencies enroute or at our destination. So, somewhat reluctantly, our ship turned northward at 3:15 p.m.

Captain Vette took the DC-10 to an altitude of about 10,000 feet and cruised northward at that level, paralleling the coast of Victoria Land. The ensuing half-hour must have been the "greatest glacier show on earth." We had seen this great array of the Admiralty Mountains and many glaciers earlier, of course, from 35,000 feet on our southward journey. But seeing them "eyeball-to-eyeball," so to speak, from a much lower altitude, gave us a whole new dramatic perspective. The glacial rivers of ice flow through the mountains in such numbers and size it was astounding. Imagine the latent energy of a 10-mile wide glacier! With the afternoon sun angle, shadows and contrasts and frequent glints reflecting from the ice created yet another treat of natural beauty.

By 3:45 p.m. we were again abeam of Cape Hallett and shortly the Antarctic continent was behind us. It was another hour or so, however, before all of the sea ice was behind us.

For the long return leg to Christchurch, Captain Vette took us up to the stratosphere again, for more efficient cruising, where the air is thin and very cold and the DC-10's big engines (50,000 pounds of thrust at sea level) use much less fuel to push us along at a speed of about 85 per cent of the speed of sound . . . well over 600 miles per hour.

In the passenger cabin, the mood became quiet and reflective. All that we had seen and experienced in the previous few hours had created a high level of excitement, and now the tempo slowed to one of relative calm. That is, except for our indefatigable cabin staff who, now able to pass through the aisles, resumed the task of looking-after our comfort and wishes. Refreshments and a good meal further relaxed everyone and led to a nap for many. It was a comfortable ride home. We didn't realize it, but there was one more unexpected treat in store for us.

Upon reaching the South Island near Invercargill, Captain Vette again took our DC-10 down to about 3000 feet above the terrain. It was nearing sundown as we flew above the rolling countryside toward Christchurch. Softly lighted by a low sun and then twilight, the farms and rivers and towns passed below us in a beautiful expanse of green -- sharply contrasting the endless white of Antarctica.

With the very last of daylight, Captain Vette gently set our DC-10 on the runway at Christchurch. It was 8:15 p.m. -- 11 1/2 hours after takeoff.

Many of our new friends departed the flight in Christchurch; the rest of us continued on to Auckland, arriving about 10:15 p.m.

It had been a day to remember. Traveling over 6000 miles, to a part of the earth only few people have seen at all, and fewer yet from our privileged perspective. It was by all odds, a once-in-a-lifetime day.

Congratulations to the people and aircraft of Air New Zealand for a truly magnificent performance.

APPENDIX 2

NZP/ZLC

1 December 1980

D. A. R. Williams, Esq.,
Messrs Russell McVeagh McKenzie Bartleet and Company,
Barristers and Solicitors,
P.O. Box 8,
AUCKLAND 1.

Dear David,

ROYAL COMMISSION OF INQUIRY INTO DC-10 ACCIDENT

I refer to our telephone conversations on 27 and 28 November,
1980.   I attach a copy of the memorandum which I personally
delivered to the following executives:

Mr. M. R. Davis	Chief Executive
Mr. J. B. Wisdom	Deputy Chief Executive
Captain A. C. Kenning	General Manager Airline Operations
Mr. C. W. Beresford	General Manager Corporate Services
Mr. G. W. Matheson	General Manager Airline Services
Mr. A. A. Watson	General Manager Associated Companies
Mr. M. A. Ramsden	General Manager Commercial
Mr. A. W. Varcoe	General Manager Corporate Finance
Mr. R. B. Keenan	Deputy General Manager Commercial
Mr. J. E. Davies	Director of Administration and General Services
Mr. P. Preston-Thomas	Director of Finance
Mr. P. P. Burkitt	Director of Corporate Services
Captain D. R. A. Eden	Director of Flight Operations
Mr. P. C. Clayton	Director of Engineering
Mr. N. R. Searle	Director of Marketing
Mr. M. R. Stanton	Director of International Affairs
Mr. I. J. Diamond	Technical Support Director
Mr. D. C. Saxton	Public and Corporate Relations Director
Mr. B. J. Patrick	Commercial Services Director
Mr. D. G. W. Marshall	Cabin Services Director
Mr. R. E. Birch	Traffic Services Director
Mr. D. G. Jeune	Planning Director
Mr. I. M. White	Regional Director New Zealand
Mr. I. G. Philip	Company Secretary
Mr. T. C. Cook	Assistant Company Secretary

All executives have advised that documents have already been produced
and that they hold no documents.   As I indicated to you, Richard McGrane
and I discovered an old file in one of the DC-10 filing cabinets and I also
discovered a little information in Public and Corporate Relations Director's
filing cabinet.   Both pieces of information were delivered to Richard.

*This is a copy of the original letter of 1st December 1980 between lawyers for Air New Zealand - Denise
Henare to David Williams at Russell McVeagh solicitors confirming that she personally delivered copies to
Morrie Davis and David Eden, with the help of Richard McGrane.*

-2-

I confirm that I have spoken to Vern Mitchell and Craig Saxton of our Public and Corporate Relations Section regarding the Brizendine article and advise that the article has not been used in promotional advertising either in New Zealand or overseas. It appears that parts of the article were subsequently reprinted in various staff news publications. We have also checked with our Commercial Distribution Centre and confirm that there is no indication that the article was used in a mail order brochure.

Finally, I attach a copy of transcript pages 791 - 1146.

Yours sincerely,

(Denese L. Henare)
ASSISTANT COMPANY SOLICITOR

APPENDIX 3

Not from 12 (No1)   4

DECEAS   Here   PORT

Full name of deceased: J   (CAPTAIN)
                          ~ o S. HELLERS
Address at time of death:

Place of death: ANTARTIC   Date: 28. 11. 79
Full name and address of next-of-kin or near relative: MARIA COLLINS
                                                           surname first
3. GRANDIAN Ro St HELLERS

INVENTORY
(Original must be attached to File)

CASH: NIL

1 PR GREY SPORTS TROUSERS WITH NAME "J COLLINS
ON LABEL - AT ROOM
1 PR BLUE SPORTS TROUSERS
3 SHORT SLEEVE UNIFORM SHIRTS
1 PR "NEW BALANCE" RUNNING SHOES
      SIZE 11½
1 PR SIZE 10 BROWN SUEDE SHOES
1 BLUE WOOLLEN JUMPER
3 PR MANS SOCKS
1 PR BLUE RUNNING SHOES - SINGLE
1 RED/WHITE/BLUE STRIDO SINGLET
1 BLUE PLASTIC RAINCOAT
1 BLK GENTS UMBRELLA
1 BROWN LEATHER SHOE POLISH KIT
1 TOILET BAG CONTAINING - TOILETRIES
1 N.Z PASSPORT No R197405 WK.
PROPERTY RETURNED TO CAPT BRUCE CROSBIE

CARRY ALL BAG DESTROYED 1/10

RECEIVED BY: W KEANE Inspector

N.B. A RECEIPT FOR PROPERTY IS PRINTED ON THE BACK HEREOF

These are copies of property reports from the Auckland mortuary showing the disposal of certain personal effects of the TE901 DC-10 Captain Collins by Bruce Crosbie and others.

POLICE DEPARTMENT *CAPT COLLINS*

DECEASED PROPERTY REPORT

Full name of deceased: 19.2B/1/6 *CAPT COLLINS*
(Surname first)

Address at date of death:

Place of death: Date: / /

Full name and address of next-of-kin or near relative:
(Surname first)

INVENTORY
(Original must be attached to file)

1. CLOTHING: 1 blue tie (ANZ) Air N.Z.Shirt
   1 pair uniform trousers (T.COLLINS,34 Grampian Road,Auck 5.

2. UNDERCLOTHING: 1 pair underpants

3. ACCESSORIES: 1 leather belt

4. DRY CLEANING & LAUNDRY MARKS (see 01)

5. JEWELLERY: 1 gold wedding ring (Maria 27.2.1962) *Found 5 PIECE DRIED oT TO free Ric 2/2/79*

6. DOCUMENTS: 1 Flight Plan form — *NOT SIGHTED Ric 1/12/79*
   YMCA Card of Hong Kong (Guests name: Mr T.J.COLLINS)

7. MONEY: U.S.Currency ($20.00)
   N.Z.Currency ($33.00)

8. MISCELLANEOUS: 1 Wallet, American Express credit card (Name Thomas
   J.COLLINS) Stamps (N.Z.) Air N.Z. Card (20+)
   Name Captain T.J.COLLINS.

BLOOD GROUP CARD RH +

RECEIVED MONEY, RING

FOR AIR NZ

DESTROY OTHER PROPERTY

PROPERTY DESTROYED DI 12/12/79

Index

C

D

Y

Z